Praise for *Origins of the Crash*

"So is it safe to buy stocks again? After you read Roger Lowenstein's *Origins of the Crash* . . . you'll have serious doubts."
—Paul Krugman, *The New York Times Book Review*

"As a premier business journalist and author, Lowenstein has the chops to deliver what this book promises: 'the definitive account' of Wall Street's latest unraveling."
—Jeffrey M. O'Brien, *Wired*

"A wide-ranging examination of the stock-market boom of the 1990s and its resounding crash. . . . Are there lessons to be drawn? Yes, many."
—*Kirkus Reviews* (starred)

"If you want to feel discouraged, outraged, and simultaneously enlightened about the current state of the stock market and the corollary issue of corporate excess, turn to Roger Lowenstein's cynical and fascinating *Origins of the Crash*. Carefully and clearly, financial expert Lowenstein explains how the American financial system got to where it is today."
—*BizEd*

"Someday, students of American business history may tear open *Origins of the Crash*, Roger Lowenstein's latest book, to learn why the last decade's bull market came to an ugly end nearly four years ago. . . . An intelligent look at what ails America's corporations. . . . Mr. Lowenstein is at the top of his own game."
—Alison Leigh Cowan, *The New York Times*

"A lively and readable account of the last thirty years on Wall Street. . . . Fresh and interesting . . . authoritative as well as informative. Recommended."
—Susan Hurst, *Library Journal*

"Lowenstein carefully picks through the threads of the 1980s to reveal the ones that connect to the excesses of the 1990s. . . . The result is an original explanation of financial events that uses familiar ingredients to bake a novel cake. . . . Lowenstein has staked out some solid ground, at once iconoclastic and conservative, and fortified it well. He has set a high standard for anyone who disagrees."
—Aaron Brown, *GARP Risk Review*

"The spellbinding story of the bubble . . . the author of *Buffett* and *When Genius Failed* vividly explains the rise and fall of the 1990s stock market in plain, easy to understand language. . . . This fascinating analysis may reveal more about the future than Wall Street would like to admit."
—Stephanie Swilley, *BookPage*

P9-CJK-117

"The ingredients are familiar: executive overcompensation and stock options, irrationally exuberant shareholders. . . . The author juxtapose[es] them so brilliantly that the twenty-year history that inflated the bubble seems not just understandable but inevitable. . . . Lowenstein's low-key ease with the most complex financial reporting makes this book both accurate and easy to read."
—*Publishers Weekly* (starred)

"Roger Lowenstein is a rare commodity: a financial journalist with no apparent ax to grind, who seems to understand the people and institutions he covers and is more often right than wrong on the big issues that matter. . . . In short, it would be hard to pick a better candidate than Mr. Lowenstein to sum up the broader lessons of the most recent boom and bust."
—Jonathan A. Knee, *The New York Observer*

"With the benefit of hindsight, it appears unbelievable that so many people, including presumed market experts, could have been wrong about so much, that such huge sums of money could have simply vanished in crazy-seeming speculations. How could this have happened? A comprehensive answer can be found in Roger Lowenstein's *Origins of the Crash*."
—Paul Gray, *The New Leader*

"A former *Wall Street Journal* reporter and the author of bestsellers about Warren Buffett and long-term capital management, Lowenstein blends detail and drama in a colorful, fast-paced narrative."
—Steven Brull, *Institutional Investor*

"Lowenstein opines with grace and intelligence . . . in his litany of wrongdoing, Lowenstein raises a startlingly basic idea—the new products and techniques that Wall Street was infatuated with had little connection to corporate profitability. . . . And so, in the end, much of the Internet effect was 'not to enhance profitability but to trim it'—a lesson that was all but lost on a euphoric and greedy Wall Street."
—Tom Goldstein, *San Francisco Chronicle*

"In *Origins of the Crash* Lowenstein steps behind the numbers to examine the culture that led to the creation and the bursting of the stock market bubble at the turn of the millennium. . . . Lowenstein tells the story of the bubble with authority, force, and just the right amount of outrage. It is a sobering tale."
—John P. Mello, *The Boston Globe*

"A fine writer with a gift for concision . . . Mr. Lowenstein captures the spirit of the era."
—Russ Mitchell, *The New York Sun*

"*Origins of the Crash* by former *Wall Street Journal* reporter Roger Lowenstein masterfully dissects the late-1990s stock boom and how it came to be. . . . A crucial account of an era of excess and folly . . . will only seem fresher with time."
—Marcia Vickers, *Business Week*

PENGUIN BOOKS

ORIGINS OF THE CRASH

Roger Lowenstein, author of the two bestselling books *Buffett: The Making of an American Capitalist* and *When Genius Failed: The Rise and Fall of Long-Term Capital Management*, reported for *The Wall Street Journal* for more than a decade and wrote the *Journal*'s stock market column "Heard on the Street" from 1989 to 1991 and the "Intrinsic Value" column from 1995 to 1997. He is now a columnist for *SmartMoney* magazine and writes for *The New York Times Magazine* and *The Wall Street Journal* among other publications. He has three children and lives in Westfield, New Jersey.

ORIGINS
of the
CRASH

The Great Bubble and Its Undoing

ROGER
LOWENSTEIN

PENGUIN BOOKS

PENGUIN BOOKS

Published by the Penguin Group

Penguin Group (USA) Inc., 375 Hudson Street, New York, New York 10014, U.S.A.

Penguin Group (Canada), 10 Alcorn Avenue, Toronto,
Ontario, Canada M4V 3B2 (a division of Pearson Penguin Canada Inc.)

Penguin Books Ltd, 80 Strand, London WC2R 0RL, England

Penguin Ireland, 25 St Stephen's Green, Dublin 2, Ireland (a division of Penguin Books Ltd)

Penguin Group (Australia), 250 Camberwell Road, Camberwell,
Victoria 3124, Australia (a division of Pearson Australia Group Pty Ltd)

Penguin Books India Pvt Ltd, 11 Community Centre, Panchsheel Park, New Delhi - 110 017, India

Penguin Group (NZ), cnr Airborne and Rosedale Roads, Albany,
Auckland 1310, New Zealand (a division of Pearson New Zealand Ltd)

Penguin Books (South Africa) (Pty) Ltd, 24 Sturdee Avenue,
Rosebank, Johannesburg 2196, South Africa

Penguin Books Ltd, Registered Offices:
80 Strand, London WC2R 0RL, England

First published in the United States of America by The Penguin Press,
a member of Penguin Group (USA) Inc. 2004
Published in Penguin Books 2005

1 3 5 7 9 10 8 6 4 2

THE LIBRARY OF CONGRESS HAS CATALOGED THE HARDCOVER EDITION AS FOLLOWS:
Lowenstein, Roger.
Origins of the crash : the great bubble and its undoing / Roger Lowenstein.
p.   cm.
Includes index.
ISBN 1-59420-003-3 (hc.)
ISBN 0 14 30.3467 7 (pbk.)
1. Business cycles—United States—History—20th century.   2. Stock exchanges—United States—
History—20th century.   3. Bankruptcy—United States—History—20th century.   4. United States—
Economic conditions—1971–1981.   5. United States—Economic conditions—1981–2001.   I. Title.
HB3743.L68   2004
330.973'0929—dc21   2003054819

Printed in the United States of America
Designed by Stephanie Huntwork

To Judy

ACKNOWLEDGMENTS

A few people deserve my heartfelt thanks. They helped me with their time, their insight, their candor, and their good spirits. Neil Barsky and Jeffrey Tannenbaum, two dear friends and now time-tested teammates, tirelessly read each of these pages. Their comments were of incalculable help. My father, Lou Lowenstein, also read (and, in many instances, reread) the manuscript, to its vast improvement. I am grateful beyond words.

This book is somewhat changed from what was planned at the outset; indeed, the original intent may be unrecognizable in the finished work. Through all of the readjustments that this entailed, my agent, Melanie Jackson, retained— or at least projected—her continuing faith; to her, I owe my gratitude as well. The change in my focus—I began the project before the collapse of Enron and so many other developments in the corporate sphere—may obscure the contribution of many people who generously agreed to be interviewed before the project's redirection. Their help is appreciated nonetheless. Finally, my editor, Ann Godoff, was indispensable in helping to set this book on its proper course—indispensable and irreplaceable. To her, more than ever, my acknowledgments and my thanks.

Contents

"Set our course by the stars,
not by the lights of every passing ship"

—OMAR BRADLEY

ORIGINS

of the

CRASH

ONE

Origins of a Culture

In the 1970s, a candidate for president advanced the novel proposition that the money in the Social Security system should be funneled into, of all places, the stock market. The candidate's name was Ronald Reagan. The incumbent president, Gerald Ford, had a good deal of fun with this evidently zany proposition. "I am not sure a lot of people would think it was a very good place to invest funds over the longer period of time," Ford declared.[1] His advisers had no trouble tarring the idea as kooky. The president likened it to "something dragged out of the sky." If not certifiably alien, then it might even be—perish the thought—an example of "wild-eyed socialism," which was no doubt something worse.

Ford did not have to explain why he thought the stock market was not a safe place "over the longer period of time." Stocks were considered simply too risky. Indeed, in 1976, the market was no higher than its level of *eleven years* before. Adjusted for inflation, the picture was far worse: the purchasing power of the average stock had fallen by two-thirds. Even over the longer sweep of a half century, stocks had managed a gain of only 3½ percent a year, so that people thought of the stock market as a place that went upwards a little but sideways mostly, with wrenching nosedives along the way. Indeed, the number of Americans who owned stock would actually fall during the '70s by seven million.[2]

Such grim statistics were reflected in a certain distance between the market and people's ordinary lives. Most newspapers carried at most a single account of the previous day's action on Wall Street, and television barely covered it at all. Today, at my daughter's middle school in New Jersey, an investing club is busily educating future market wizards, but in the '70s, through four years on an Ivy League campus, I didn't hear a mention of the stock market. Professors spoke darkly of America's "economic interests," but if any of those interests happened to be corporations with publicly traded shares, it was a detail that went unspoken.

Unlike in the '90s, when people would become accustomed to faithfully adding a little bit to mutual funds, rain or shine, every month, in the '70s, they *withdrew* a little bit, month after month, and they did so for eight long years. For Wall Street it was one long night, one long depression. Even the pros who managed pension funds were little more interested in stocks than my professors were. By 1979, of the money managed by pension funds, 90 percent was invested not in stocks but in bonds, bills, and cash, which was practically like stuffing it under a mattress.[3] That summer, *Business Week* sized up America's non–love affair with the stock market in a morbid, instantly famous cover story—"The Death of Equities."[4]

But equities were not dead, only dormant. And the renaissance began in short order. Three months after the article, mutual funds—finally— took in more money from investors than they redeemed. The net addition was a trifle—a mere $12 million. But deep in the giant furnace room where the economy is engineered, a long-stuck wheel had emitted a creak, shaken off its cobwebs, and, finally, turned. People were buying stocks.

Over time, this little shift, this rediscovered habit that ripened into a passion, affected far more than the Dow Jones average. When investors awoke, executives found that they, too, inhabited a different world. The rules soon changed for auditors and analysts and ordinary savers as well—an entire culture was retailored. By the late 1990s, America had become more sensitive to markets, more *ruled* by markets, than any country on earth.

This was the culture that led to prosperity and also to Enron. Markets became virtually sovereign—unchecked by corporate watchdogs or by government. Distortions followed, and with the temptation of wealth that distortions brought, corruption. But in the late '70s, no one was thinking of markets as powerful or pervasive. The country's problem was that it was too *in*sensitive, too *un*responsive, to markets. They were not hyperactive or feverish then but—potentially—a cure.

The bullishness and greed of the '90s had their origins in the very different environment of the '70s and, in some sense, much earlier. The financial culture had for most of the twentieth century suffered from a deficiency in what is known, rather antiseptically, as corporate governance. Since most executives owned no more than a nominal amount of stock, their interests were less than precisely aligned with those of the stockholders. It is no wonder that many a corporate CEO took home a large salary and enjoyed the perks of "success" even while his stockholders grew poorer.

Of course, the CEO was nominally supervised by the directors. But the typical board was larded with the CEO's cronies, even with his golfing buddies. They were generally as independent as a good cocker spaniel. It is true that textbooks spoke of shareholder democracy and that, in theory, the shareholders could vote the directors out. But proxy challenges virtually never succeeded—indeed, they were rarely attempted.

The electoral mechanism was too cumbersome and management's advantages too numerous. Some other means was needed of holding managers' feet to the fire.

This had been evident in a crude sense since the 1930s, when Congress held hearings into the roots of the great market crash, and it was in the '30s that the basic rules for protecting investors were put in place. A string of scandalous revelations had left a clear impression of Wall Street as unsavory and, indeed, untrustworthy. In one episode, the National City Company (a predecessor of the present-day Citigroup) peddled foreign bonds, issued by Peru, to naïve investors while concealing from the public information that left no doubt as to the dubious nature of Peruvian credit. "No further national loan can be safely issued . . ." wrote the bank's agent in Peru, all the while as its salesmen in New York were lustily hawking three distinct issues of Peruvian bonds.[5] And there was widespread evidence that, during the 1920s, stocks had been secretly manipulated by powerful insiders. The most notorious was Albert Wiggin, president of Chase National Bank, who, without bothering to inform his shareholders, was privately dealing in his own stock and, indeed, helping to drive it down.

In retrospect, it is startling how similar these stunts were to episodes of the '90s. National City might have been the Internet analyst of its day, and Wiggin was merely a harbinger of Dennis Kozlowski, the quick-fingered chief executive of Tyco International. So much recurred that one almost wonders if the government had adopted any protections at all.

But of course it had. The New Deal's response was extensive, but it can be summarized in one word: "disclosure." Legislation created the Securities and Exchange Commission as a cop on Wall Street, but the SEC could never have the manpower to go poking into every single company's files. Instead, the burden of preventing would-be Enrons, Tycos and WorldComs would rest with the companies and their auditors, who were now required to disclose all the material facts that an investor would want to know. The real policing would be done by *markets*.

The theory was that a CEO, knowing that markets were watching, would keep his hands clean. Disclosure was the least intrusive form of supervision—like a mother's telling her child to keep the cookie jar in plain sight. Or as Louis D. Brandeis had explained, "Sunlight is said to be the best of disinfectants; electric light the most efficient policeman."[6]

It worked, but only to a point. As long as a CEO made proper disclosure, a poor performance—even a poor record over a long period of time—generally did not result in his ouster. In other words, the requirement to disclose motivated a CEO *not* to do ill and generally not to violate the law, but it did not ensure that he would build value for the owners.

By the 1970s this had become painfully clear. CEOs such as Harold Geneen of International Telephone & Telegraph (ITT) had built huge conglomerates that, while enhancing their fiefdoms (and their regal lifestyles) had done precious little for their shareholders. Executives in industry after industry had been so complacent they did not see the oncoming freight train of international competition. Detroit saw its share of the world auto market plunge from 75 percent in 1950 to an abysmal 20 percent. At IBM, too, dominance bred smugness. So satisfied was the computer giant with the fat, 60 percent profit margins on its flagship mainframe that it was asleep to the tectonic shift unfolding in computing, which dislodged mainframes in favor of the personal computer.[7] For some reason, at these and at many other companies, the market check—the need of executives to perform for their investors—wasn't working.

Not surprisingly, the generation that ran these companies had come of age after World War II, in an era of fixed exchange rates and government regulation. They were programmed for stability, not change—for gradual evolutions planned by managers, not for chaos wrought by markets.

But chaos found them anyway. By the end of the '70s, stocks had fallen far enough to scream "cheap." The values inherent in stocks inspired a new and distinctly American phenomenon: the hostile takeover. The phrase refers to the practice of acquiring a company over the objection of management. Instead of waiting for their intended to say, "I do," raiders simply asked the stockholders to tender (sell) their shares, though there was nothing tender about it. Most of the early hostile bids involved companies in the same line of business, frequently energy (Conoco Oil was a celebrated target). With prices so compelling, so the saying went, the cheapest place to drill for oil was on the floor of the New York Stock Exchange.

By the early 1980s, Wall Street had spawned a new occupational class: the raider or takeover artist for hire—the gunslinger without portfolio. Carl Icahn, Henry Kravis, Irwin Jacobs, and a host of lesser gunmen were financiers as distinct from operators; they went after whole companies in diverse industries, typically offering premiums of 30 percent to 40 percent above the market price. People's interest in stocks naturally began to revive.

Takeovers had a similarly energizing effect on managers, in particular on CEOs. Previously, theirs had been the safest jobs around; now, their fortress was under siege and their pulse rate was on the rise. Given the dreadful state of their companies, a little anxiety was no bad thing. To escape a buyout, CEOs felt they *had* to raise their share price. This was a significant departure. Previously, stock prices had been seen as a long-term barometer. Prices in the short term were notoriously unreliable (this was the lesson of the Great Crash). But with a Henry Kravis lurking, the long term might not exist. Or as John Maynard Keynes liked to say, in the long run we are dead. Now CEOs had to demonstrate that they (and not T. Boone Pickens) had the shareholders' best interests at heart. They began to think more often, and more urgently, about their stock price. Willy-nilly, takeovers had become a tool of corporate governance.

A new phrase crept into the argot: "shareholder value." It was painfully redundant. After all, *any* value in a corporation is shareholder value; a CEO has no other constituency. But more and more, when a CEO did something—anything—to get his company on track, it was cloaked in the flag of the shareholder. A computerized search found five references to the term in the entire decade of the '70s, six in 1982, and steadily more thereafter. By 1985 there were ninety-nine, after which it becomes ubiquitous.

When underachieving companies such as Walt Disney and ITT promised to boost shareholder value, in the mid- to late-1980s, they meant something other than pursuing their usual business of shooting films or managing hotels. What they were really intent on pursuing was their share price. The distinction was intuitively understood by the public, even if it were not articulated. "Shareholder value" became a rallying cry; CEOs who resorted to the cliché quickly cultivated a following among investors. In a prescient piece in 1984, *The New York Times* observed that takeovers "had put renewed emphasis on stock price."[8]

But takeovers did not cure the patient, not immediately at any rate. The early '80s were even gloomier than the '70s. The Federal Reserve, hoping to squelch inflation, let interest rates soar to the midteens, which sent the economy into not one but two recessions, back-to-back. Bankruptcies were widespread, and the mood was somber. A spate of articles and books forecast a coming depression, a runaway inflation, a catastrophic energy shock, or worse. Consultants predicted that in the "next" crisis oil would rise to $100 a barrel, choking off the country's growth and even threatening democracy![9] A private economist with a flair for phrase-making—Alan Greenspan—termed it "The Great Malaise."[10]

. . .

Some of the problems ailing business seemed to be cultural as much as economic. Many of the companies getting pounded hardest, such as Xerox and Kodak, were losing out to rivals from Japan, a more consensual society. The notion of Japanese shareholders' launching a hostile takeover—a hostile anything—was preposterous, but perhaps that was Japan's secret. Japanese executives did not have stock market worries or the threat of takeovers to make them jumpy. They could focus on the longer term—on making quality products.

By the mid '80s, a new despairing expert—the Nippon-phile—began to crusade for a wholesale imitation of Japanese ways. This crowd tried to steer American executives in the *opposite* direction from takeovers—toward relationships, not markets; toward deeper strategy, not daily stock quotes. In fact, if Japan's soaring stock market was any clue, the way to get industry as well as the market moving was to *disregard* the clamor from myopic investors.

Consultants returning from Tokyo bemoaned America's obsessive short-termism, its low rate of savings, its lack of team spirit. Michael Crichton's *Rising Sun* warned of a new Japanese supremacy. Articles such as "Meeting the Japanese Challenge" became common, and a few were openly defeatist. Imagine, only a generation after Pearl Harbor, American book buyers swarming to a volume entitled, *Japan as No 1: Lessons for America.*[11]

Eager to see the light, American companies experimented with quality circles, with fostering more contact between workers and managers, with forming partnerships as opposed to unceasing competition. There was a vogue for so-called stakeholders, a dissonant term suggesting that a corporation existed to serve not just its stockholders but a nest of related interest groups—its workers, its community, its suppliers.

The stakeholder movement, essentially an attempt to plant the Japanese model on American soil, emphasized a company's ongoing relationships, whereas in a market system, workers might be sacked, suppliers might be replaced, whole divisions might be sold, depending on what was most advantageous at the moment. Incorporating the needs of stakeholders, it was said, would resolve the age-old dilemma of governance by aligning American companies with the interests of society. At the very least, it would soften free enterprise—tame its Darwinian edge.

But the movement was slow to gain steam, not only because the notion of a stakeholder was fuzzy and lacking any legal basis but also because it was, in a profound sense, un-American. Whatever the ideals of reformers, individualism was simply too central to the country's spirit. Admiration for the Japanese miracle was fine, but in America, innovation was the result of heated competition; it occurred precisely on the Darwinian edge. The question for faltering companies was how to restore that edge.

Takeovers alone hadn't worked, but the raiders had a new weapon, even a new idea. The idea was leverage. It may sound absurd, now, to think that companies could borrow their way to health or that investors could lend their way to prosperity, but then, investors had once been eager to lend to Peru. Leveraged buyouts (literally, buyouts financed by debt) had always been around, but in the late '70s and especially in the '80s LBOs became the rage. Much of this, of course, was due to Michael Milken.

Milken, in the '70s an obscure bond trader at Drexel Burnham Lambert, had theorized that junk bonds (meaning bonds that were issued by distressed corporations, and hence were of lesser credit quality) often traded at excessive discounts. Milken thought these bonds offered high-enough interest rates to *more* than compensate investors for the risk of default. For a bond trader this was a fine theme, and it certainly made Milken money.

But Drexel (and Milken) soon found they could make higher profits by underwriting *new* junk bonds rather than merely trading existing ones.[12] He thus began to float bonds for low-rated borrowers who, previously, had been shut out of Wall Street. Some of the borrowers used the money for internal expansion or for paying off prior debts—but others saw that junk bonds could fund a war chest for acquisitions. For instance, Ronald Perelman, an ambitious deal maker who had started at his father's metal fabrication company, managed, at thirty-five, to buy his first business, a jewelry distributor, with precisely $1.9 million in borrowed funds.[13] After meeting Milken, Perelman could borrow not merely millions but billions. In an episode that set the tone for the latter half of the '80s, Perelman, still a little-known financier in 1985, launched a bid for the cosmetics giant, Revlon, run by Michel Bergerac, a courtly Frenchman and an icon of the establishment. When Perelman, a crude, cigar-chomping newcomer with seemingly smaller resources, prevailed, it triggered anxious spasms among CEOs everywhere. Executives who had slept while Japan and Europe retooled could not sleep now, for with the raiders armed with debt, no company was safe.

Could LBOs, then, be the tonic? There was always an element of fantasy about this. After all, the deal money could not be endless; it had to come from *somewhere*. Not that this was a problem during the '80s. Ordinary investors were flocking to mutual funds that indiscriminately purchased every junk bond in sight. The lure, of course, was the huge interest rate—12 percent, 14 percent, sometimes more—that junk-bond issuers promised. The notion that investors could earn high returns from borrowers that were on the verge of bankruptcy was remarkably innocent, not to say naïve. Just as equity investors forgot about risk a decade later, so bond investors in the '80s ignored the possibility of default. Milken had conditioned them not to worry, for when a bond did run into trouble Milken would sponsor a *new* batch of junk bonds to re-tire the earlier, troubled issue (in other words, companies would encum-ber new debts to pay off the old). By such a circularity, junk bonds obtained an aura—altogether pleasing to the investor—of inevitability.

It was easy to say that the mania couldn't last but hard to resist the trend (just as, later, people who recognized the insanity of the dot-com mania participated in it). LBO artists were appearing out of the woodwork, their pockets swollen with cash with which to bid up shares. What was a CEO to do? Even raiders who had not announced a target had no trouble raising blind money to use in an LBO—any LBO—if they should find one.

As the LBO trend gained momentum, corporate managers grew des-perate. There was no time for holding the workers' hands and improv-ing the product—they had to get the stock up. The only defense was to imitate the raiders and borrow. Thus, under the unlikely rubric of share-holder value, companies such as Harcourt Brace Jovanovich and West-ern Union hollowed out their balance sheets by adding mountains of debt, the better to buy back shares and, they hoped, boost the stock. Managers at R. H. Macy and many other corporations went, so to speak, all the way and bought out (with borrowed funds) all of their own share-holders.

Improbable as it may sound, given the desperately mortgaged condi-tion of their companies, such managers were hailed as saviors. The no-tion that owner-managers would run a business more efficiently than hired salarymen had intuitive appeal. And let a man buy a company on borrowed funds, with either fortune or bankruptcy hanging in the bal-ance, and his incentive was profound. Indeed, the fact that LBOs were financed with debt added to their mystique, for the operators truly ex-isted on the edge.

By the latter part of the '80s, every investment bank—not just Drexel Burnham—was underwriting LBOs, often with management participating. Many of the early buyouts succeeded, and there is no doubt that some achieved efficiencies and that corporate America had been in need of a belt-tightening. But the deals became steadily, then recklessly, more leveraged. Finance has its own Peter Principle, by which a successful model will be adapted to progressively riskier cases until it fails. Ultimately, borrowers such as Federated Department Stores (acquired by the blustery Robert Campeau) promised to pay far more in junk bond interest than they had earnings. These later LBOs were—by simple arithmetic—doomed to fail.

Nonetheless, LBOs were now, uniformly, winning the warm praise reserved for an elixir, a cure-all for corporate America.[14] The fact that the buyers could afford to pay a premium for the stock was seen as proof that a leveraged company was *inherently* more efficient. (Conveniently overlooked was the possibility that the raiders were overpaying.) Michael Jensen, a prominent theorist at Harvard Business School, even suggested that the commonplace public corporation might be an anachronism.[15] His "Eclipse of the Public Corporation," published at the height of the LBO craze, argued that LBOs had led to efficiencies apparently beyond the grasp of companies with public shares. Jensen's argument was based on a premise, known as the efficient-market hypothesis, beloved to academics: that stock prices were ever as rational and correct as they could be. Thus, if raiders were paying more for stocks, it must be because stocks were worth more in their hands.

Thinly buried in the praise of Jensen and others was the suggestion that the raiders were a throwback to the industrialists of a century ago— the Carnegies, Morgans, and so forth. Takeover artists were championed as the vessels of a provident Invisible Hand, weeding out the slothful corporate bureaucrats and restoring America's entrepreneurial spirit. This was a theme that the acquirers, naturally, did nothing to discourage. Henry Kravis, the architect of the RJR Nabisco buyout, the decade's largest, reaped hundreds of millions of dollars in buyout profits and fees and, indeed, lived in the Park Avenue building that once was home to John D. Rockefeller Jr. Not surprisingly, he argued that LBOs were "restoring" America's competitive edge, sweeping away "stagnation" and so forth.[16]

Nelson Peltz, one of the more affected of Milken's raider-clients, who divided his time among an oceanfront home in Palm Beach, Florida (complete with hydraulically operated glass panels to protect his pool from winds), a twenty-two-room estate in Bedford, New York, and an apartment in Paris, actually likened himself to a Carnegie. "The industrialists of the nineteenth century were highly paid and highly criticized," Peltz observed, "and I guess we'll have to bear that burden too."[17]

The recession of 1990 put paid to the raiders' pretensions, though not to their mansions and sliding panels. Scores of LBOed companies filed for bankruptcy; dozens of others, notably Perelman's Revlon and Kravis's RJR, were permanently weakened by their improvident levels of debt. Milken, by then, was gone from the scene, convicted of securities fraud. Like embittered soldiers, a band of free-market ideologues have ever since complained that his prosecution was a willful stab in the back to the junk-bond business. But no healthy market ever depended on a single trader.

And the junk bond market, stripped of its excesses, revived. What died was the notion of LBOs as a governance vehicle—a tool of natural selection that pruned the poorly run (and thus, cheaper) companies, "the corporate deadwood."[18] In fact, when financing had been so easy, good managements had been vulnerable too.

Moreover, since the buyout artists had *not*, mostly, used their own money, there was a gaping hole in the idea that Kravis, Perelman, et al.

were instruments of Adam Smith, wielding society's proxy. When an LBO failed, society was the poorer—jobs were lost, innovations were foregone—but the raiders simply went on to the next deal. The LBO operators bore a moral hazard, for they had nothing to lose. What they had was a free ride: heads they won big; tails they tried again (while the lenders got wiped out).

As we will see, this also describes the equation for a corporate executive endowed with a stock option. And it was no coincidence that as the LBO era neared a crescendo, options were granted with increasing largesse. Since it was clear, by 1990, that LBOs were not a universal answer (piling on ever more debt was simply suicidal), attention reverted to public company executives. What could be done—what carrot could be bestowed—to make them more like the idealized owner-managers of academics' dreams?

CEOs had already embraced much of the raiders' agenda. They were buying back shares, cutting costs, selling divisions. They had bought into shareholder value. What was needed, it was said, to make CEOs truly behave like owner-managers was to make them *owners*. Soon, a new model of governance, a new elixir, and not incidentally a new culture was born, and it revolved around the stock option.

TWO

Early Nineties—
A Culture Is Rich

In 1990, Michael Jensen, the Harvard professor who had championed LBOs as an antidote to corporate America's ills, published a
call to arms in the *Harvard Business Review* for boards to revamp the
way in which CEOs were paid. Jensen and his coauthor, Kevin Murphy,
were interested in the incentives imparted by specific pay formulas.
They acknowledged that their recommendations would probably lead
to higher absolute levels of pay, but this was not their concern. "It's not
how much you pay, but how," the authors advised.[1]

The problem with the "how," in their opinion, was that CEOs did
not own enough of their companies' stock. In words that later reverber-
ated in the counsels of compensation consultants, Jensen and Murphy
wrote, "On average, corporate America pays its most important leaders
like bureaucrats. Is it any wonder, then, that so many CEOs act like
bureaucrats . . . ?"

The way to get CEOs to act less like bureaucrats was for them to own a "substantial" amount of stock. Since most CEOs were not independently wealthy, this could mean only that they should be granted options.

Stock options had been around in a minor way since before World War II. In 1936, Ben Graham, the father of modern security analysis, had raised an eyebrow at companies that tried to "pay" their employees with scrip rather than cash. In what he intended as an impossible hyperbole but what in fact described the business model that flowered in Silicon Valley in the 1990s, Graham wrote a mock press release for U.S. Steel that purported to announce a "sweeping modernization scheme" that would, among other changes, shift all wages and salaries to options. "The almost incredible advantages of this new plan are evident," Graham wrote in his best deadpan. "The payroll of the Corporation will be entirely eliminated."[2]

For several decades, Graham's satire remained only a spoof, and option awards continued to be only a modest component of pay. In the '70s, with the market dead, executives were not exactly clamoring for stock. Only one out of two companies granted options, and the grants were typically small. Part of the reason was cultural. Options were still thought of as a perk—not the main event. They were icing on the executive cake that would do no harm and might at least get the CEO thinking about his investors.

In the '80s, that began to change. For one thing, executives could hardly help but notice that the raiders and investment bankers were making more than they were. It was one thing for a twenty-six-year-old in suspenders to declare that you should sell your company. It was another to see him get rich from giving you the sack. To mollify their managers, boards began to promise "golden parachutes" in the event that execs were tossed from their jobs. By and by, executives began to push for—and get—more money for staying on the job, too. With the stock market rising, these executives allowed it would be okay to get some of their added compensation in options after all. And wonder of wonders, they now found that their demands—far from being rejected as greedy—were welcomed as a sign of their enlightened approach towards shareholder value. The mantra was on every consultant's lips—the more enlightenment the better—and woe to the consultant or corporate director who did not pay it homage.

The example of Silicon Valley made stock options seem especially fashionable. If California has been a laboratory for social experiments from tax revolts to pot, so would Silicon Valley be the advance guard of the stock market bubble. It would rise first, crack first, and be a sort of weather vane of Americans' financial expectations. In the Valley, companies granted lots of options. Robert Noyce, the coinventor of the computer chip, started the trend. In 1968, he bolted from Fairchild Semiconductor, a New York–run company that had refused to give options to its talented engineers on the West Coast. Noyce, subsequently, founded Intel, which along with launching the microchip revolution made options a central tenet of its culture. In the '80s, companies such as Oracle, Sun Microsystems, and Microsoft followed Intel's lead. Soon, Silicon Valley was known as a place where nerdy, postadolescent programmers worked for modest wages but got rich on stock options—just as Ben Graham had imagined.

Traditional managers envied the Valley's stock market riches, of course, and they coveted, too, the fawning praise that was heaped on the Valley's risk-taking culture. Stodgy blue chips began to plumb their entrepreneurial selves, loosening up on dress codes and organization charts and especially loosening up on stock options. Before the decade was out, Michael Eisner at Disney and Charles Lazarus at Toys "R" Us had each reaped multi-million-dollar bonanzas. As each man had turned around a moribund organization, no one begrudged them. By the end of the '80s, the percentage of corporate stock reserved for options had doubled to 5 percent of the total outstanding, which at bigger companies amounted to a sizable chunk of potential wealth.[3]

Protests that pay was getting out of hand were not unknown in the '80s; in fact, they were rather common. CEOs who earned more than $1 million frequently drew fire (Lee Iacocca allowed to Larry King that *no* exec was worth that much). Peter Drucker, the management consultant, fretted that it was unhealthy for CEOs to be making more than twenty times what their workers earned.[4] The standard for health was Japan— where (as in Europe) the ratio was far lower.

Protests grew louder when the first President Bush and a dozen CEOs visited Japan, early in 1992. The climate was inauspicious. America had just been through a recession and United States companies were (still) closing plants and sacking workers. The United States' trade deficit with Japan was a staggering $40 billion. Not surprisingly, the trade mission became a pitiful exercise in American pleading that the Japanese agree to sell us fewer of their goods or at least buy something—anything—"Made in the USA." During the trip, it was reported that the visiting CEOs had earned a combined $25 million in a single year. Though the average for the group, about $2 million, was not a lot by American standards, it was far more than was paid to the heads of Japanese companies, even as the Americans were begging the latter for help. The revelation caused a tempest. As if to demonstrate the embarrassing weakness it had revealed in American culture, Bush, who had intestinal flu, vomited in plain sight at a state dinner.

Executive pay remained a hot topic in the '92 campaign. Patrick Buchanan, who was running a redneck challenge to Bush within the Republican Party, stood outside a factory in New Hampshire and declared, "You can't have executives running around making $4 million while their workers are being laid off."[5] He didn't have to add that Japanese workers weren't getting pink slips. Congress picked up the ball, and was soon preparing a bill to ban tax deductions on salaries above $1 million. The limit, which was passed in 1993 at the urging of President Clinton, backfired; since stock options weren't covered under the cap, boards interpreted the rule change as an implicit encouragement to grant more options.

But despite their increasing prevalence, options drew little scrutiny. Commentators in the early '90s usually focused on the cash that CEOs took home, not on their options. When Tony O'Reilly, the chief executive of H. J. Heinz, did cash in a package worth $71 million, in 1991, Wall Street was shocked,[6] but such jackpots remained rare. Most executives were still seeding the ground, accumulating options that would be valuable later if their stocks rose. The point that option grantees did not bear risk—did not, in this crucial sense, bear any similarity to entrepreneurs—was glossed over, drowned out by a thousand repetitions of the chestnut that options promoted shareholder value.

For Jensen and Murphy were having a profound influence on American boardrooms. "The Jensen article was seminal," according to Graef Crystal, who consulted to boards on compensation. "All the consultants ran with it, and all of them said, 'You've got to give 'em more stock.'"[7] According to Jensen, the Drucker idea of holding CEOs to a ratio of their workers' pay was the worst possible fix. The notion of *any* limit was antithetical to growth: one might as well tell an engineer to limit the number of circuits on a chip or tell a slugger to cap his home run totals. And Jensen was correct: though CEOs were already very well paid, rigid boundaries would, indeed, tend to produce bureaucrats rather than entrepreneurs.

However, he then made an unsupportable leap that was to have drastic consequences. "What really matters," Jensen argued, "was the percentage of the company's outstanding shares [that] the CEO owns."[8] As evidence, Jensen admiringly pointed to Warren Buffett, the nonpareil investor and student of Ben Graham, who owned roughly 45 percent of the public company that he managed, Berkshire Hathaway. While not all CEOs could own 45 percent, Jensen admitted, "the basic lesson holds." In other words, get all CEOs up to 45 percent, or as close as one could, and we would have a race not of bureaucrats but of Warren Buffetts—of managerial supermen.

But Jensen overlooked a key aspect of his "basic lesson." It wasn't only Buffett's percentage that distinguished him as a shareholder-oriented manager, nor even his inherent sense of fairness. At least, if one hoped to replicate the Buffett approach in other CEOs, the key point was that *Buffett had acquired his stock with his own money*. A poker player will bet aggressively when he is playing with the "house money." In contrast, an executive with his own capital on the line will identify with his company more closely—much more closely—than will a CEO who has simply won the options lottery. And the latter was the path suggested by Jensen.

He did not much worry that CEOs might try to pump up their stocks, and thus the value of their options, by manipulating their companies' disclosures. "Manipulation is an enormously difficult thing to do," he remarked. "It's difficult to fool investors."[9] The academic doctrine that investors were not easily fooled—that stocks prices were generally right—was an important underpinning for options, for it implied that a CEO who raised his stock had created genuine and enduring value. In fact, Jensen fretted not that CEOs would be overpaid but that corporate boards, with their acute social sensitivity, would be too embarrassed to offer sufficient rewards.

In any case, by the time of the Clinton inauguration, in 1993, American companies had less to be embarrassed about. For one thing, Japan was well into its grim collapse: its stock market had been cut in half. Japan's vaunted stability did not look so attractive; now it looked more like stagnation. Its social harmony had come at a price in creativity lost. It had coddled workers but also protected its entrenched elites. Seen through the lens of Japan's distress, America's CEOs—even with their fat paychecks—looked more entrepreneurial. In fact, Japan began to look like a liberal version of the former Soviet Union—a perfectly stable (and perfectly stultifying) society in which people accepted a fixed reward in return for a fixed output.

America was growing again because it was doing the opposite: it was paying people to excel. "Pay for performance" had become the universal corollary to shareholder value. When Lou Gerstner was given 500,000 options—in 1993, an almost unheard-of quantity—to turn around IBM, no one, then, suffered from indigestion or emitted a peep of protest. In fact, people applauded. Investors said it would be good for IBM's stock.

I t would be fruitless to speculate on whether stock options did more to generate public enthusiasm for stocks or the reverse. It is simply a fact that ordinary Americans were encouraged by the sight of a Gerstner and that a Gerstner reaped greater profits thanks to the ordinary Americans who had begun to buy his stock.

And more investors *were* ordinary. The bull market of the first half of the '90s had a broader base than previous markets did. One reason was that the 1980s, specifically the spectacular crash of 1987, had already occurred. The market's subsequent and speedy recovery had given rise to an enormously seductive aphorism: "Buy on the dips." This implied a universal license: Buy on *every* dip. And thus far, such a strategy had paid off handsomely. From the crash to the Clinton inaugural, a little more than five years later, the market had practically doubled.

As the United States rebounded from the recession and the first Persian Gulf war, the economy improved and corporate profits surged. Stocks in the early '90s did offer attractive values. However, the popular refrain emphasized the "dip"—not the value—as the reason to invest. It dangerously conditioned investors to think about stocks as one-dimensional numbers, irrespective of the underlying businesses.

The trend toward indexing subtly reinforced the notion of a market as a thing unto itself. However strange it may seem now, until the early

'80s few investors could have told you how "the market" had done. They followed their own investments, they knew whether they had lost money or made it, but that was it. My grandmother faithfully served Oreos because (for decades) she owned shares of National Biscuit. But she would not have known whether the stock, in a given year, had risen 5 percent or 10 percent and certainly not whether it had outperformed an index. The game was not so scientific.

By the early '90s, people were being inundated by advisers, talk shows, and newspaper columnists all urging them to compare each investment against a market index—and better still, to buy a fund that tracked an index itself. Nor were such comparisons done only at quarter's end, when fund statements were mailed. (Believe it or not, investors used to wait for the postman to track their returns.) Now, local newspapers as well as the *The Wall Street Journal* were publishing daily fund results, so that investors could compare their own funds with others and, when the spirit (as well as the fund industry's unceasing promotions) moved them, switch—not only every year or quarter but by the month, the week, the day. Knowing little about the substance of their investments, people largely thought of them as disembodied, as "stocks" or "funds"—mere quotations in a sea of numbers.

Investors became number junkies, increasingly hooked on the effluvial tide of data that emanated from Wall Street. (Investors *love* numbers when stocks are going up; it is only when they are falling that people turn to the business, the Oreo behind the stock.) Countless gurus encouraged them, including, in particular, the managers of mutual funds, who were presumed to have a deep expertise in investing. Investors, generally, were not aware that the guru who truly examined a security was rare; most simply parroted the accepted wisdom that stocks were a sure thing and that, therefore, a representative sampling of stocks would be sure. "Stocks," according to Jeremy J. Siegel, the author and academician, "should constitute the *overwhelming* proportion of all long-term financial portfolios"—advice he dispensed in multiple editions of a best-selling book without regard to the price or valuation at which stocks were trading.[10] These experts prophesied an unblemished future, a golden market, an American millennium (the precise opposite of what was forecast by the depression-mongers of the early '80s). John and Jane Doe were told again and again to buy the index, to follow the trend— and to keep following it.

Reinforcement was everywhere. People talked about stocks in their homes and offices and wherever they went; they could scarcely escape. A little electronic ribbon began to appear at the bottom of the television, to flash across the windows of banks, to flicker in airport waiting rooms: the ribbon that was the ubiquitous presence, the daily barometer.

In the mid-'90s, I happened to listen to a Joe Smith address an evening crowd at the public library in Millburn, New Jersey. The mural on the wall, which depicted an eighteenth century town meeting, re- minded me of a civic debate—of a public gathering like the one I was at- tending. But since this was the '90s, Smith, a marketing manager and off-hours investor, wasn't meditating on war or peace or education; he was talking about the stock market. And his message to the neophytes in the audience was that they could be like Peter Lynch, the fund manager at Fidelity who had earned a return of 2,700 percent over thirteen years. Smith said this without irony. As in the Roaring Twenties, it was com- monly held that everyone could become, ought to become, rich— rich!—merely by investing in, and remaining in, common stocks.[11]

The most effective envoy for this view was Abby Joseph Cohen, the market "strategist" at Goldman Sachs. Cohen had turned bullish on stocks in 1991, and, what is noteworthy, she had stayed bullish—for the entire decade. That single call, and her clock-like repetition of it for a decade, made her the country's most lionized pundit. A modest woman who rode the bus from Queens, Cohen endeared herself to investors by translating the market into homey metaphors—an interest rate hike was a "flu shot"; the economy's supposed potential for stretching rendered it like "Silly Putty" (a simile inspired by her school-age daughter's toy).[12] Her demeanor was plain; her optimism was cautious rather than bold. This suited her perfectly not merely to Goldman's clients but to what became her larger audience of ordinary investors. The true purpose of a Goldman strategist—or one at Merrill or Morgan—after all was not to strategize or educate but to reassure, and by repeating her bullishness so doggedly, so faithfully, Cohen became a beacon to millions. She made higher prices seem assured.

The illusion of inevitability was heightened by the spread of 401(k) retirement plans. As the nomenclature suggests, 401(k)s owe their startling success to an administrative accident. In 1980, Congress added a short paragraph—letter "k"—to Section 401 of the Internal Revenue Code. Essentially, it said that taxes could be deferred on profit-sharing plans that were open to lower-paid employees as well as executives. Congress's intent was modest—it was tweaking the rules that applied to existing plans, which typically applied to year-end bonuses. However, a benefits consultant in Newtown, Pennsylvania, named Ted Benna grasped an unseen potential. Benna thought 401(k) would also permit employees to defer (and shelter) regular salary; what's more, he saw that the statute would not prevent employers from chipping in more money, thus encouraging workers to save. Benna proposed such a plan to a client, a local bank, but was turned down. For a while, the only Americans with a 401(k) account were the fifty employees at Ted Benna's consulting firm.[13] However, as the advantages of 401(k)s became known, they appealed to corporations, which were able to shift the responsibility of providing for retirements to their employees. As the stock market rose in the '80s, employees—even those with no financial expertise—began to think of managing their retirement portfolio as a basic part of being a literate American, like knowing how to buy insurance or select a mortgage.

centric lens.[17] The theory was that unfettered markets and "technological determinism" would create more jobs, educate more poor, and build more low-cost housing than any public policy.[18] And the economy of the early- and mid-'90s did boom, though it did not exactly raise all boats. Even as corporate profits soared and investors prospered (CEOs, of course, did much more than prosper) average wages did little more than track inflation, and poverty rates remained abysmally high for a rich Western nation.[19]

But the dogma of free markets went unchallenged. Academics pushed it; executives felt reassured by it; overseas Americans, like missionaries, extolled it. The theory was so seductive, especially when stocks were rising. (The Dow had risen from roughly 800 when *Business Week* reported the "death" of equities to over 3,000 by the early '90s.) If companies were run for their shareholders, if shareholders were free to buy and sell, if executives could tabulate their "votes" by the market price—what could possibly go wrong? What other referendum could better allocate society's capital? For markets were *never* wrong. As a popular business school textbook declaimed, markets did not succumb to "illusions"; rather, they unfailingly and "unromantically" gauged a security's proper worth.[20] They "discovered" value, they did not assess it; they were as perfect as a human institution could be. The triumph of the faith was virtually complete.

The administration's free-market apostle was Robert Rubin, the former trader and co-CEO of Goldman Sachs, who consistently pushed to open developing nations to the free flow of capital, and just as consistently pushed for bailouts when such nations ran aground. Rubin had an ally in the conservative Federal Reserve Board chairman, Alan Greenspan. The Fed chief had at once an implacable faith in markets and a tender concern for their well-being. Having come on board just before the harrowing crash of '87, he was ever wary of upsetting traders. Markets increasingly revered Greenspan—the journalist Bob Woodward virtually deified him.[21] At times, the surging stock and bond markets seemed to be validating not the prices of securities but the Fed chairman himself.

But it would vastly understate the trend to chalk it up to one official, or two, or even to an entire administration. Washington had been deregulating in fits and starts since the mid-'70s, beginning with the liberalization of banking rules and interest rates. Much of this was a response to computer technology, which put power in the hands of individual traders and even consumers (a trend that culminated with the online brokers and research services of the late '90s). Markets were a vehicle for this democratization; they trumped central decision-makers as parliaments had trumped kings. Thus, bond markets rather than secretive bankers now determined mortgage rates. The market for corporate loans was similarly democratized. Once, the commercial banker had been omnipotent, unilaterally aggregating deposits and deciding which companies to lend to; now, investors decided for themselves in the bond market.

There were plenty of parallels outside of finance. Airlines now continually adjusted seat prices according to passenger demand; shoppers dictated fashion rather than the other way around.

Corporate CEOs experienced the devolution of power in acute form. They were beholden to the stockholders—to the market—as never before. Of course, we want executives to work for investors, just as we want politicians to represent voters. But markets hold referendums not every four years but around the clock. Often, the process by which markets arrive over the long term at a reasonable conclusion amounts in the short term to a series of very irrational ups and downs.

No sane man could heed their every verdict. With Wall Street scrutinizing them so closely, the focus of CEOs became immediate and obsessive. Executives became acutely sensitive to what would make their stocks rise, not over the long term but by the hour. In 1992 and '93, a string of highly prominent CEOs were forced to retire—John Akers at IBM, Paul Lego at Westinghouse, James D. Robinson at American Express, and Robert Stempel at General Motors. The sackings were certainly justified (even overdue), given the companies' foundering records. They were also unprecedented. What forced the boards to act was the support, in some cases the outright rebellion, of shareholders, such as, in the case of GM, the California Public Employees Retirement System. To avert a coup, CEOs felt a dire pressure to move the stock.

This was, to repeat, a monumental change. In the memoir of Alfred P. Sloan Jr.,[22] who ran General Motors from the 1920s until the 1960s, there is no mention of GM's share price as a factor in his decision-making. Sloan was almost wholly engaged with GM's car divisions, its corporate structure, its competitors, and so on. That the stock price would follow was implicit, but the stock was merely a derivative yardstick. In the 1990s, a CEO would no more ignore his stock price than he would his cholesterol.

Their heightened sensitivity was amplified by a reform that had an unfortunate side effect. Starting in 1994, the Securities and Exchange Commission required companies to publish a chart of their stock performance in the annual proxy statement, which is where the CEO's pay is disclosed. Though the chart was useful for shareholders, the CEO now saw his pay linked explicitly, and also quite publicly, to this one barometer. As the adage goes, "You manage what you measure."

Execs intent on "managing" their stocks became hypersensitive to a single number: quarterly earnings per share. From an economic perspective, quarterly numbers are virtually irrelevant, because it typically takes years—not months—for business strategies to bear fruit. They are important only on Wall Street, where traders myopically focus on the next scrap of news, the next bit of data—on each ensuing bit of ephemera. CEOs began to hear too much of this minutia—they began to drown in it.

William Smithburg, the longtime chairman of Quaker Oats, was in many respects typical. Until the '90s, his record had been unblemished. Then, Quaker's stock began to lag. It wasn't his fault: oatmeal wasn't exactly a growth industry. But Smithburg was eager to keep the stock aloft, and in 1994, Quaker announced a $1.7 billion acquisition of Snapple, an iced-tea company. Smithburg had visions of new flavors and new markets. The acquisition turned out to be a disaster. Smithburg admitted as much to Wall Street investors in a conference call. It had the ring of a show trial, a ritual confession. "I am, as you are, very disappointed in the stock price and I intend to move every mountain to improve it," Smithburg said.[23]

Smithburg became yet another CEO casualty of an underperforming stock. He discovered (too late) that the arbiters of Wall Street fashion were pushing not for mergers but deconglomeration—for simpler corporate bloodlines and fewer Snapples. CEOs were forced to pay heed. Executives who had once thought only of acquiring new subsidiaries now rang their bankers and begged them to, please, please, divest them of their ill-fitting pieces.

So craven were executives that various multiline companies issued additional stock certificates to provide the appearance of the separation the market wanted even while in substance they remained whole. These second stocks, known as tracking stocks, did not confer any ownership; they merely allowed for a public referendum on individual units, such as the wireless business of AT&T or the baking division of Ralston Purina.* It was as if frightened executives wanted to give over to Wall

*Other companies with tracking stocks included General Motors, Circuit City, and Sprint.

Street their direct proxy on every business, every decision—baking, wireless, why not the company cafeteria?—lest there remain somewhere a shareholder who felt disaffected and unpersuaded by the stock and who might be moved to sell.

John H. Bryan was illustrative in a different way. Son of a Mississippi hog butcher, he had sold the family business to Sara Lee and, by and by, found himself running a publicly owned conglomerate that was known for a delectable frosted chocolate cake and also made sausages, briefcases, brassieres, T-shirts, socks, and shoe polish. Bryan was not a guy to bend to Wall Street. At the height of the LBO craze in the '80s, *BusinessWeek* had published a story entitled, "Sara Lee: No Fads, No Buyouts, Just Old-Fashioned Growth."[24]

But the '90s were different. Old-fashioned growth wasn't good enough. And Sara Lee's share price, too, had started to sag. This being the unpardonable crime, the unfaddish Bryan opted to remake his company.[25] He decided to sell the tangible assets, the textile plants and the slaughterhouses. In the future, Sara Lee would merely contract out for cakes and brassieres that were made by somebody else—foreigners maybe, or private companies that didn't have a stock—and slap on one of Sara Lee's well-regarded brand names. A press release quoted the hog butcher's son as declaring, "Slaughtering hogs and running knitting machines are the business of yesterday." But really, they were yesterday only for Sara Lee. *Somebody* was going to make that stuff—a somebody not beholden to the stock market.

Bryan let his hair down just a little. "This is what they want," meaning the guys in the suits, he said. "Wall Street can wipe you out. They are the rule-setters, and they have decided to give premiums to companies that harbor the most profits for the least assets. I can't argue with that."[26]

The hollowing-out of Sara Lee reflected the market's desire for fleet and nimble profit centers, for businesses liberated from the burden of assets. It is no accident that Coca-Cola was, similarly, divesting itself of bottling plants or that gas companies such as Enron were pursuing similar steps. There was a fashion for asset-light and streamlined ships, a certain intellectualization of the concept of business and even of profit.

For profit was obtained not only from selling goods above cost but also from trading, restructuring, and financial maneuvering—from any operation that Wall Street recognized as profitable or that could be booked as a profit in the quarterly number. The game was to keep earnings rising, but never by too much, so as to save more for the next quarter. CEOs were encouraged to engage in such legerdemain, because investors rewarded them with higher stock prices.

Not surprisingly, within the corporation, the role of finance was quietly elevated. In Sloan's day, finance was merely a support service. It supported GM's manufacturing by providing capital, and it supported sales by extending credit. By the '90s, finance had become a profit center. Companies once content to park their surplus cash in Treasurys now engaged in all manner of complicated derivative deals to juice up the bottom line. Financial engineering obtained a premium. At its simplest, chief financial officers hastened to buy back shares, irrespective of their price or value, with the blunt intention of goosing the stock. At its more complex, companies set up complicated vehicles to strip assets from the balance sheet and achieve the slimmed-down look the market craved.

The notion of a fixed asset became somewhat unfixed; everything was fungible and disposable—more dependent on markets. Even people were disposable and, indeed, in the early and mid-'90s announcements of layoffs at AT&T and such were routinely greeted by a rally in the stock price, much as several years later a press release declaring a "dot-com strategy" could be counted on for a one-day rally.

The big commercial banks were exemplars of the shift from fixed operations to more fluid ones. Once, they had maintained a portfolio of loans to customers. They had dealt in relationships. Now, the banks were mere trading houses that shuffled loans (or tiny pieces of them) and a mind-numbing array of derivatives. Banks had become traders, and ordinary companies had largely become banks, for manufacturers, marketers, and high-tech companies too were hiring squadrons of financiers and traders.

The rise of corporate finance sparked a parallel rise to prominence of the chief financial officer. Once a mere administrator—a number cruncher—the CFO became a front-line executive, the person most responsible for "making" the quarterly earnings number. The CFO's elevation brought Wall Street ever nearer to the corporation's heart.

In their eagerness to win the Street's approval, corporate finance departments subscribed to newfangled measuring tools, some so esoteric they were trademarked by consultants, such as Stern Stewart's EVA (equity value added). EVA added a new wrinkle to the relatively straightforward business of evaluating corporate performance. It was based on a seemingly simple idea, that a company's returns should be graded according to the precise cost of its capital. It was said, then, that if companies invested only in projects that returned more than their cost of capital, nirvana would be theirs. And corporations including Coca-Cola, Eli Lilly and, indeed, Quaker Oats beat a path to Stern Stewart's door, the better to boast to the market of their newly sophisticated appreciation of value.

The small problem with EVA is that no one number for the cost of equity capital exists. It is one of the inherent riddles of finance. Stern Stewart tried to square the circle by assuming that the cost (for each company) varies with the volatility of its stock—that is, with the extent to which the stock jumps around.[27] This was supremely, almost incestuously, self-referential. Executives were supposed to divine their target returns based on the ups and downs embedded in their own stock charts. As in so much else, the stock drove the strategy instead of the reverse.[28]

The larger problem with EVA and with other such yardsticks is that it endowed finance with a faux precision and, what's more, a pointless one. The questions that determine the success of an investment project yield to common sense much more than to the slide rule. (Dot-coms discovered this in spades.) Planners who can predict whether a market will exist for some intended innovation, or how much competition it will face, are worth more than any number of consultants' fancy elixirs. But the consultants reassured the Street, just as Abby Cohen reassured investors. And the bull market reassured everyone. Insofar as there being room for doubt, the loop was closed.

THREE

Enlightenment
Gets out of Hand

It was in 1986 that Ivan Boesky, who had never been to college, declared in a commencement address at the Berkeley School of Business Administration, "Greed is all right, by the way.... I think greed is healthy. You can be greedy and still feel good about yourself." The students cheered. But his remarks were viewed less charitably when, six months later, the financier was arrested for insider trading. And Gordon Gekko, the Boesky character in *Wall Street,* who famously paraphrased Boesky ("Greed is Good"), was seen, when the movie was released the following year, as the incarnation of evil. Not even Gekko really believed that trading on inside information was good; he was merely being ironic.

However, during the '90s, his reputation gradually improved. If not exactly a candidate for canonization, Gekko came to be seen as at least a pragmatic realist, someone who did the dirty work that made society's wheels turn faster and, ultimately, made all of us the richer. Greed was to be praised, even if it sometimes went off the tracks; it was the instinct that moved the Invisible Hand. No less than the economic correspondent of *The New Yorker,* in a generally perceptive piece on the '90s, wrote, "Economists from Adam Smith to Milton Friedman have seen greed as an inevitable and, in some ways, desirable feature of capitalism."[1]

What is interesting about that statement, given how plausible it sounds today, is that it isn't true—not with respect to Adam Smith at any rate. The premise of Smith's Invisible Hand is that people will be driven by self-interest, a concept far less mean than greed. Smith recognized that greed was omnipresent, but it was to be combated, not encouraged. It certainly was not desirable. To Smith, born in 1723, the son of a Scottish customs official, the proper engine of capitalism is what we, today, would describe as enlightened self-interest. In his famous passage, "Every individual [who] employs capital [and] labours neither intends to promote the public interest, nor knows how much he is promoting it . . . he is . . . led by an invisible hand. . . ."[2] The reason the hand points toward good, and not toward some Gekko-like villainy, is that, in order for a person to sell his goods or transact business, he must satisfy the party on the other side as well. Thus, "He will be more likely to prevail if he can interest their self–love [self-interest] in his favour."[3] Smith had been trained at Oxford in moral philosophy, which was the subject he taught at the University of Glasgow. Economists today are trained in applied mathematics, not morals, but in the eighteenth century the dismal science did not yet exist as a separate discipline. Economics was simply another tool to examine the human experience. In an age when commerce was often controlled by government, Smith believed that free trade could be a force for good, since a man whose livelihood depended on his reputation would be ill advised to resort to "frauds." Smith championed open markets (much as we do the principle of disclosure) because he thought of an open market as a fair one, less likely to promote the rapaciousness that he knew quite well was ever lurking.[4]

The distinction between self-interest and greed is worth retaining, for it is a distinction that, in the '90s, was utterly lost. Greed was not only good; it was to be promoted, feted, satisfied, and enabled, all to bizarre excess. Moreover, greed was ennobled as never before. The urge to get rich was practically sanctified in the financial press; market mavens attained the status of demigods. What virtue was to Cotton Mather and industriousness was to Calvin Coolidge, greed now was to the man on Wall Street—the purported engine of social welfare. In a specific sense, this is why the stock option came to be accepted as a tool of governance—a vehicle for promoting the corporate good. And perhaps, if used in moderation, it would have been. So we must now look, more closely, at how options were actually employed.

Nelson Peltz, the Milken-financed deal maker, is a fine place to start, for no one moved from the leveraged buyouts of the 1980s to the stock options in the 1990s with more aplomb. In the late '80s, Peltz had used junk bonds to gain control of Triangle Industries, a packaging company. Then, in what Peltz later described as a most fortunate coincidence, he bought out most of the public's interest in Triangle just days before he was to start talks with a French bidder who eventually bought the entire company at a huge premium.[5]

By 1993, public shares were à la mode, and Peltz remained a man of the times. He duly purchased control of Triarc Companies, a publicly owned but struggling conglomerate that owned Arby's Restaurants, RC Cola, and other interests, and immediately took options on 600,000 of Triarc's shares. Now, the mathematics of options, for those who may be unfamiliar, is simple: Triarc's stock was trading at $18, and Peltz had an option to buy the stock at that price over the next decade. This was the standard formula for executives (though the size of the grant was unusual), and Peltz's steady accretion of more options became, in many respects, a model for the age.

We have noted that executives such as Peltz were in a favored position over cash-paying shareholders, as they had nothing to lose. Their potential gains, too, were hugely disproportionate. If Triarc's stock had risen by, say, 5 percent a year, a rate less than that on Treasury bonds, the shareholders would have been sorely disappointed. In economic terms, their capital would have been squandered. But Peltz would have snared a $7 million profit. Because options do not require any capital, they reward the holder not just for the part of a stock's rise that reflects superior performance but also for the part that reflects what might be termed normal business progress or even very mediocre progress.[6] Thus, even at substandard rates of return, an executive with enough options can reap a fortune.

As it was, during the first year of the Peltz epoch, Triarc manifested no progress whatsoever, and the stock sputtered. Unbowed, in March 1994, Peltz took 75,000 more options; then, the following month, he hauled in his truly big catch—2.1 *million* options.[7] Now if a million options established Peltz as an enlightened servant of the shareholders, 2 million qualified him as their patron saint, or such was the view at the time. Indeed, so sensitive was Peltz to the hoary duties of noblesse oblige that he pledged, in return for his mammoth grant, to accept no more than $1 a year for his labors. In the dry letter of the proxy, Triarc stated that Peltz's options were granted "in lieu of base salary, annual performance bonus, and long-term compensation," for a period of six years.

Gordon Wolf, a principal at Towers Perrin, a consulting firm, gushed with pride over his client's willingness to stake his future, rudder and mast, to that of the shareholders. Peltz, truly, was an "extraordinary" version of the new executive man, willing to put his "entire compensation" on the line, or so Wolf allowed to the *The Wall Street Journal*.

Triarc's businesses continued to stumble, and no sooner was the ink on the proxy dry than the stock fell by half, leaving Peltz's options well under water. And so, later that year, Peltz took 240,000 more options—at a lower price, of course—and in 1995, 150,000 more. This was Peltz's fifth grant in the span of two years, a pace that scarcely allowed for his sundry other activities, such as tending to his wind-protected swimming pool in Palm Beach or even, perhaps, managing the affairs of Triarc.

And yet, these bequests were anything but frowned upon, for each new grant, it was said, provided Peltz with yet more incentive to rise from his chamber and toil on the shareholders' behalf. And that much were true, if the grants were considered individually. But the point that was missed, in particular by journalists who tend to assess compensation in any one year without regard to what had been awarded in previous years, was that the *collective* impact of so many grants was altogether skewed. For now that he was getting grants at frequent intervals, Peltz could get rich—er, even richer—if the stock merely rose above its level at the time of any *particular* grant. Since stocks fluctuate, some of his grants would tend to be at depressed prices, as likely to recover as are the hands of a clock to return to twelve, meaning that his option to turn a profit became a virtual certainty.

Peltz's two most recent grants, for instance, were awarded at prices significantly lower than when Peltz had taken command. These latter options would do nothing less than reward him for recouping the ground he had already lost—for running on a treadmill. This plainly subverted the supposed principle of pay for sustained long-term per-formance. And in the mid-'90s, as large awards proliferated in corporate America, such a subversion became increasingly common.

Now, lest one think that Peltz, in taking more options, had violated his promise to forgo additional long-term compensation, Peltz explained—after checking with his lawyer, for such men depend on lawyers—that he had meant to say that he would forgo long-term *cash* compensation. In 1996, therefore, it came as a surprise that Peltz collected a $2 million bonus, in cash, which the new proxy referred to as a special bonus, exempt from his pledge. This was awarded for "special" accomplishments, such as paying down debt, selling assets, sharpening the company pencils perhaps—that is, for what in fact were routine parts of the job. And as the stock, by now, had swooned to 11½, a 36 percent loss for investors, one might have questioned whether Peltz's pay was not a wee bit out of line with his performance, save that, the proxy mercifully explained, no "single measure" (stock price, earnings, etc.) was determinant; therefore, no single form of pay was sufficient. But then, the company may as well have quoted Gordon Gekko.*

In the variety of his compensations, too, Peltz was a man of his times, for executives were not merely awarded many more options; they demanded, and received, princely sums that were spread over many and sundry categories. Each tended to be based on a different yardstick—one on share price, another on earnings, yet another on qualitative achievements, such as leadership, effecting a merger, or meeting the extraordinary challenges of reporting to work, not to mention of hanging one's hat and doing the job—so that, as a general rule, if a CEO were deprived in one pocket, he was amply rewarded in another.

Consider the case of Edward E. Whitacre Jr., the chairman and chief executive of SBC Communications.[8] Whitacre, a six-foot four-inch Texan, had signed on with SBC, then Southwestern Bell, in 1963, and risen through the ranks to the CEO job in 1990. Since then, Whitacre had got-

---

*From Peltz's initial option grant of April 1993 through the close of 2002, a ten-year stretch, his stock advanced a paltry 4 percent a year, netting his shareholders less than half the return of the market average. Nonetheless, Peltz continued to grab immense compensation, including $36 million in 1999–2001 alone.

ten bigger option grants in virtually every year. In addition, Whitacre got a salary as well as a bonus, which invariably amounted to millions of dollars. Nor was that all. Whitacre also received so-called restricted stock—meaning outright grants, which are valuable whether the stock goes up or down. He also got money under a long-term incentive plan—as if his shares and his options, too, were not an incentive. Nor was that all. Whitacre got cash (for certain expenses) in a category known as "other," and he got more money still in a category that, the inventiveness of his pay consultant apparently having been exhausted, was simply deemed "all other." A shareholder who wanted to know what Whitacre had earned had to add the sums from seven different pockets. This was one reason the multipocket approach was employed—no one subtotal would appear too big.

Whitacre, admittedly, was an earnest executive, who through a series of mergers transformed a regional Baby Bell into a nationwide colossus. Over time, however, the growth strategy did not pay off in earnings, and over the length of Whitacre's tenure, his investors have merely tracked the market averages.[9] Nonetheless, the board kept finding reasons to up his pay. In 1995, he got $5 million a year *not* including the enormous value of his options. By 1997, the figure had rocketed to $15 million. That year, the board cited Whitacre's "excellent leadership" in fashioning a merger with Pacific Telesis. This mimicked a trend of paying extra for work once rightly considered a part of the job. After all, if the Telesis merger succeeded, Whitacre would benefit (from his stock options), as would his shareholders. The bonus was merely a double dip. However, what truly raised eyebrows was his "special retention grant" of $8.7 million. Why raised eyebrows? Almost absurdly, Whitacre was to get a comparable retention grant the next year and in each of several succeeding years, as if the chief executive were at once both an indispensable captain and a notorious flight risk.[10]

· · ·

A company spokesman defended Whitacre, arguing that he had in no way "abused the system" or gone "off the reservation." And that was true: Whitacre was smack in the middle of the reservation. His arrangement consciously mimicked that of other CEOs, for it was a staple of consultants that any arrangement could be justified as matching an equally generous arrangement of some competitor. A game of leapfrog ensued. The SBC directors judged that Whitacre should rank among the top quarter of his peers, thus his package raised the average for all that followed him, as did that of each succeeding CEO.

By such an escalatory spiral, pay for performance was transmuted into a gilded sinecure. This was glaringly apparent in the case of Whitacre's competitor, AT&T's Michael Armstrong, who got stock with a value guaranteed—even if it fell—of $10 million.[11] Now, the notion of an investment that is guaranteed no matter the performance seems so twisted as to be from some Marxist caricature of capitalism, but it was, increasingly in the '90s, the picture that capitalists were painting of themselves.

It is fair to wonder why directors went along with such abuses, and the answer has its roots in the distinct culture of America's boardrooms. In all likelihood, the reader little reflected on the description of Whitacre, a few paragraphs above, as Chairman and Chief Executive, for in American companies this twinning of positions is nearly universal. But think how inappropriate would the description President and Chief Justice sound, or Head Coach and Quarterback. The board's job, like that of the coach, is to monitor those on the field. This is why, in Britain, the chairman of the board and the CEO are usually distinct. Indeed, the merging of these roles in America stands out as a unique institutional mistake. It inflated the CEO's already considerable power and elevated his status within the body that nominally oversees him.

Boardrooms are in any event fraternal places—modern oases of gentility. Warren Buffett once wrote that to stand up and criticize the CEO felt like "belching" at the table.[12] Directors frequently served for many years, becoming gradually more cozy with the chairman. Even worse, the moral hazard of interlocking boards—a black spot in J. P. Morgan's day—remained through the 1990s. Thus, two of Whitacre's directors ran companies where Whitacre, in turn, was a director, so that his watchers were also the watched. Armstrong of AT&T and Sandy Weill of Citigroup were a powerful example of such an interlocking couple.

The boardroom conflicts were even more egregious in the case of Michael Eisner, Disney's CEO, who stacked the deck by putting on the board his personal lawyer, the principal of the elementary school previously attended by his children, and the president of Georgetown University, to which Eisner had donated more than $1 million.[13] These so-called independent directors, of course, were chosen for their loyalty to Eisner, as distinct from any loyalty to Disney.

Generally, CEOs did not need to be such blatant fixers. Gerstner simply seeded the IBM board with fellow big-company CEOs, who were hardly blind to the fact that Gerstner's pay would figure into the averages on which their own pay was based. In a less specific, perhaps unconscious, sense, Gerstner's fellow directors shared the same mind-set as to the CEO's role and, also, his entitlements; they not only hired the same consultants, they also golfed at the same country clubs, flew in similar Gulfstreams, had their boardrooms furnished with the same mahogany.

If any misgivings over compensation remained, the directors eased their consciences with the nostrum that stock options were free—so why not issue another million? Of course, as every economist since Adam Smith could tell you, nothing of value—not even lunch—is free. In fact, when executives exercised options, many companies turned around and repurchased an equivalent number of shares at the higher prices prevailing in the market, an expenditure that cost corporations such as Microsoft billions. But since it did not appear in the earnings statement, it had no effect on the number watched by Wall Street. Stock options were not costless; it was just that their cost went unaccounted for.

The group that is the arbiter of accounting issues, known as the Financial Accounting Standards Board, recognized the problem, which became more pressing as the size of awards mushroomed. In 1993, after years of debate, FASB recommended a rule to require companies to deduct the cost of options from their reported earnings. Arthur Levitt, the new chairman of the SEC, supported the change as consistent with honest accounting. However, success did not come so easily.

Corporate America embarked on a lobbying extravaganza to stop the rule. In Silicon Valley, where, as we have seen, options were the mother's milk of progress, high-tech executives, led by John Doerr, the venture capitalist, went into overdrive. They even engineered a public rally to demonstrate the supposedly grassroots support for stock options. Kathleen Brown, the California treasurer and the daughter of a storied Democratic governor, shouted to a cheering crowed, "Give stock a chance!"[14] (It was, presumably, the first mass rally against an accounting standard since the birth of double-entry bookkeeping). The accounting industry, plugging the interests of its corporate clients, lobbied, if anything, more vociferously. We will not belabor their arguments save one—that the new standard would primarily hurt the little guy by depriving him of his slice of the American dream.* Joseph Lieberman, the Democratic senator from Connecticut, where the FASB is headquartered, sponsored a Senate resolution asserting that the accounting standard posed "grave consequences" to entrepreneurs. Mil-

---

*Accountants also argued that companies could not expense options because they could not be valued precisely. This was a canard. In the first place, earnings statements rely on a multitude of other estimates, none of which has ever spurred a mass rally or a lobbying blitz. Moreover, traders on options exchanges have no trouble arriving at a value, as they buy and sell thousands of options every day.

lions of ordinary workers would now be cast into a cold, optionless world. No doubt, it would be back to breadlines and hawking apples.

Lieberman, a pragmatic Democrat if ever there were one, was a big recipient of Wall Street and accounting industry contributions.[15] That he could make such an argument, even cynically, says much about the increasing sway of America's wealthy, to say nothing of that of the accounting industry. For FASB had not proposed to outlaw, or even limit, options—only to require companies to book their cost. This was the essence of American corporate governance—disclosure.

Lieberman's larger point, that workers would suffer—in effect, that options had become a middle-class entitlement—was simply untrue. Although many companies were distributing a small number of options to the rank and file, 75 percent of options went to people who ranked in the top five in their companies. More than half of the remainder went to the next fifty managers. Only three million real workers—about 2 percent of the country's workforce—got stock options, and the slice they divvied up among themselves amounted to only 10 percent of the pie.[16]

It does not take a genius to discern that the people who were lobbying to preserve the fiction that lunch was free were the people scarfing down most of the meals—the senior executives. And the total number of options—most of which went to this select group—was rising during the '90s, from 5 percent to, approximately, 15 percent of the ownership of corporate America—an unprecedented accumulation of private wealth.[17]

Actually, even corporations were on record that the free-lunch treatment was a fiction. In the accounts that companies filed with the IRS, they routinely deducted options as a cost, saving billions in taxes. It was only when reporting to their own shareholders that executives maintained otherwise. And they would not give in. Ultimately, Lieberman and some like-minded cohorts threatened to strip FASB of its power. This was a gun to the head. Late in 1994, Levitt, the SEC chairman, reluctantly advised the accounting board to back down, and the rule change was shelved.* The whole episode was of a piece with the Republican campaign, a few years later, to repeal the inheritance tax—the bulk of which is paid by the wealthiest one-sixth of a percent of all estates. (No tax was paid by any estate outside the top 2 percent.) Yet the estate tax was masterfully, and deceitfully, savaged on Capitol Hill as a threat to the family farm. In both cases, politicians wrapped themselves in red, white, and blue to do the bidding of the ultrarich.[18]

Properly organized, markets should be an engine of general prosperity. In theory, as share prices rise, the common man should reap a dividend through the stimulative effect on growth and jobs. But the shareholding culture of the '90s made a grander claim—that the ownership of stocks themselves was disseminating through society. Employee 401(k)s and other forms of employee participation were, it was said, democratizing capital. The relentless upward march of stocks was thus invigorating the middle class. Stocks were a leveling force, bringing ordinary Americans into the economic mainstream much as the automobile had done in the era of the Model T.

That was the theory, and it is a prime reason why markets won such favor from politicians. But the leveling was a myth, as was the notion that the market was dispersing wealth throughout society. Many people owned a small portfolio but very few had a large one. As late as 1998, the eighth year of the boom, half of the households that owned stock of any kind (mutual funds, retirement accounts, direct shares, and so forth) had a total portfolio worth less than $25,000.[19] Even among relatively afflu-

---

*The surrender was not complete. FASB did require companies to state the effect of options in a footnote. Although the earnings number that was disseminated to Wall Street thus remained unaffected, investors who wanted to know the cost of options and derive their own earnings number now could do so.

ent families—those with household income of more than $100,000—the median stock portfolio was only $150,000. So the million-dollar portfolios that were glorified in the popular culture were limited to a very thin crust.

As the *New York Times* columnist Paul Krugman wrote, it's remarkable how little of the boom did trickle down. Despite the riches on Wall Street, those on the bottom, and also in the great middle of society, were essentially treading water. Median family income, adjusted for inflation, grew in the '80s and '90s by only a half a percent a year—and that only because many families were now sending two people to work.[20] In other words, the Americans who constituted the lower half—not the lowest tenth, not just the jobless or the people on society's margins but the lower *half*—librarians, checkout clerks, forest rangers, and so on, did not participate in the boom at all.

Despite its pretensions, America was becoming a far less egalitarian society than it had been before the market boom. By the mid-'90s, celebrity CEOs such as Sandy Weill of the Travelers (later Citigroup), Roberto Goizueta of Coca-Cola and Jack Welch of General Electric, and also a goodly number of lesser-known studs, were pocketing many tens of millions annually—in some cases, more than $100 million annually. Lawrence Coss, chief executive of Green Tree Financial, a little-known company that financed mobile homes, took a bonus in 1996 of $102 million. That was simply for that one year. The total was so hyperbolic—so weirdly excessive—as if greed were truly good, as if boards were hoping to induce not the work that greed might inspire but simply "greed," the Herculean compensation, itself. By 1997, CEOs on average were taking home *326 times* what a factory worker was making (compared to a ratio of 10 or 15 to 1 in Europe).[21] This did not even include their lavish pension plans, which were worth additional tens of millions and which, in many cases, rewarded CEOs for many more years of service than they had actually worked.[22]

· · ·

Once the accounting controversy was out of the way, boards felt freer to disperse stock options, and million-share awards—so-called megagrants—began to proliferate. In 1994, the year of Peltz's megagrant, only Enron's Kenneth Lay and a handful of others got comparable awards. But within a few years, dozens of executives were getting a million and then some.[23] Michael Eisner, in 1996, got options on 8 million shares. Henry Silverman, the CEO of Cendant, got 14 million. Bernard Ebbers, chairman of WorldCom, established what is, in this particular and most dubious category of self-enrichment, a world record; megagrants *five years in a row.* Even moguls such as Ted Turner, Sumner Redstone, Michael Dell, and Larry Ellison, who already owned billions of dollars of stock in the companies they had founded and/or built, claimed such monster grants. (Bill Gates, notably did not.) Such alms for billionaires suggested a mindless, or perhaps a conspicuous, flaunting—for what other purpose could they have? Jensen had feared that embarrassment would restrain the level of compensation; rather, publicity fed a gaudy competition to top one's neighbor.

In part, this was due to the faintness of any protest from investors, who of course were the ones paying the tab. With stocks moving ever upwards, people were not of a mood to rock the boat. In 1997, when CEO compensation vaulted 35 percent, the market gained 31 percent.[24] It was also the third straight year of better than 20 percent gains, so something for investors was going right. And investors were repeatedly advised that the market's ebullience was a direct result of the incentives given to executives. Indeed, the idea of setting any limit was heretical. When *Fortune* dared to question whether some level of pay could be "too high," the consultant Ira Kay, who ran the executive compensation practice at Watson Wyatt, took umbrage at the very thought. "The minute you ask that, you damage the market,"[25] he replied, a comment that presumably did not displease his executive clients. Of course, the consultants, who were hired by friendly managers or directors, had little trouble discerning where their interests lay.

The press was remarkably gullible on this score, tending to treat pay consultants as impartial experts rather than hired guns. As late as 1999, *Forbes* wrote, "there is plenty of evidence that seven-figure pay is in line with free-market value for executive talent," a strange comment in that *Forbes*'s own list of top earners were making *eight* and *nine* figures, not seven, and that the corporate boardroom where pay was determined was anything but a free market.[26] The flaw in corporate governance, visible in the Depression and ever since, had never been mended. Directors were simply too cozy, too conflict-ridden. And when it came to setting the boss's pay, the shareholders were inadequately represented and ill informed, except in the case of some of the big institutional shareholders, who had yet to show even a modicum of interest in corporate governance. So Jensen's notion of a market for CEO services was illusory. The market for welders, druggists, and journalists was brutally efficient, but the same could not be said of the market for CEOs.

For an incentive to function properly, there must be a prospect of pain as well as gain. Jensen knew this, but he missed the point that the huge scale of option profits trivialized the possibility that, in some future year, pay might be withheld. In any case, it rarely was. Bonuses and other cash payouts established, in effect, seven- or eight-figure floors. CEOs adopted the pose of risk-takers, but they were sheathed in a golden cocoon and reimbursed for every conceivable expense of living—financial planning, personal loans, entertainment, and so on. Frank Newman, of Bankers Trust, collected $1.1 million to relocate to New York, as if he were moving from the Arctic Circle rather than, in fact, Washington, D.C.[27] There were, for so many others, sumptuous apartments, pampered travel in whispery jets, European art, and gilt-edged retirements.

At a more fundamental level, CEOs' incentives were distorted by the problem alluded to earlier, namely, the frequency with which options were dispersed. Jerry Sanders, the wealthy founder of Advanced Micro Devices, took options in 1994 at a price of 26⅞. As he had ten years in which to exercise them, it might have been supposed that his options would alleviate any urgency he felt about his personal portfolio. However, two years later, when the stock plunged, Sanders grabbed 2.5 million more options, this time at a price of only 14¾. Similarly, when Cendant, a franchising company, made an ill-considered merger (its partner was cooking the books) and the stock plunged from $40 to $7, Henry Silverman, the CEO responsible for the deal, simply helped himself to millions of new, much cheaper options—an opportunity not available to the shareholders who had paid $40.

CEOs with up-and-down records became bizarrely wealthy thanks to their ability to sow annual crops of options and harvest them over short-term intervals. Increasingly, they were permitted to start peeling off profits from ten-year options after only the first year. This severed a crucial link, because over the short term a stock's performance may be wholly unrelated to business performance. Moreover, because of the lopsided scale of awards, executives who were successful early in their careers amassed fortunes that far, far, eclipsed their performance over longer time frames. A case in point was Disney's chief, Michael Eisner, who in the '80s had been a celebrated success. Disney's gains continued in the '90s—for a while, anyway. From the start of the '90s to the end of 1997, the stock practically quadrupled, from approximately $8½ to $32. That was when Eisner cashed in an extravagant option package worth $565 million, believed to be an all-time record. Thereafter, Eisner continued to pocket hefty sums, but the business—and the stock—went into a prolonged slump. Disney's shares ultimately fell to $16, wiping

out much of the profits for his shareholders that were the supposed justification of his personal take. Over the entirety of the '90s and the first
three years of the new millennium, a thirteen-year-stretch, Eisner collected more than $800 million, during which time his investors earned
less than a Treasury-bond return.[28] Never has a CEO reaped such a fortune from such prolonged mediocrity.

As the examples of Sanders, Eisner, and many more attest, CEOs
were rewarded for success over discrete intervals but went unpun-
ished for failure. Under such conditions, a gambler would bet on every
horse he could. And that, essentially, is what CEOs began to do. Normally, before embarking on an investment, a businessperson tries to cal-
culate both the possible gain and the potential for loss. The fear of losing
is the cutting edge of the Invisible Hand, for it restrains society from
overinvesting. But the Hand had been deformed by the easy money
from options. Since CEOs had nothing to lose, they began to make increasingly risky bets—with their shareholders' capital, of course. This
was especially true for the CEOs with the most stock options. World-
Com's Ebbers and, as we will see, his peers in telecommunications, were
prime examples. From the mid '90s on, telecom execs, larded with millions of options, began to invest enormous sums in the highly speculative premise that revenues would skyrocket virtually forever. The
deluge of options simply corrupted their personal calculus.

From the executives' point of view, even an investment that ultimately failed could bear juicy fruit, for as long as the market was temporarily enthused, the executives would have time aplenty to reap their
personal harvest. And what executive, with his or her power to talk to
the media, to Wall Street, and so on, could not incite at least a brief excitement in the stock? Linda Wachner, the formidable CEO of Warnaco,
the apparel company, harvested $16 million in pay, in addition to cashing

a previous option package worth $76 million and receiving a fresh megaaward, all in 1998.[29] By then, Warnaco was already on a path to bankruptcy (and the stock was on a path to zero). Similarly, Stephen Hilbert made $170 million while he was running Conseco, a company he left in tatters and which in 2002 filed for bankruptcy.[30] As the bull market rolled, executives who reaped eight- and even nine-figure rewards were legion; the money stuck but not necessarily the stock prices on which the rewards had been based.

As dubious as was the connection between performance and pay in cases where, at least, some fleeting success was registered, it was thoroughly sundered in the numerous cases in which failed CEOs were shown the door with tens of millions of dollars to ease their paths. Frank Newman of Bankers Trust ($100 million), Jill Barad of Mattel ($50 million), and Douglas Ivester of Coca-Cola ($25 million), were examples.[31] It is hard to think of any other society in which failure pays so well.

Why, then, did the outsized awards keep coming? We have spoken of the "entitlements" of the CEO, and the phrase has a pejorative ring, for it is usually applied to welfare payments and the like. But the truth is that, aside from those with inherited wealth, CEOs in the '90s became not just a gilded class, as Krugman argued, but the most entitled class in America's history. They were less like Adam Smith capitalists than Soviet bosses, promoted to a rank where plunder was a privilege. Warmed by the adulation of markets, the notion that CEOs deserved to be paid for performance morphed, quite simply, into the notion that they should be *paid*. They were as if ennobled. When Kodak granted two million options to George Fisher, in 1996, his second megagrant in three years, the board explained that it had extended Fisher's contract—*for two entire years*—as if his every waking hour was a precious resource.[32] So lordly was the CEO, so scarce his presumed talents, no sum for his services was considered too great. Disney awarded Eisner a bonus even for the two years following his eventual retirement, as if to spare him any sordid financial cares for his truly golden years.[33]

A kind of reverence drew around the CEO, even a kind of cult—a deference that owed to their lavish compensation and also contributed to it. CEOs were rich because they had raised their stocks; the money was a token of their power, of their vaunted talent to move markets. Executives of a previous generation, including Sloan, tended to be understated and faceless. They were the men in the gray flannel suits, the businessmen who to the noncorporate world oozed an insufferable dreariness. Now, they were vigorous, sporting—exuberant in the manner of football coaches—and, of a turn, public personae. In 1980, *Business Week* had published but one issue with a CEO on the cover. Now, chief executives were household names. Seemingly whole forests were razed for the publication of CEO biographies, CEO memoirs, CEO how-to manuals, and even collections, Chairman Mao–style, of CEO quotations. And CEOs strove to be as visible as possible; they flocked to appear on CNBC and to engage the public, for they knew that, ultimately, their power came from the stock price.

It became common to speak of how much an individual CEO had raised "his" share price—as if General Electric had not two hundred thousand employees but only Jack Welch, as if Eisner had not inherited the library of Disney cartoons but had personally drawn them. Investors, board members, security analysts—began to believe that these executives were titans, capable of whatever target was articulated, any transformation. CEOs became the role model, the highest aspiration for an American, the embodiment of the national mission, as becoming president or fighting communism was in an earlier day. They had the arrogance that once was government's, jetting from their crystal palaces to wherever a contract beckoned with a retinue of handlers, vice presidents, and aides-de-camp. They spoke on darkened stages, waltzed through slick presentations. They were pampered and attended to; their calendars kept, their time carefully apportioned. When they donated to charities, they were feted at black-tie dinners; they joined the boards, saw their names emblazoned on the walls of hospitals, galleries, music halls. They dined in private rooms, vacationed in restricted settings, spoke to private audiences (what did reach the public was carefully filtered by corporate spokesmen). Their employees deferred to them, tensed when they approached, breathed deeply when the boss moved on. It was not for CEOs to share the pain—to suffer a pay cut when workers were sacked, when profits slumped, when share prices fell. Nor did they offer any apologies over their unseemly pay. Tony O'Reilly, the CEO of Heinz, declared of his stock options, "There could be no more honorable or fairer way in American capitalism." Shortly after, O'Reilly stepped from a blue Bentley to a white pavilion set up by the swanky Leopardstown racetrack near Dublin, where a crowd of Heinz people, assorted politicians, and fellow tycoons smilingly awaited him.[34] It was a pleasant summer's day in 1997, the festivities undarkened by the news in Pittsburgh, Heinz's hometown, where the company was in the midst of laying off 2,500 workers. Since the start of the '90s, O'Reilly's company had managed to increase its earnings at merely one-third the pace of its closest rival, Campbell Soup. Its once-blazing stock was now distinctly mediocre. Yet O'Reilly, an Irish-born, globe-trotting bon vivant, had pocketed $182 million during the previous six years, and he had just received yet another monster option award. He had stuffed his board with subordinates, beneficiaries of his philanthropy, and long-time friends, one of whom, Donald R. Keough, a former Coca-Cola president, was to remark, "Tony is larger than life, and he knows it." This comment was more sage than it might appear. If anyone had propagated the cultish dimension of the CEO, it was the CEO himself.

FOUR

Number Games

The standard for shareholder value was set by Jack Welch. He came from Salem, Massachusetts, a tough, hot-headed son of a Boston & Maine Railroad conductor who had, as *Fortune* magazine described it, a primal need to win.[1] He laid off so many people that his own son was once beaten up by the son of a man he had fired. That was Neutron Jack. A chemical engineer who hadn't been able to get into an Ivy League school, he started his career, in 1960, in plastics in General Electric's facility in Pittsfield, Massachusetts, and within a year he was so frustrated by the company's bureaucracy he nearly quit.[2] Two decades later he was CEO. General Electric, a sprawling conglomerate with assets in everything from locomotives to refrigerators, was a company where, as Welch described it, tradition meant everything. To Welch, tradition meant nothing. If a business wasn't first or second in its industry or didn't have a good chance of getting there, Welch unloaded it. This knocked GE for a loop. In fact, it upset bureaucracies all over the country. In 1981, corporate America was in its dark days. Welch was a perfect antidote. With Welch in charge, no Japanese *keiretsu* would overtake General Electric. The thing about change, Welch declared, was that it never stopped.[3] You kept inventing, kept redefining. It would be hard to think of a philosophy more attuned to the market—to shareholder value. By the '90s quite a few other CEOs wanted to be like Jack, too. Year after year, *Fortune* named him its most-admired CEO. The magazine ran glowing articles just for the purpose of letting Jack talk about how he did it. His annual reports, artful sermons on the beauty of a "boundaryless" company, on defeating bureaucracy wherever it lurked, on retaining the soul of a small company inside of a big conglomerate, inspired generations of managers.

Welch and his underlings collected plenty of stock options, and few executives made more of their incentives than GE's did. In a ten-year stretch, Welch earned $400 million in salary, bonuses, and options—an extraordinary fortune for a hired hand.[4] Most of it derived from the rise in GE's stock. Over Welch's entire two decades as CEO, adjusting for later splits, GE's shares rose from $1.20 to roughly $50. How did Welch orchestrate such a phenomenal rise? First, he cashiered businesses he deemed unattractive, even the division that made GE's famed toasters, and redeployed their capital into more profitable businesses, such as broadcasting and financial services. Second, he demanded relentless improvement in the quality and productivity of the businesses that he did keep. His unceasing focus on profits helped to raise GE's reported earnings eight times over.

But if GE's earnings rose eight times, why did its stock rise *forty-two times* over the same span? Why were investors now willing to pay five times more for a dollar of GE's earnings than they had been in the past? That was what analysts really meant by shareholder value—getting a higher value in the stock market. And nobody did that better than Welch.

The secret of GE's perennially rising stock was not just the growth of

its profits but the consistency of its growth. Through war, through recession, through market crashes, its bottom line kept growing. In fact,
GE's earnings from continuing operations rose a phenomenal one hundred quarters in a row.[5] Investors gladly paid for that consistency. It
saved them from sleepless nights, from having to analyze the company
themselves. They could simply rely on Jack.

Welch liked to talk about "stretch," meaning imposing seemingly
impossible targets on managers and getting them to deliver. He also
talked about making growth consistent—"with no surprises for investors."[6] Of course, the businesses that GE managed had plenty of surprises. Every business does. Over the years, Kidder Peabody, GE's
brokerage unit, took a billion-dollar loss. GE Capital, its huge financial
arm, suffered numerous hits to its portfolio. GE's turbine business was
ever riding up and down with the cycle of aircraft manufacturing. The
list could go on and on.

But you wouldn't know it from GE's smoothly rising bottom line.
GE was said to enter every quarter with a specific profit goal in mind—
and to do "everything in its power" to make the number, regardless of
whether its actual performance turned out to be better or worse.[7] The
idea that a company has discretion over its reported earnings might
sound strange. Companies never announce earnings of "somewhere between 50 cents and 60 cents a share"—they announce a single figure as
though it had been chiseled in stone and was beyond the power of management to influence.

But in fact, modern accounting is as much art as science, and one is
allowed a great deal of discretion in deriving the earnings for any one
quarter. To take a simple example, when should a company recognize
revenue—when it ships a product to a store or when the product is sold?
For that matter, when *is* it sold—when the customer orders or when he
pays? And if the customer buys on credit, when should the retailer con-
clude that the loan is bad—and if so, how much of the receivable should

be written off? These and a hundred similar issues yield to judgment, not to an absolute answer.

This doesn't mean that anything goes. The object of accounting remains to present a true economic picture of the underlying business and to permit useful comparisons of earnings from year to year and from company to company. Auditors may honestly differ, but if a product is stacking up in the warehouse, the numbers ought to reflect it. Otherwise, disclosure is worse than meaningless—it's misleading.

Unfortunately, as corporate activities became more complex, the range over which auditors could invoke their discretion widened. Stephen Key, an accountant and later the chief financial officer at both ConAgra and Textron, recalls that when he entered accounting, in 1968, it was possible to read the entire rulebook in a day. At recent count, however, the rulebook had grown to 4,750 pages. "When you have 4,750 pages," Key explained, "you start salami slicing. The rules become a cookbook."[8]

One way GE used the cookbook was to adjust the reserves that GE Capital maintained against problem loans, adding to the reserves in strong quarters so as to save income for a rainy day and reducing them in weak quarters, when the income was "needed." GE Capital was so complex it was considered a black box to outsiders, even those who were financial experts. In any given quarter, depending on the assumptions it made about its multitudinous assets, loans, and derivative deals, GE Capital could report almost whatever earnings number it pleased.[9]

Naturally, bad news could not be put off forever. But whenever GE suffered a major loss—say, from a restructuring—in one part of the empire, Welch inevitably found an unusual gain in another part. And these offsetting items always seemed to occur in the same quarter. For instance, in 1999, GE booked a huge paper profit from selling assets to its Internet baby, NBCi. Instead of reporting the extra profit, GE used the occasion to add to reserves, giving it a cushion to draw on in the future.

The following year, GE Capital took a $200 million charge when one of its borrowers, Montgomery Ward, filed for bankruptcy. GE offset the loss by selling part of its stake in the broker PaineWebber. The size of these onetime items could be substantial.

None of these maneuvers was illegal, and any of them might have been adopted for the right reasons. But in the aggregate, they helped to depict a business that was inherently rife with the normal business fluctuations as preternaturally smooth. It suggested that when Welch's efforts to win were insufficient, he ordered his managers to prettify the scoreboard, much to the betterment of his stock options.

Moreover, Welch, like other CEOs, used the pension plan to significantly inflate reported income. In an economic sense, pension plans are a black hole. By law, once money goes into a plan it can never be used for the benefit of stockholders. Nonetheless, the plans can be used to create an *appearance* that is favorable to the stock. When pensions earn a surplus, the parent company can book a credit to its earnings, the size of which is highly dependent on management's assumptions. At GE, which relied on such adjustments to keep its earnings streak going, about 10 percent of the profit reported to Wall Street was actually money safely locked in the pension plan that neither Wall Street nor shareholders could ever touch.

Robert Friedman, a certified public accountant with the rating agency Standard & Poor's, deconstructed GE's earnings by stripping out gains from its pension plan, adding a tiny charge for stock options, and netting out the gains and losses from unusual items. The result was what Friedman termed core earnings. As you would expect, core earnings were a lot lower than reported earnings—over six years, anywhere from 1 percent to 20 percent lower. They also grew at a slower rate. Most interesting, perhaps, is that GE's core earnings didn't grow smoothly at all. One year they grew 39 percent. Another year they fell

4 percent; in another, 8 percent.[10] This is not as desirable as a steadily rising slope—it just happens to be how business in the real world works. People do not increase their consumption of every product and service by identical increments in each twelve-month interval.

Friedman didn't publish his findings until after GE's shares (as well as the market generally) had lost their luster, but the thrust of his argument was well known before. In 1998, SEC chairman Levitt gave an impassioned speech at the Stern School of Business at New York University, warning that the reporting of corporate earnings had become "a numbers game." Levitt blamed the zeal of managers "to satisfy consensus earnings estimates and project a smooth earnings path." What's more, he said, "trickery is employed to obscure actual financial volatility," and not just by smaller companies. "It's also happening in companies whose products we know and admire."[11] As a government official, Levitt didn't name names, but it's a good bet that GE was on his list. In the private sector, though, GE was anything but scorned for managing earnings. Indeed, Welch was admired for it. Executives *wanted* that steadily rising slope and, given the structure of their option packages, they certainly wanted the stock price that went with it. The long boom, the yawning sense of a modern Babylon, of a world of easy profits without accountability, was eroding people's standards. Though deception was at the core of creative accounting, the ethical distinctions of another generation were being whittled away.

Almost unnoticed, executives who played number games became less candid with their investors. Their moral basis was undermined. Executives who consistently relied on accounting contrivances to sugarcoat their results came to respect the process less, and ultimately, they respected the shareholders less. At times, their contempt was plain. Al Dunlap, the cost-cutting executive at American Can, Scott Paper, and Sunbeam, glorified his supposed concern for shareholders in a bestselling book, *Mean Business:* "The most important person in any company is the shareholder. I'm not talking here about Wall Street fat cats. Working people and retired men and women have entrusted us with their 401(k)s and pension plans for their children's college tuition and their own long-term security."[12] While his concern for pensioners, university students, and other investors seemed touching, at Sunbeam, an appliance maker, Dunlap coldly betrayed them. According to an SEC complaint, the "revenue growth" that Dunlap reported to investors was actually achieved by "stuffing the channel," meaning that he was secretly offering huge discounts to get dead inventory out the door. He also established phony "cookie jar" reserves to inflate profits. Sunbeam filed for bankruptcy in 2001, and the shareholders were wiped out.

More commonly, accounting artifice encouraged, if not outright fabrications, a more casual relationship with the truth. Corporate disclosures—which, it bears repeating, are the heart of America's system of governance—became tainted by a cynicism in which companies resorted to legalisms. They reported results in a way that was lawfully permissible as distinct from a way that would openly answer the question that Mayor Ed Koch used to ask of himself ("How'm I doin'?").

IBM was asked by various news organizations about its practice of lumping onetime asset sales with administrative expenses, which had the effect of making it appear as though its costs, which Wall Street watched closely, were lower than they were. The computer giant replied that its accounting was "within the letter of accepted industry practice" and was "fully compliant with regulatory standards."[13] One wants to groan. What dedicated employee would defend a misleading entry by telling the owner that he was "fully compliant" with government standards? The more it played the game of touching up the numbers, the more IBM forgot what shareholders were—owners who deserved its complete candor. And it was hardly alone.

. . .

As Levitt feared, number games were becoming a pervasive part of the culture. The total of companies forced to restate earnings because of accounting errors rose from a handful a year in the early '80s to more than 150 a year by the late '90s.[14] And restatements only scraped the surface; most companies, including IBM, were clever enough to manipulate the numbers without running awry of the rules. Microsoft flattened its results by deferring (until, presumably, a rainy day) billions of dollars in revenue. PepsiCo resorted to the well-known artifice of a "big bath"—a one-time charge that would enable it to report higher quarterly earnings in the future.[15] According to an intriguing study, the number of companies that either met or just topped their previous quarter's earnings far surpassed the number that fell just a penny or two short—a result inconsistent with mathematical chance.[16] In other words, many companies were, like GE, doing some "stretching" to meet the numbers.

Lucent, thought to be one of the fastest-growing big companies in America, was using every revenue-enhancing trick imaginable. The context is important, for the pressures at Lucent were felt, to a varying degree, at most other companies as well. In the three and a half years following Lucent's spin-off from AT&T, in 1996, its stock rocketed from $9 to $75. Lucent was the toast of the country's market subculture, a must-own for institutions and parlor investors alike. In retrospect, Lucent wasn't growing at all—it was only managing the numbers to keep up with Wall Street's spiraling expectations. In various calendar quarters, Lucent booked revenue from Third World customers that had scant ability to pay, then boosted income by reducing its allowance for doubtful accounts even when its receivables were sharply *rising*, changed its pension plan assumptions, resulting in huge reported profits, and took a multibillion-dollar bath enabling it to reduce depreciation and inflate profits later.[17] Lucent's incoming chairman, Henry Schacht, was so alarmed by the company's accounting that, late in 2000, he warned a group of fifty senior managers that Lucent had moved "uncomfortably close to the edge of respectable behavior."[18] In fact, it had moved well over the edge and had to restate its results.

But executives had no reason (other than whatever sense of ethics) *not* to move to the edge because, typically, the SEC did not catch up with corporate miscreants until many quarters later—if ever. In the meantime, the stock price would benefit from the appearance of earnings. And, significantly, an executive who exercised options and sold stock prior to a restatement was almost always able to keep his gains. Virtually all accounting cases were resolved by civil suits, not criminal prosecutions. The lack of an effective deterrent, combined with the perverse structure of options, meant that, the rhetoric of pay for performance notwithstanding, many executives had an incentive to cheat.

It is hardly a coincidence that they increasingly broke the rules in the late '90s. As with Lucent, scores of companies had seen their stocks soar, meaning that executives suddenly had tens of millions of profits embedded in their options. But options do not vest at once; typically, executives may exercise only a portion every year. And underlying growth, especially in high technology, had begun to cool. For executives with unexercised options, keeping the stock high for as long as possible became an urgent concern. The problem, as a chastened Jensen later reflected, was not that options hadn't worked to motivate but that they had worked too well.[19]

As companies became more anxious to avoid offending Wall Street, their disclosures became less transparent. In particular, the growing use of private contracts known as derivatives made their finances harder to decipher. Generally, in such deals, companies agreed to exchange streams of cash that were derived (hence the name) from the performance of other indicators, such as interest rates, the value of the euro, and so on. This enabled banks, corporations and others to transfer virtually any risk without having to make the usual balance-sheet disclosures. Moreover, companies could book the ups and downs of their derivative deals into earnings well before the contracts expired, which greatly enhanced their ability to rely on estimates and, indeed, to fudge. As Frank Partnoy, a former derivatives salesman, observed, the regulations on how to account for derivatives considerably lagged the ability of practitioners to work around them.[20] Thus, one upshot of the derivatives revolution was that annual reports grew steadily thicker, yet a careful reader understood less and less about the companies behind them.

A related development was that, by the late '90s, most public corporations were using so-called special-purpose vehicles, often for the avowed purpose of shielding assets and obligations from public view. These special vehicles—or SPVs—were something like the side pockets of a wallet: they were stitched to the main purse but were legally separate.

Companies might use SPVs to free up capital (by shunting some of their assets into other compartments) or to reduce their costs—a totally legitimate function. Many companies could get better credit terms by borrowing against a circumscribed portion of their activities—that is, the activities in just one section of the corporate wallet.

For example, a retailer such as Kmart might borrow against its credit card receivables, securing a loan against the money owed to it by customers. To arrange such a borrowing, Kmart would sell its receivables to a distinct legal entity—the SPV, which was a partnership created just for that purpose. After the transaction Kmart will have cash, but it will no longer have an asset (the credit card receivables) on its balance sheet.

Other companies created SPVs more for this latter purpose—to take assets off the balance sheet, in the hope of making their shares seem more attractive. Dura Pharmaceuticals, for instance, used an SPV to move the cost of research and development off its books, so that investors saw only the benefits of selling drugs, not the burden of developing them.[21] The line between substance and window dressing became increasingly murky.

Beginning in the late 1980s, the SEC and also a few maverick accountants began to worry that SPVs were being abused. It was simply too easy to use SPVs to mask one's true appearance; indeed, to some degree, that aim was implicit in every such vehicle. Walter Schuetze, a partner at KPMG, one of the big accounting firms, especially voiced concerns. Naturally, this did not make Schuetze's clients happy. Citicorp, KPMG's biggest client, observed that Coopers & Lybrand, among other accounting firms, was perfectly content to let clients account for SPVs as they wished. This suggests the problem for honest auditors: the client can always shop around for another accountant—one more willing to provide a rubber stamp. Thus, on the matter of SPVs, Schuetze, who later became the SEC's chief accountant, warned the agency that unless regulators quickly established a rule, each of the Big Eight would attempt to win clients by adopting a more lenient approach than its rivals.[22]

FASB, the accounting board, did fashion a rule in 1991. It decided, reasonably enough, that for an SPV to be considered independent, some party unrelated to the parent corporation had to invest in it. In other words, if Kmart was going to claim that its credit card receivables no longer belonged to Kmart and therefore should be off its books, there had to be some other, independent party that *did* own them.

But how much independent ownership was enough? Clearly, the lower the standard, the more deals companies could do. By the early '90s, banks were organizing scores of SPVs with only 3 percent equity. In other words, if Kmart wanted to sell $100 million of receivables, a Merrill Lynch or a Citicorp would arrange for an SPV to borrow $97 million and then find a private client who would invest the other $3 million. The big accounting firms thought 3 percent was plenty for independence. (Of course, their clients were the ones doing the deals.) Lynn

Turner, the ranking accountant at the SEC, protested. "Gee," he said when alerted to the 3 percent standard, "that doesn't sound like a lot of equity to me." Turner followed up with a letter urging a tougher standard, but the accountants ignored it.[23] And by the mid '90s, billions of dollars of corporate America's assets had been shunted into thousands of SPVs and had, from the point of view of public investors, disappeared. More ominously, the SPVs had become largely invisible even to their creators. In 1994, Citicorp undertook a survey of its off-balance-sheet activities. It was shocked that the total amounted to $45 billion, more than the total assets of all but a handful of banks.

One of the most clever practitioners of off-balance-sheet financing was the thirty-seven-year-old chief financial officer at Enron, Andrew Fastow. In 1999, *CFO Magazine* gushed that Fastow had pioneered "unique financing techniques" to transform a once sleepy pipeline company into a multifaceted trading company.[24] That was not quite accurate—Fastow was an adapter more than an innovator. But he was typical of the new breed. Traditionally, the CFO's job had been held by accountants. They were glorified controllers, who balanced the books and made sure companies had the liquidity to operate.[25] Fastow, like many of his peers, was an MBA, not a CPA. He was an ambitious strategist who focused on enhancing earnings and raising the stock, not a curmudgeonly, old-style number cruncher.

Fastow managed to reduce the debt that was on Enron's balance sheet, thereby raising its credit rating, while Enron was simultaneously *doubling* its asset total. In plain terms, Enron was remaking itself into an enterprise at once riskier in fact and staider in appearance. This was thanks to Fastow's adroit use of SPVs. "Our story is one of a kind," he boasted, little suspecting how right that remark would prove to be.[26] In 1999, Fastow won one of *CFO Magazine*'s prized Excellence awards, one of which had gone the previous year to WorldCom's Scott Sullivan. In 2000, the magazine honored Tyco International's Mark Swartz.

That all three winners were eventually indicted testifies to Wall Street's weakness for (too-) clever financiers. And it hints at a serious problem with creative accounting: it can lead to outright violations and fraud. Few corporate miscreants set out to break the law; more often, they are guilty of a trifle bit of fudging, which they attempt to cover temporarily, much like the bank teller who borrows a few dollars with every intention of promptly repaying it. In finance, alas, the fudged earnings report, like the goosed-up revenue number, raises—not lowers—the temptation to cheat again, for the prettified quarterly result raises the bar for the next quarter. Moreover, the CFO or CEO who becomes accustomed to stretching becomes, with experience, habituated if not hooked, and the subtle distinctions between managing earnings and fraudulently distorting them are apt to be ignored in his increasing desperation to satisfy the Street.

The incestuous dance between public corporations and Wall Street, a curious facet of late-twentieth-century capitalism, became, like the arcane rituals of some ancient religion, highly routinized in the latter '90s. Executives developed an obscure language to forecast results. Usually, this was in the form of private guidance to security analysts, who by a series of questions, prompts, and other genuflections, were able to forecast precise earnings-per-share numbers for the ensuing quarters. These practitioners became less like true analysts than clerks, a transition that was strangely accompanied by a vast increase in both their profiles and their bonuses.

It has often been noted that analysts were too conflicted to weigh in with negative judgments. The analyst who covered General Electric for, say, Merrill Lynch, was compensated in part on the basis of the banking business that GE brought to Merrill. And GE was more inclined to seek an underwriter whose analyst had spoken kindly of it. This conflict had, as we will see, damaging repercussions. But there was another, equally important factor in eroding the analyst's mission.

The increasing focus on the short term made real research all but irrelevant. Wall Street has always been a place of fleeting passions; this time its myopia infected the general shareholding culture as well. As the public infatuation with stocks mounted, the incessant national chatter became a dull thunder, a frenzied conversation over the fate of every stock, the outlook of each next trade, that stretched from backyards to brokers' offices to, increasingly, the Internet. And the more prices rose, the more investors went on alert. They invested more, but they trusted less; their time horizon shrank. They were concerned not with the longer-range prospects of a business but with whether it would make its next quarter. This was the age-old virus of public markets, but in the '90s—thanks to the country's passion for stocks, to technology, to the faster pace of life, perhaps—the virus became epidemic. Let a company miss by even a penny a share and its stock would sink by 10 percent, sometimes by 20 percent. As it happens, a true analyst is better equipped to appraise the medium-term future in rough terms than he is to forecast the here and now with precision. He may know that Microsoft's products and prospects for the coming years look bright; he cannot predict with exactitude its earnings for the next quarter. For that, he needs guidance from the company. So analysts were gradually transformed into dutiful reporters who traded on their closeness to the CFO.

Executives deluded themselves into thinking that the analysts who relayed their outlook to the Street performed a useful service. In reality, it entrapped them. Making the publicized estimate became the executive's only goal, and CEOs adapted their policies to whatever would produce the quarterly number. This was by no means a formula for long-term, or enduring, shareholder value. Nortel Networks was a disastrous example; under the pressure of analysts' expectations, it acquired nineteen companies between 1997 and 2001 in a quest to transform itself from traditional telephony to data networking. The stock steadily climbed—until investors realized that Nortel had issued $32 billion in stock for largely worthless assets—whereupon Nortel's stock collapsed from $80 to $2.[27]

The effect of the game on divisional managers was, if anything, more insidious than on CEOs. As Michael Jensen, who was increasingly skeptical of the pay for performance culture he had championed, later wrote, most line managers realized that the budget process was "a joke"—it had been tainted by the desire of senior managers to impose a high target. Welch's notion of stretch, also referred to as stretch planning, had been widely adopted. Division managers were commonly told to forecast optimal results so that the CFO could publicize the most optimistic forecast to Wall Street. Thus, Jensen said, the line managers ". . . go to a lot of meetings, scope the extent of their problems, submit budgets they know will be unacceptable, then scramble to redo budgets to reflect the new level of earnings stipulated by senior management who are, in turn, driven by the earnings game . . . with Wall Street analysts."[28] The angry title of Jensen's paper, "Paying People to Lie," suggested the impassioned extent to which this historically sympathetic scholar felt betrayed by corporate executives.

It is common to suppose that investors were merely victims of managers who massaged the numbers, but, in fact, their relationship was symbiotic. We have used the term game, and the game was played by both sides—corporations and investors, especially professional investors, such as mutual funds. In fact, these investors *wanted* the numbers that were disclosed to them to be managed; in some sense, they wanted to be misled. None would have phrased it that way, of course.

But investors knew that when GE's earnings rose in lockstep or when Pepsi contrived a big bath, gamesmanship was involved. And their reaction, inevitably, was to bid up the stock. They happily bought numbers that had been doctored for their collective benefit—numbers for the sake of numbers often profoundly at variance with the economic substance. Investors had been conditioned—even indoctrinated—by the likes of CNBC to invest on such a basis. The anchor people treated each jot of corporate news, each incremental bit of data (no matter how short term) as profoundly significant. And investors, being greedily focused on the short-term price action, were generally more concerned with how the other investors who they knew were also watching would react than with the intrinsic merits.

In April 1997, an analyst at Oppenheimer, Roy Burry, wrote that Coca-Cola had "absolute control over near-term results," meaning through the end of the following year.[29] On its face, this seemed preposterous. The drinks had yet to be poured; the economic and climatic conditions that inevitably affect soft-drink sales could not have been known. What *was* known was that Coca-Cola, which had been managing its growth around an 18 percent to 20 percent target, was committed to delivering the right numbers regardless. Investors considered this a good thing.

What was worse—or more venial—was that the mutual fund managers stood to profit even if Coca-Cola didn't ultimately pour those drinks—that is, even if its stock eventually retreated. For in the interim, the fund would rise, and the fund promoters would hawk their performance numbers to attract more investors.

It was, of course, to the detriment of investors that mutual funds traded into and out of stocks so rapidly—because the investors were stuck with the higher tax burden that results from short-term sales. But it was not to the detriment of mutual fund managers, because their results were reported, and generally evaluated (by Morningstar and such), on a pretax basis. This reinforced their tendency to speculate.

In the case of high-growth stocks, particularly in technology, the cycle became fatally self-reinforcing. Fund families such as Janus, Van Wagoner, and Putnam would stuff their portfolios with Cisco, Qualcomm, JDS Uniphase—the hottest stocks—which purchases would drive the stocks and thus the fund prices higher. Thanks to the innumerable newspaper surveys of mutual funds, which reported performance by the month, investors were ever aware of who had the hot hand; moreover, top-performing fund managers—Paul Wick of the Seligman Communications & Information Fund, Jim McCall of PBGH—were only too happy to grant an interview to the readers of *Barron's* or the viewers of CNBC. No sooner did word of their success filter out than their funds attracted more capital, which the managers used to buy still more of the favorite and already overpriced stocks and keep the cycle going. And so to return to the question of whether a company had doctored its earnings—such chicanery would not be manifest for so long (presumably, not until after the fund managers had cashed their bonuses) as to be of less than immediate concern. Indeed, it was not in the narrow self-interest of such momentum-minded managers—who were really more like brokers in investors' clothes—to see an earnings number questioned; a conspiracy of silence served them better.

The conspiracy thus gained a dangerous momentum; from the vantage of corporations it was hard to break. "It would be better if we could go back to where the focus was on long-term performance," Paula Norton, vice president of investor relations at Terra Industries observed, as if speaking of the rituals of a long-lost civilization, "but we're expected to manage to the penny."[30] Managers became trapped in expectations of their own making. Ultimately, of course, investors did become their victims.

One company that consciously imitated General Electric's numerical consistency and, in a fashion, raised it to an art form, was Tyco International, a little-known conglomerate with assets in butterfly valves, fire alarm systems, medical equipment, and a hodgepodge of much more. Its chief executive, Dennis Kozlowski, was often said to be another Jack Welch and, like Welch, Kozlowski was a self-made executive. He was raised in the tough Central Ward of Newark, New Jersey, the burly son of a news reporter and boxer turned investigator and political ward heeler (Kozlowski frequently misrepresented his father as a police detective, a fib that suggested that, unlike Welch, Kozlowski was not above resorting to outright falsehood.[31]) Jonathan Laing, a usually skeptical writer for *Barron's,* hailed him as a paragon of efficient management and pay-for-performance who admirably resisted spending on perks, such as first-class air travel, country club memberships, and the like.[32]

From the time Kozlowski became CEO, in 1992, until the end of the '90s, Tyco's earnings rose at an even smarter pace than GE's, thanks to Kozlowski's proficiency in acquiring and, it was said, improving lackluster companies. Over eight years, in fact, Kozlowski made no fewer than two hundred acquisitions.

Acquisitions have always held a mystique for the would-be builder of an empire. The new acquirer of a business, instantly expanding his domain by a degree that would require years if left to normal operational growth, is apt to feel a surge of adrenaline, an effusive giddiness. Managing an existing business day to day is often tedious, all toil and detail; a fresh acquisition is as light as first love.[33]

After the business is acquired, the honeymoon is apt to be short. Whatever the problems were that dogged it before—after all, something drove the previous owner to sell—these ills will most likely reappear.

Soon, the acquired business begins to feels old, and the CEO begins to yearn for rejuvenation—perhaps, indeed, for another acquisition.

But whatever the complications mergers pose in fact, they offer unique opportunities on paper, in particular to those adroit in the art of accounting. A big acquisition can blur the comparison between this year's numbers and last; management can thus paint the picture as it chooses. Further, new management often takes a charge against the acquired unit—which, as we have seen, will provide a shot in the arm to earnings down the road. In the hands of an executive with a high-priced stock, mergers are a veritable elixir. The stock can be used as a currency, and each acquisition tends to add to earnings, perhaps levitating the share price further still. The game was a kind of alchemy, but a manager as astute as Kozlowski had to know that it never goes on forever. Thus, he began to manage the numbers with a heavier hand than his idol at GE. In May 1999, Tyco agreed to acquire Raychem, an electronics manufacturer, for $2.9 billion. Immediately, Tyco ordered its soon-to-be subsidiary to accelerate the payment of any bills, add to its reserves, and execute similar maneuvers to depress Raychem's cash flow and profitability before the acquisition date. The next year, the depressed profit could be recaptured, and to all the world it would appear that Tyco had magically fixed yet another new business.[34] This is known as spring-loading.

Tyco did it again when it acquired CIT, a commercial finance company. In its last five months as an independent outfit, CIT earned $81 million. Then, in its first four months under Tyco, CIT earned $252 million—a sensational increase, except that it was stage-managed by Tyco, which ordered CIT to book a massive provision for credit losses before the closing. Tyco's spring-loading was investigated by the SEC and resulted in no action, even though an independent analyst deemed it "one of the most startling examples of financial engineering you can hope to find."[35]

Alas, spring-loading, like any form of earnings management, provides merely a temporary fix, a onetime boost to earnings. The next quarter, Tyco would need yet another shot, hence its desperate pace of acquisitions. In the late '90s, Tyco crossed an ethical line, ordering dealers for ADT Security Services, one of its subsidiaries, to venture into drug-infested slums and sign up any customer with a pulse, without regard to his ability to make payments. "Tyco kept pushing. They wanted numbers," a manager with ADT told *The Wall Street Journal*. "They didn't give a crap if the accounts fell off the books later."[36]

The legality of such tactics, borderline at best, is almost besides the point. Tyco had become engaged in a pattern of deception that enabled the executives, through their options and performance bonuses, to profit at shareholder expense. A moral line had been crossed. The later disclosures of massive looting by Kozlowski and his underlings was merely a fuller blooming of the corruption that its deceptive accounting nurtured.

Xerox was a more conventional case, in that executives did not resort, as far as is known, to criminality. The copier maker, based in a bucolic, twenty-five-acre setting in Stamford, Connecticut, had had a long history of disappointments. It invented the technology for the graphic interface—the mouse—but failed to exploit it. It was asleep to the threat from Canon, its Japanese rival, which captured the low end of the copier market. It was late to grasp that office PCs would stimulate a demand for small desktop printers. It let Canon get a foothold in big corporations—once Xerox's exclusive turf—by being the first with a digital copier. However, in 1997, Paul Allaire, the chairman and chief executive since the early '90s, promised that Xerox was, finally, turning around. The stock began to revive, much as it was rising at Lucent, where Allaire was a director. At Xerox, Allaire consistently encouraged Wall Street, and he did not seem to realize the perilous nature of their tango.

The next year, 1998, Xerox made a change in the way it accounted for equipment leases that added $250 million in pretax income over the

next three years. In the scale of things, the effect was modest. It accelerated revenue, as distinct from creating it.* However, in reporting its results, Xerox did not disclose that it had made the change.[37] Meanwhile,
on the strength of Xerox's "turnaround," Allaire pocketed $6 million
plus a quarter of a million stock options. In 1999, Xerox made its earnings number only with the help of a onetime sale of receivables—which,
again, was not clearly disclosed.[38] But that seemed to suffice for traders.
By early 1999, Xerox's stock had doubled, and management was por-
traying itself as a resilient role model for recovering industrial titans.
(The front page of *The Wall Street Journal* approvingly asserted, XEROX
RECASTS ITSELF AS FORMIDABLE FORCE IN DIGITAL REVOLUTION.[39])

In fact, its sales were under pressure from more nimble competitors,
and executives were increasingly concerned. Xerox's receivables and inventory had risen to worrisome levels by the end of '98, suggesting that
customers were becoming slow to buy and even slower to pay.[40] Allaire's real appraisal of Xerox's turn may be glimpsed by the fact that, in
February 1999, he unloaded 24 percent of his stock.[41] Privately, Xerox
officials spoke of "closing the gap"—the chasm between the stretch
targets it imposed on divisions and the results the divisions actually
achieved.[42]

Allaire, who briefly relinquished the CEO's job but remained chairman throughout the period, could have admitted there was a gap, but
that would have been like stopping a dance in midnumber—too abrupt,
too likely to alienate Wall Street. And, no doubt, he still believed, or at
least greatly hoped, that the turnaround would come—eventually. But
the fund managers were so insistent—so impatient. In the meantime,

---

*The accounting issue is simple. If a customer leases equipment, its future payments may be sorted into two
types: money related to the equipment's value and money for service and supplies. (Somewhat analogously,
a mortgage payment includes money for both principal and interest.) Accounting rules stipulate that the les-
sor—Xerox—can recognize the first stream of payments immediately, as if the machine had been "sold" all
at once. But payments for servicing and for paper, ink, and so forth may be recognized only as delivered.
What Xerox did was to increase the portion of revenue booked immediately.

Xerox merely wanted its bean counters to close the gap.[43] The second fudging was easier than the first, the third time easier than the second. Thus, Xerox would resort to accounting tricks—the term was used at headquarters—in eleven of twelve consecutive quarters. Meanwhile, the execs were calmly unloading more than $30 million of their personal shares.[44]

In 2000, Xerox continued to lose ground to Canon and suffered a loss. What's more, it revealed that it had a problem with unpaid bills in Mexico—one that Stamford, over the objection of local managers, had previously suppressed.[45] Xerox depicted the problem as localized and insignificant. It fired some workers in Mexico, hoping to depict the trouble as the work of a few rogue *empleados*. But bad numbers started to pop up in other territories as well.

Then, an assistant treasurer, a fifteen-year veteran named James Bingham who had been doing some quiet sleuthing, warned his bosses that the problem was systemic. Xerox, he said, had been inflating revenue by improperly accounting for leases, using reserves to spike future profits, and otherwise misstating results. Bingham said the problem stemmed from a "win-at-any-cost" mentality at headquarters—not from Mexico. His immediate superior, the company treasurer, was unresponsive.

Bingham then directed an e-mail to the company's chief financial officer and president. He was ordered to "destroy" the e-mail. When this language became public, a spokesman called it an "unfortunate selection of words." In fact, it was an honest expression of management's anxiety over the slow unraveling of its cover-up. Finally, Bingham met with senior executives and presented his findings. Two days later, he was fired.[46]

Despite the serious criticisms Bingham had leveled against management, Xerox's board did not bother to debrief him.[47] As we have seen, directors were culturally disinclined to question management and were often conflicted. Two of the directors, George Mitchell, the former senator, and Vernon Jordan, the Washington lawyer and political insider, served on, respectively, seven and twelve boards. The notion that they could have the time—much less the desire—to seriously monitor management was a joke. Mitchell and Jordan were there for the $75,000 stipend, in return for which management got well-known, and dependably supportive, directors. We may also appreciate that Paul Allaire, the Xerox chairman, who happened to be chairman of the audit and finance committee at Lucent, may not have been the best possible person to push for rigorous accounting there.

In 2001, as Bingham had predicted, Xerox did modestly restate its results. The company's public pronouncement sounded oddly celebratory. No "fictitious" entries had been found—any mistakes, it asserted, had been inadvertent. Once again, Xerox predicted a speedy return to profitability. But the steady growth in computer printers was cutting into the market for copiers and, for the third year in a row, Xerox's revenues were falling.

The odd fact about cooking the books is that a day of reckoning always comes. In retrospect, one always wonders, "What else *could* they have expected?" Xerox's outside auditor, KPMG, began to balk at the company's accounting. KPMG got the same treatment as Bingham; it was fired. By now, the SEC was on the trail. In 2002, the SEC charged Xerox with massive accounting fraud, which the company did not contest, and of having "misled and betrayed investors." The SEC levied a $10 million fine, the biggest penalty ever in an accounting case. It detailed many of the abuses alleged by Bingham, emphasizing that they were often "approved, implemented, and tracked" by senior management. Techniques to accelerate revenue and other undisclosed practices accounted, in some periods, for 30 percent of Xerox's reported profit.[48] Thus, Xerox was forced again to restate its numbers, this time for a period of four years. Meanwhile, the stock had cascaded from $60 all the way to $6.

. . .

Allaire retired, having pocketed $10 million in additional compensation (since the aforementioned $6 million) and, incredibly, with a fresh load of options, priced at $4.75—a bargain that became available only because of his failed stewardship. The new CEO, Anne Mulcahy, was a twenty-five-year insider who had been on the scene throughout the company's attempts to deceive investors. Mulcahy continued the pattern of dissembling by belittling the settlement with the SEC, saying that Xerox was "best served by putting these issues behind us."[49] Wayward souls seek redemption through contrition; wayward corporations are taught to sidestep responsibility. Mulcahy did not discuss the issues that Xerox was putting behind it; she did not admit that they arose from management lies and distortions and, indeed, from a culture of lying at headquarters. Just so, executives up and down the Fortune 500 played their number games to the inevitable and bitter end. They had been trained by lawyers and accountants; they had been schooled by the culture not to communicate openly with the shareholders whose very name they invoked with each new transgression.

FIVE

Doormen at Noon

The first chairman of the SEC was Joseph P. Kennedy. The gregarious son of a Boston saloon keeper and Democratic Party activist, Kennedy had amassed a fortune running the stock department for Hayden Stone, an investment firm. He claimed to have earned his money in administrative work, "not in market operations," which was as bald a fabrication, the historian Joel Seligman has pointed out, as his subsequent assertion that he had "no political ambitions" for himself or his children.[1] In fact, Kennedy had made much of his money running pools, the Jazz Age term for the shadowy rings that manipulated stocks at the expense of small investors. This was precisely the sort of activity that the new SEC, launched in the Depression year 1934, was intended to prevent. New Deal reformers were stunned by his selection, but Franklin Roosevelt laughed them off, joking, "Set a thief to catch a thief."[2] The president rightly figured that Kennedy, having already made his money, would be more interested in earning public respect than in protecting old friends on Wall Street.

Kennedy's task was to establish the SEC as a lasting watchdog, one that would endure after the market revived and after the public's memory of the Crash faded. To appreciate the challenge, one has to recall how radical the SEC was considered. Wall Street, led by the chairman of the New York Stock Exchange, Richard Whitney, huffed that *any* regulation would preclude markets from raising capital—grass, as they said, would grow on Wall Street. This was more than idle criticism; investment bankers had effectively gone on strike against the new agency, and in 1934—admittedly, it would have been a slow year anyway—underwriting ceased.

The Democrats' control of Congress and the public's disenchantment with Wall Street gave Kennedy a mandate, but his approach toward the bankers was conciliatory. In his first address as chairman, he reassured Wall Street: "We of the SEC do not regard ourselves as coroners sitting on the corpse of financial enterprise."[3] He pushed the Street to work with the agency, an endeavor that benefited from the common perception (which the chairman did nothing to discourage) that Kennedy was an intimate of Roosevelt. Kennedy also recruited a glittering group of lawyers, including William O. Douglas, a future SEC chairman and Supreme Court justice.

Respect came slowly, but it did come. The SEC was generally able to police Wall Street without sapping its vigor or distorting free-market incentives. After World War II, when business revived, even bankers came to acknowledge that markets were benefiting from the reassurance the agency afforded to the public. Its main tool, recall, was disclosure, and as one observer has noted, transparency is the American way, "an eleventh commandment of American life generally, not just of financial markets."[4] During the Eisenhower years, none other than the Stock Exchange lobbied for an increase in the SEC's staff—a recognition that Wall Street could survive, even thrive, under the glare of a tough-minded regulator.[5] In short, the SEC was the very rare New Deal institution that retained both its relevance and its luster.

Arthur Levitt Jr. was, surprisingly, only the second of Kennedy's many successors to hail from Wall Street.[6] A fluky coincidence was that Levitt, who had joined a small retail brokerage in the early '60s, had risen to be president of Shearson Hayden Stone, the successor to Kennedy's old firm. Raised in Brooklyn, Levitt was the son of a longtime, highly regarded New York State comptroller. Not unlike Kennedy, he had an easy charm that suited him for politics. He also had experience with Wall Street's avaricious side. Levitt had seen firsthand that brokers' recommendations were often conceived with their commissions—not their customers' accounts—in mind. Indeed, Levitt had been complicit in such behavior.[7] This triggered a latent reformist impulse. In the late '70s, he quit his firm to run the American Stock Exchange, which he used as a pulpit on behalf of small investors. (Shearson was left to the eager hands of one of Levitt's original partners, Sandy Weill.) Levitt's success in raising money for Clinton in 1992 won him appointment as SEC chairman the following year.

Initially, he focused on individual shareholders. With millions of new investors having entered the market, Levitt was worried that many would not appreciate the risks inherent in investing. Thus, he directed mutual fund companies to rewrite their disclosures in plain English. Also, he ended the collusion among Wall Street dealers, thereby lowering expenses on the Nasdaq shares that small investors favored. An instinctive politician, he held a series of "town meetings" with investors around the country.

However, as their portfolios swelled, investors became less interested in fine-print warnings from Washington. Inevitably, Levitt began to focus on the flow of information on which the little guy—whether he knew it or not—depended. The SEC began to examine more closely the auditors who prepared the corporate reports, the board directors who monitored them, and the security analysts who interpreted them. Each of these groups may be thought of as essential gatekeepers who exert a check on the system. But many of the gatekeepers were, as we have seen, conflicted, and as the bull market progressed, they were less gatekeepers than doormen. Levitt became increasingly concerned about what he termed the "unholy alliance" of executives, accountants, and bankers.[8] In retrospect, his eight-year tenure was an exercise in trying to force or cajole each of these gatekeepers to live up to their statutory, and also their moral, responsibilities.

Though initially tame, Levitt turned out to be a harsher critic of his industry than Kennedy. But Levitt did not have Kennedy's mandate. For one thing, markets were on a roll, and bankers, being human, are naturally reluctant to submit when times are flush. Driving at thirty miles an hour a man accepts the speed limit without hesitation; at eighty miles per hour he yearns for freedom. Unfortunately, this is when regulation is needed most. History has shown that Wall Street is most apt to cross an ethical line when seven-figure bonuses abound. But good times are precisely when the public is least interested in regulation. And Levitt's political support was minimal. Clinton had entered the White House with a long agenda, ranging from health insurance to campaign reform (neither of which he achieved); securities regulation was well down his list.

After the Republicans won control of Congress in 1994, Levitt was effectively marooned. Unlike in the '30s, Wall Street could point to its recent record with pride and argue that, but for the dead hand of Washington, it would be growing all the faster. The next year, Congress (overriding Clinton's veto) enacted a law to discourage shareholder lawsuits. The law extended a new layer of protection to executives and also to their accountants—even those who had signed misleading reports. Its effect was magnified by two U.S. Supreme Court decisions in the early '90s, one of which shortened the statute of limitations on securities fraud and the other which ended implied causes of action for aiding such offenses.[9] Fueling the permissive climate, the Justice Department showed little interest in prosecuting cases of accounting fraud, which was not considered a major problem.

These developments gave executives, accountants, and corporate lawyers a general sense that the risks to themselves had diminished.[10] Veteran investors detected a new swagger in the executive suite. As the fear of lawsuits receded, executives grew cocky. A Stephen Wiggins (of Oxford Health Plans) would boast of great results to come, brazenly sell his stock, then coolly admit to a devastating problem within the company.[11]

On its face, restricting the freedom of shareholders to sue argued for greater regulatory supervision. So did the surge in households that owned mutual funds (from 5 million in 1980 to roughly 50 million by the end of the '90s). The swelling army of individual investors, virtually all of them novices, was especially vulnerable to deceptive marketing, phony reporting, and other abuses. This argued for giving Levitt more staff, not less. But congressmen and their sugar daddies on Wall Street saw it differently.

By summer 1995, Congress was awash in proposals to reduce the scope of regulators, freeze the budget of the SEC for five years, eliminate some of its commissioners, and reduce disclosure requirements. Stephen Blumenthal, Republican counsel to the House Commerce Committee, fulminated that SEC regulations made it "frighteningly expensive to raise capital."[12] This was the black scare from the 1930s—grass growing on Wall Street—strangely resurrected during a boom. The very day Blumenthal raised the alarm, Netscape Communications, an Internet company with a sensational product—a browser for surfing the Web—but with only two quarters of sales history and no profits, went public. Demand for its shares was so hot that Morgan Stanley, the underwriter, was fearful of inciting a panic. Scott Sipprelle, the young head of the syndicate desk at Morgan, urged Netscape's CEO, Jim Barksdale, to show some restraint in pricing the shares, though he acknowledged that, given the animal spirits on Wall Street, it would be up to Barksdale—not to the buyers—to keep the price reasonable. "Jim—You're at the senior prom. Your date is drunk," Sipprelle noted. "Whether you're a gentleman is up to you." [13]

The public, if not yet drunk, was certainly giddy. In Levitt's maiden year, investors had purchased a then-record $60 billion of initial public stock offerings. As the boom picked up steam, the agency gradually became overwhelmed by the growing burdens of vetting IPOs, of monitoring Internet trading, and of scrutinizing ever more complex disclosures. During Levitt's tenure, investor complaints grew at a clip of 13 percent a year; staffing at only 1 percent a year. [14] Budgetary pressures on the agency were truly crippling. Just when its vigilance should have been mounting, the SEC had to lengthen the cycle of corporate reviews, from every three years to every six. The practical implications were telling: Enron, whose annual report was reviewed in 1997, would not be due for another checkup until well into the next millennium. [15] But in an era of such faith in markets, government shortcomings were generally ignored, as were Levitt's pleas for deputies. Like Gary Cooper in *High Noon*, Levitt was the unloved marshal, abandoned just as the fearsome Miller gang saunters into town.

In his first years, Levitt had a tendency to compromise. Over time, sensing he had little to lose, he grew more forceful. In particular, he waged a series of battles aimed at what he termed the "dysfunctional relationships" on Wall Street. [16] As was clear, even then, most securities analysts had become shills for their firm's clients, a fact made plain by the almost complete lack of sell recommendations. Their role was really

that of promoter. The analysts could be seen at plush investor confer-
ences touting client stocks like carnival barkers. CNBC and *Wall Street
Week* were forever asking analysts to reveal their top picks to viewers,
few of whom were aware of the inherent conflicts. Salomon Smith Barney raked in tens of millions in underwriting fees from companies that
had been touted by its aggressive telecommunications analyst, Jack
Grubman. Asked if that mightn't pose just a tiny conflict, Grubman
shrugged: "What used to be a conflict is synergy now."[17] Of course, it
wasn't synergistic for investors—only for investment banks. Buy recommendations were handed out like golf trips or other business favors.
Shareholder value, supposedly the analyst's prime concern, had become
tainted by cronyism and greed.

As Levitt understood, all too well, the system was *designed* for
cronyism. Analysts were not rewarded for being right, so few tried to
be. "There is little payback for doing research," as one said. "There is
no incentive."[18] Consider, for a moment, the singular report on Oxford
Health, then a hot stock, by a little-known analyst named Ann K. Anderson. "Sell," the report fairly shouted: "Signs of Trouble Ahead."
Anderson had seen worrisome discrepancies between the numbers that
Oxford filed with state insurance regulators and those it disclosed to investors. However, all of the twenty-nine other analysts who followed
Oxford were bullish. Uniformly, they ignored Anderson's report, and
the stock, then $67, continued to rise. In the fall of 1997, Oxford re-
vealed serious internal problems of the nature suspected by Anderson,
and the shares fell from $76 to $23 in a day. Tellingly, Anderson worked
for an independent money manager, not a broker or underwriter.[19] In
other words, of thirty analysts, only the one whose firm was not conflicted saw fit to publish a negative conclusion. That did not seem like
coincidence.

But what could the SEC do about it? It was not a crime to be wrong
about a stock, and to prove that an analyst was *intentionally* misleading

would be exceedingly difficult. Levitt tried to prod television executives to inject a little balance into their financial shows but got nowhere. That is not their business. He suggested that Wall Street's self-regulatory body devise a code of conduct for analysts and was, similarly, rebuffed.[20]

The one lever at Levitt's disposal was in the area of disclosure. Executives, as we have seen, routinely confided in analysts, who frequently leaked to favored big investors. Even execs who disliked this little game often went along, feeling essentially extorted. Adam Smith had recognized that chicanery flourishes under cover; so, on Wall Street, illegal trading must often have resulted from private chats. Stocks all too often moved in *advance* of company news, evidence that pros were acting on tips.

In 1999, Levitt proposed a Regulation Fair Disclosure to require companies to disclose to the public whatever material information they disclosed in private.[21] Though individual investors naturally favored the idea, Wall Street loudly protested. Henry Paulsen, the chairman of Goldman Sachs, called Levitt from China to urge him not to promulgate the rule.[22] He, and others, argued that Reg FD would stifle executives from talking at all. The flow of information would cease, increasing volatility. This concern is worth a little pondering. When a CEO whispered to an analyst, the news would get out to certain select investors and the stock would gradually respond. If the same CEO simply issued a press release, the stock would adjust all at once. On that day, it would indeed be volatile—an entirely appropriate response to a news flash. The absence of a gradual adjustment hurt only the pros, who were deprived of their opportunity to profit (at the public's expense) along the way. Insiders were so accustomed to being tipped that they lost sight of its essential unfairness. George Gilder, a doctrinaire supporter of markets, complained that *all* rules against insider trading stifled the inherent desire of information to "bubble up"; information, he intoned, "wants to be free."[23] Of course, Gilder, who published a technology-stock tip sheet, was precisely the sort of insider who was in the loop of analysts and company conference calls. And when Reg FD was adopted, the conference calls did not stop; they were simply opened to the public, leveling the field. The reform hardly turned analysts into objective sleuths, but it moderated the unseemly interchanges among analysts, corporations, and quick-fingered pros.

A more harmful lapse in the gatekeeper function involved the corporate director. Here, too, the SEC had little authority. The rules that govern boardrooms and also the internal affairs of corporations are mostly a matter of state law, a relic of the regionalism of the nineteenth century. In practice, Delaware, Nevada, and the rest competed to see which could write the most notoriously lenient rules—what one former SEC chairman aptly termed a "race to the bottom."[24] And public companies—regardless of where they did business—simply incorporated in states where the rules were sufficiently lax. By the late 1960s, it had become obvious that statutes written for robber barons were irrelevant for multinational corporations and that corporate boards were failing to provide real supervision.

Two episodes drove this home. In 1970, Penn Central, the nation's sixth-biggest industrial company, collapsed. Its directors were practically the last to learn of the railroad's troubles, a not uncommon state of affairs. *Dun's Magazine,* in words that seem to prefigure the later Enron affair, observed, "The sad case of Penn Central is worth mentioning, not because it is unique, but because it is not. Many another U.S. corporation has gotten into trouble because its directors did not do what they were supposed to do—that is, keep a warily inquiring eye on management, and ask the right question at the right time."[25] Then the Watergate investigation led to a series of corporate scandals involving payoffs to politicians and bribes of foreign officials.

Suddenly, everyone from Ralph Nader to law school professors were proposing federal laws to reform the boardroom. No one disputed that directors had been derelict. On most boards, directors did not even get the information they needed had they wanted to exercise a check. Nor did the independent directors meet in any systematic way and behind closed doors to review the managers under their charge. But one must remember, most directors were picked by management from old boy networks. As Seligman observed, management slates ran unopposed 99.8 percent of the time and were elected 99.9 percent of the time, majorities that would have been the envy of political candidates of that era in Moscow, Warsaw, or Prague.[26]

Successive heads of the SEC demanded reform; the Achilles' heel of shareholder democracy, its weak directors, was, it seemed, finally to be mended. But the SEC never took the crucial step of offering legislation. The agency had always been chary of overstepping its turf—especially in the forbidden zone of governance. Whatever the reason, the impetus for reform died, and the deficiencies in the mahogany jungle continued to fester.

So Levitt had to pick his target with care. A good candidate would be the board's audit committee, which is responsible for making sure that management reports the numbers cleanly. However, on many boards, the committees included members of management or perhaps the CEO's lawyer or banker—monitoring themselves, as it were. Some of the audit members were unqualified in another respect—their utter lack of financial expertise. (At the risk of making a point by hyperbole, the audit committee of Infinity Broadcasting once included O. J. Simpson.[27]) Most committees subjected the books—and the auditors—to at most a casual, even a perfunctory, review. At Cendant, in the year before a massive accounting fraud was uncovered, the audit committee met but once. The compensation committee met four times.[28] Not surprisingly, given the weakness of audit committees, accountants thought of themselves as working for management, not for the board—and certainly not for the shareholders.

Lacking direct authority over boards, Levitt decided to put pressure on the New York Stock Exchange and Nasdaq.[29] After agreeing to study the issue, the exchanges tightened their standards for listed companies. They clarified that outside auditors reported to the audit committee of the board—not to management. And they demanded that committees question not just the technical accuracy of the numbers but also the spirit of a company's disclosures. These were substantive changes. But as they were adopted only in the final month of the 1990s, their impact would not be felt until after the boom's peak.

Audit committees hinted at Levitt's most urgent concern: the accounting industry itself, which *does* fall under SEC jurisdiction. Over eight years, he and the industry waged a running and often heated battle. Their conflict reflected a disagreement over how to interpret America's financial prosperity. To the accountants, rising stocks were proof positive the system was working; to Levitt, they began to suggest deception of epidemic proportion. Some of their skirmishes concerned the proper way to account for specific transactions, such as mergers and, of course, stock options. Others were over the larger issues of independence and oversight. Ultimately, the disputes cut to a question at the profession's heart: whose interests did accountants serve?

We have noted the alarming rise in companies that were manipulating results, especially with big bath losses or (à la Lucent and Xerox) improper revenue recognition. But the outside auditors' willingness to endorse such tricks seemed to bother Levitt even more. As he wrote in a memoir of his chairmanship:

> I came away from these back-channel brawls with one overriding impression: accounting firms were passive when it came to standing up for investor interests. It wasn't surprising that chief financial offi-

cers would fight for standards that let them understate expenses and exaggerate profits. But I was shocked when I saw how the auditors behaved. . . . They had become advocates.[30]

In fact, the accountancy—the most essential gatekeeper—was a changed profession. In some ways, profession was no longer the right word. Beginning in the 1980s, the industry had undergone a fierce consolidation (by a series of mergers, the Big Eight became the Big Five). In their thirst for revenue, firms turned to consulting, a fertile field that grew with corporations' increasing need for help with computer systems and so on. The change was especially pronounced at Arthur Andersen where, in 1989, the partners organized consulting as a separate, though mutually owned, business. Andersen Consulting became considerably more lucrative than auditing, and the auditing side soon rebelled by launching its *own* consulting practice, hoping to leverage its relationships with auditing clients. In the industry, consulting grew to 51 percent of the accounting firms' revenues, up from 13 percent at the beginning of the 1980s.[31]

Meanwhile, auditing seemed a diminished craft. The number of high school students planning to major in accounting dropped precipitously, from 4 percent at the beginning of the '90s to 1 percent at the end.[32] And no wonder: Big Five firms were hiring starting CPAs at merely $35,000 a year. The prestige business schools, awash in future consultants and investment bankers, didn't even bother to train CPAs, considering the profession beneath their dignity.

As traditional auditing business took a backseat, accounting firms metamorphosed into, in effect, sales organizations. Their partners keenly understood that while you can audit a client's books only once a year, there is no proscribed limit to proffering advice. And consulting was simply sexier. The changes in the accounting industry's mission, even its self-image, were palpable on the cover of Arthur Andersen's marketing literature, known as its highlights report. Published in 2000, it featured an Andersen partner in a black leather jacket, his knees straddling a red Ducati motorcycle. The partner had helped Ducati design a Web site. Noticeably absent in the report were images of people at Arthur Andersen doing any accounting.[33]

The big firms still did audits, but it was discount work. Scrutinizing the books—the business on which their venerable reputations had been based—became a hook for becoming intimate with the client, the better to pitch consulting work. The American Institute of Certified Public Accountants, the industry trade group, made this plain in a manual that it bluntly (and crassly) entitled, "Make Audits Pay: Leveraging the Audit into Consulting Services."[34] Individual auditors who did not generate consulting fees (like securities analysts who failed to generate investment banking business) were consigned to the slow lane. A partner and veteran auditor in the Buffalo office of Ernst & Young was dispatched to training classes to learn how to drum up consulting work. Then, he was ordered to fulfill a quota of consulting revenue from the companies whose books he scrutinized.[35] It was degrading—like a priest being told to solicit donations in the confessional.

Although the firms denied it, auditors that performed extra services for an audit client were in effect taking a payoff. Few clients understood this as well as Waste Management. In the early '90s, Waste Management told Arthur Andersen, its auditor, that it was capping the fees it would pay on audits. However, Waste officials added, Andersen could earn additional fees by performing "special work"—an almost transparent invitation to acquiesce in cooking the books.[36] And from 1991 to 1997, while Andersen performed $7.5 million of audit work for Waste Management, it raked in $18 million from consulting.[37] This was not atypical; according to a survey, public corporations were paying their auditors close to $3 in consulting fees for every $1 of audit work.[38]

. . .

Andersen's auditors frequently objected to the way that Waste Management calculated its income. Disagreements between auditors and audited are inevitable—even healthy. However, Andersen believed that the trash hauler was systematically, and improperly, eliminating or deferring numerous expenses to inflate reported profits. The company refused to depreciate the value of its aging garbage trucks, for example, and similarly suppressed many other costs.

But when Andersen objected, Waste Management officials insisted on sticking with their numbers. As a sop to its compromised accountant's conscience, Waste Management offered to write off its accumulated errors over a period of ten years, thus repaying the "borrowed" earnings in small, unnoticeable increments. Incredibly, Andersen agreed to this blatant scheme, which was codified in a secret document known as the Summary of Action Steps. Publicly, Andersen certified Waste Management's disclosures as conforming to generally accepted accounting principles (GAAP).[39] The student of human behavior will not be shocked to learn that the corrective Action Steps were never implemented. However, in 1998, Waste Management, under pressure from the SEC, announced the biggest restatement of earnings—totaling $1.43 billion—in history.[40] Three years later, Andersen was charged with "knowingly or recklessly" issuing false and misleading audit reports and was fined $7 million.

The difference between Waste Management and, say, Xerox, is that Waste Management's accountants, those leather-jacketed fellows at Arthur Andersen, *knew* that its client was breaking the rules. And it is impossible to believe that Andersen's fervent desire for consulting dollars had no effect on its willingness to acquiesce on audits.

The year after the Waste Management restatement, in 1999, Levitt floated a proposal to ban accountants from selling many types of consulting services to their auditing clients.[41] It sparked an all-out war—an eruption in Levitt's long-simmering conflict with the accountants. The industry unleashed a barrage of letters, phone calls, lobbying, and none too subtle arm-twisting. Among those who protested was Kenneth Lay, chairman of Enron, who wrote Levitt that his company, a diversified and as yet still solvent energy concern, had benefited from the expertise of its outside auditor, Arthur Andersen, in areas beyond "traditional financial statement . . . work."[42] Andersen and others in the industry hired high-priced lawyers, who made ready to sue should the SEC go ahead. Meanwhile, an industry white paper disputed the need for any controls. Its author was Harvey Pitt, a Washington lawyer who represented both the industry and each of the Big Five firms and who, barely a year later, would be Levitt's successor.

Most of all, the industry spent bucketfuls of cash. It showered politicians with $10 million during the 2000 election cycle and spent an additional $22 million on lobbying.[43] The money was well spent. Incensed congressmen practically stormed Levitt's office to protest the threat to the beloved free market. Ultimately, they threatened the agency itself. Forty-six members from both sides of the aisle wrote letters. Senator Charles Schumer, a New York liberal, protested that the SEC would be "limiting auditing firms' expertise just when auditors appear to need it most . . . to assess today's sophisticated new economy companies." Actually, the SEC would not be limiting the volume of consulting work at all but simply unraveling the industry's conflicting strands, so that, for example, firms other than Arthur Andersen would now be free to consult with Andersen's audit clients and Andersen could go after theirs.

Representative Billy Tauzin, a Louisiana Republican, removed the iron from the velvet. Tauzin was so outraged by the SEC's interest in auditing that he threatened to hold hearings to determine if "the SEC's oversight of the accounting profession [is] warranted." Texas Senator Phil Gramm similarly warned Levitt that Senate Republicans were preparing a rider to the SEC's funding bill that would block it from implementing the rule.[44] As a result, Levitt relented and implemented a watered-down compromise that left the door to consulting with audit clients very much—if not completely—open.

Levitt's frustrations were indicative of a broad downsizing, to use a word beloved of CEOs, in the role of Washington. As *The Wall Street Journal* observed, in 1999, "the balance of power has shifted this decade in favor of the markets' rule."[45] Industries from energy to telecommunications to large areas of finance were being swiftly and reflexively deregulated. No one knew then, of course, that each of these epicenters of deregulation would be the site of a future debacle. But in airlines, which had been deregulated in the '70s, a precedent existed. Since deregulation, more than 130 airlines had filed for bankruptcy. And the problems of airlines were hardly an accident.

In industries capable of standing on their own, competition breeds variety and innovation and, thus, improved choices for consumers. (The fashion and software industries are good examples.) But in air travel, people don't want choices—they want reliable service. Airlines were less like software companies than "flying utilities;"[46] competition in the skies simply drove fares below the threshold of profitability. One might have seen a portent for telecommunications. Would a deregulated market really support scores of new telecom service providers? (Do *you* want two dozen ways to make a phone call?)

Such questions weren't asked in the '90s. The faith in markets was so rigid that deregulation was seen as ever on the side of the angels. People forgot that markets do not fulfill *every* economic purpose. If consumers wanted groceries with expiration dates printed on the label or cars that would be reliably safe, then, according to market purists, industry would provide them. In fact, the market wasn't that perfect. It didn't always hear. But a drumbeat of propaganda attributed unceasing miracles to the private sector while blaming its every lapse on Washington. Even in April 2000, when the Nasdaq finally began to slide, the writer James Glassman accused the government of "strangling" the new economy, as if only a Beltway bureaucrat could make a stock go down.[47]

This attitude was reflected in a pervasive mean-spiritedness toward government agencies. The Internal Revenue Service was, to be sure, never very loved, but during the '90s it was essentially handcuffed. Congress starved the IRS of funds and simultaneously enacted scores of tax law changes to safeguard the rights of taxpayers, which in practice helped many (usually rich) people avoid paying taxes and even avoid the scrutiny of an audit. This cost the Treasury billions.[48] Some members of Congress were surely interested in helping their wealthy constituents, but starving the IRS served a larger, more general antifederalist purpose. It was a de facto route to cutting taxes—to starving government itself. This attitude peaked in 1995, when Newt Gingrich, the Speaker of the House, threatened to trip the Treasury into default. Rubin, the treasury secretary, stopped him, but the antifederalist spirit remained entrenched on Capitol Hill.

The lone government organ that remained overwhelmingly popular was the Federal Reserve, thanks to Alan Greenspan's oft-demonstrated touch for soothing the markets. Just as CEOs were perceived to be responsible for their company's every result, Greenspan was said to be "in charge" of the entire economy, responsible for its long success and especially for the market's rise. Had it not been for Greenspan's concurrence, it is impossible to imagine deregulation moving ahead; with it, nobody worried, for it was assumed that no financial foolishness would escape his eagle eye.

But Greenspan was remarkably trusting. He was especially enamored of derivatives. To Greenspan, these innovative, off-balance-sheet contracts were a sort of do-it-yourself gatekeeper, for an entity that wished to reduce (or enhance) its exposure to the price of oil, or whatever, could do so seamlessly, by means of a pen stroke. The catch was that some other entity—the party on the other side—was conversely more exposed.

The private banks that dominated the derivatives industry fiercely lobbied against regulation, and their success demonstrated the too easy conduit that often existed between Washington and those it regulated. In 1993, just before Clinton took office, Wendy Gramm, the departing chair of the Commodity Futures Trading Commission and the wife of the Texas senator, signed an order exempting most private derivative contracts from regulation. The industry's appreciation may be judged from the fact that a few months later, Gramm was named a director of Enron, a big trader of energy derivatives.[49]

By 1998, these unregulated loops amounted to an astonishing $29 trillion.[50] No one reading a bank's (or GE Capital's) financial statement could hope to know how much risk it bore, and isolated derivative blow-ups, such as those of Procter & Gamble or Orange County, California, were occurring every year or so.[51] Regulators increasingly worried about the possibility of a major blowup.

However, Greenspan repeatedly sided with private bankers to inhibit controls and even to suppress disclosure.[52] In the spring of 1998, when a successor to Gramm at the Commodity Futures Trading Commission proposed a study—a mere study—to revisit the question of whether to regulate derivatives, Greenspan, along with Rubin, quashed the idea.[53] Remarkably, even after the hedge fund Long-Term Capital Management imploded at the end of that summer, prompting a rare Fed intervention and stunning markets (thus demonstrating that disclosure had been inadequate), Greenspan called for *lessened* regulation.[54]

The Greenspan-Rubin duo pushed deregulation on numerous fronts. Glass-Steagall, the Depression-era law that separated banking, insurance, and underwriting was erased at the particular urging of Rubin. Given the degree to which conflict of interest had become standard op on Wall Street, it was, to say the least, rather naïve to think that banks would not exploit the opportunity. J. P. Morgan was already pushing the envelope by extending loans to customers who might reward the bank with underwriting fees. As Joseph Stiglitz, chairman of the Council of Economic Advisers, later wrote, "One cannot simultaneously claim that it is important that banks be integrated, to take advantage of what economists call economies of scope . . . and also that it is important for the parts of a bank to be compartmentalized, to avoid any conflicts of interest."[55] After burying Glass-Steagall, Rubin left the government to become a senior official at Citigroup—a financial superconglomerate made possible only by Glass-Steagall's repeal. This is not to suggest that Rubin had engineered repeal for personal reasons—only that Rubin, like other government officials, lived in a world that was saturated by free market views.

Overseas, American officials became especially preachy about the wonders of the market. At meetings of the G-7 allies and such, U.S. representatives boasted that the U.S. economy was enjoying sustained, even unending, growth—which others could duplicate if only they, too, would adopt the American model. Greenspan declared that "only free-market systems" (meaning only America's) could satisfy human nature. Mort Zuckerman, a wealthy real estate developer and publisher, was even less subtle. In an essay in *Foreign Affairs,* Zuckerman forecast "A Second American Century." The London-based *Economist,* though generally admiring of America, was moved to protest America's "triumphalism": its "hubris" and "superiority."[56]

It had only been a decade earlier that the twenty-first century was said to belong to Japan, and even more recently to a newly unified Europe. But it is in the nature of people to ascribe a permanence to the latest trend, no matter how numerous the previous trends that have since collapsed. And there was no disputing that in the late '90s, America's economy was superior. Europe was stuck with high unemployment; Asia's various economies were successively imploding. America, meanwhile, was blessed with a holy trinity of high growth, low unemployment, and falling inflation. It was easy to overlook that the cronyism of which Asian capitalists stood so accused also ran rampant on Wall Street.

Feeling ever more smug about their markets at home, American officials put unrelenting pressure on developing countries to open their doors to the free flow of capital. A distinction here is important. Private *investment* is crucial to development, and it was not controversial. Free *capital flow* is something else. One relates to direct investment in factories, industry, and so forth. The other relates to trading, often short-term and speculative, in financial assets, including local currencies. Imagine that the United States had looked at the wheat fields of Argentina or the rice paddies of Thailand and declared, *"What you really need is a wheat futures exchange or a rice futures market,"* and you will not be far off. In other words, the United States wanted to turn their economies into the equivalent of overseas financial exchanges, with all the liquidity—and, also, the instability—of the stock market. This latter

approach *was* controversial. Various Clinton advisers, principally Stiglitz and Alan Blinder, feared that the likes of George Soros could place
such big bets that they would overwhelm local markets.[57] (Soros was
famed for having broken even the British pound.)

However, the Rubin approach, which was also the approach of the
International Monetary Fund and, of course, of American bankers,
prevailed. The market model was adopted. Capital flows were liberal-
ized, even in East Asian countries that, given their high savings rates
and long-lived booms, had no shortage of capital.[58] Speculators would
turn wildly optimistic over the prospects of, say, Thailand, and flood
the country with dollars. Mercedeses and BMWs careered through the
streets of Bangkok and real estate prices soared, giving the capital the
appearance of a nascent Houston. Factories were begun, skyscrapers
erected—far beyond the needs of the local economy. When this became
obvious, the short-term capital fled—for Brazil or for Russia or for
wherever was the next international miracle. The Thai baht was deval-
ued, the economy collapsed, unemployment soared. And the damage
was enduring. Even several years later, close to 40 percent of the loans
in Thailand were nonperforming and 2 million of its telephone lines
were unsubscribed.[59]

Currency crisis was, of course, an itinerant curse of the '90s, a monetary plague that was spread electronically by traders. It infected Britain
and Sweden in '92; Mexico and Argentina in '95; Thailand, Malaysia, In-
donesia, and South Korea in '97; and Russia and Brazil in '98. The common thread was a disconnect between financial speculation and business
on the ground—an exuberance of markets that overstimulated capital
investment.

When Asian markets buckled, Wall Street shuddered over the potential fallout at home. Headline writers (and also traders) nervously asked
if America would catch the Asian flu. But the question was misplaced.

The flu did not originate in Asia, and, in many respects, America had already caught it. True, the U.S. dollar was secure. But its soaring stock market was redirecting capital in amounts, and toward purposes—principally, the burgeoning Internet community in Silicon Valley—that, as in Bangkok and São Paulo, had no real basis in the working economy anywhere else on the ground.

SIX

New Economy,
Old Errors

It was in September 1998, just as the currency crisis in Russia was roiling markets, that eBay, the Internet auction king, went public. The stock was offered at $18. After a full day of trading, it closed at $47⅜. By year-end the stock was at $241. It strains credulity to report that eBay was trading at 1,800 times its previous year's earnings, but at least eBay *had* earnings. Nothing of the sort could be said for other Internet issues, such as theglobe.com, a tadpole of an enterprise begun by two twentysomethings who operated a Web site where people could build home pages. Theglobe had, over its nine months of existence, anemic revenue of only $2.7 million. Yet when it went public, that November, its stock was swept up by small investors. It soared from $9, the IPO price, to $97, within five minutes, at which point theglobe was valued at $1 billion. In all of the 1980s, there had been seven IPOs that had doubled on their first day of trading. In just the two months, November and December of 1998, there were seven more.[1]

The only person who had even a plausible chance of halting such an insanity was Alan Greenspan. In a speech at Berkeley, just up the freeway from Silicon Valley, the Fed chairman had observed that, as "Human nature appears immutable," soaring stock prices were not necessarily attributable to any miracles of the "new economy"; they could also be the product of "market bubbles."[2] Perhaps; had he acted immediately to prick the bubble?—but it was Greenspan's nature to trust the market. Even now, when the market was turning manic, Greenspan was reluctant to choke it off. It was his greatest error.

A mania may be defined as a mass refusal to acknowledge reason—even a mass *indifference* to reason. In the same week as Greenspan's speech, Jonathan Cohen, a securities analyst at Merrill Lynch, urged investors to unload shares of Amazon.com, the Internet bookseller. At Merrill, sell ratings were printed in salmon pink, a tone intended to convey alarm.[3] A functionary at Merrill, having never seen a pink report before, hurriedly called Cohen, demanding an explanation. Cohen replied, simply enough, that given Amazon's lack of earnings, its stock was too expensive. While Amazon's revenue was exploding, Cohen observed that bookselling, even on the Internet, was "an inherently competitive and low-margin business."[4] What's more, Amazon was being valued at $4 billion, twice the value of Barnes & Noble, a profitable concern with vastly higher revenues.

Nonetheless, over the ensuing three months, Amazon tripled. It was now, in mid-December of '98, a $12 billion stock, trading at $240. One price evidently being as good as another, Henry Blodget, a lesser-known competitor of Cohen's at CIBC Oppenheimer, predicted that within the year, Amazon would be trading at $400. At another time, Wall Street would have ignored such vacant prognostications, but with the Street in the grip of a mania, Blodget had the aura of a diviner. CNBC reported his forecast as if it were, indeed, news, and Amazon began to rise further. (John Doerr, the venture capitalist who had funded Amazon, ran to the trading desk, shouting, "Who the hell is Henry

Blodget?") Blodget, an affable history major at Yale and a former free-lance journalist, was not a financial expert. More nearly, he was a reader of trends. But even he had underestimated this one. For Amazon required not a year to reach $400 but a mere three weeks, after which Cohen was shown the door at Merrill Lynch and Blodget replaced him. Internet mania had now reached the stage in which people cease to think and simply imitate each other without any regard to the underlying economics—in other words, a bubble.

Investors had slowly traveled such a road since the mid 1980s. They had fallen in love with stocks—with the idea of stocks. They had looked past dubious accounting, bid up multiples of earnings, and come to confuse long-term business value with the nebulous, manipulable concept of shareholder value. By the fall of 1998, these sundry speculations had stretched, with nary a break, for eight long years. The Nasdaq index and the Dow Jones average had tripled over this period to, respectively, 1,720 and 8,000.[5] This steep ascent might have impressed upon investors the need for caution, but its effect was otherwise. If General Electric could trade at forty times earnings, who was to say what the limit was for Amazon? True, Amazon *had* no earnings, but in the wonderland of the late '90s, the lack of profits was a boon. It freed investors to speculate without the deadweight anchor of numbers; it allowed their native optimism to ripen into something larger and dreamier.

And the new economy was among the gaudiest conceits of American business. Though the name recalled the New Era of the late '20s, which had come to such grief in the Depression, it was as much a cultural phenomenon as a financial one; it followed in America's long tradition of utopian communities, social improvement schemes, and even religious cults. Technologists such as George Gilder did not deny that the new economy required a leap of faith; to the contrary, Gilder boasted of it.

To grasp the transforming power of fiber optics marked one as a visionary, whereas skeptics—the faithless—were "enemies of the future."[6] To doubt technology's promise, to insist on evidence one could see, was to insult the new religion; it was to be trapped in old-world precepts. Had Columbus seen America before he sailed?

Gilder conjectured not just a new economy but a new world, hyper-connected and irreducibly efficient, in which each of us would be forever downloading, by microthin optical fibers, any and all information onto wafer-sized computers. It was the stuff of a missionary, not a financial analyst. "Faith is central to every process of innovation," Gilder adjured. "The act of creation is a religious act," and "the investor who never acts until the financials affirm his choice [is] doomed to mediocrity by [his] trust in spurious rationality."[7] *Spurious* rationality. The Internet economy was something greater; it existed on a higher plane than the merely rational.

"By dissolving the inhibitions and obstacles, the blinders and ballasts of economic locality, the Internet will essentially make the globe transparent," Gilder wrote at the turn of the millennium. "In much the way Albert Einstein's theory of relativity transformed . . . classical physics . . . the Einsteins of Internet communications are now transforming the time-space grid of the global economy." So what if no one was making *money* on the Internet? What did the price-earnings ratio matter when it was stacked up against the time-space grid, against *Albert Einstein*?

Utopianism was distilled for the broader public by less highbrow writers, including two who unhesitatingly forecast (in 1999) that the Dow Industrials would reach 36,000, most likely in "three to five years."[8] To any protest that such an advance was illogical and without precedent, the authors of *Dow 36,000* chillingly asserted, "History can become tyranny."[9] The new economy, according to this popular and widely reviewed book, was outside of history. As the Nasdaq rocketed that year by a stunning 86 percent, such views permeated the financial mainstream. Merrill Lynch, which had once contented itself with analyzing balance sheets, explained its bullishness on technology stocks as follows: "The Internet revolution is allowing for creativity like never before, perhaps putting more of us in touch with the meaning of life."[10]

Wall Street had seen this—all of this—before. New products and technologies ever give rise to waves of enthusiasm—even utopianism. It is only human to get worked up over the wondrous technology, the life-saving drug, and this buoyancy can lead to fantastic assertions about the future. Daniel Pearl, a *Wall Street Journal* reporter with a flair for exploring fanaticism (he was a perceptive correspondent in the Middle East until, tragically, he was killed by Muslim terrorists in Pakistan) recalled at the onset of the Internet boom that the telephone, too, had spawned Toffleresque predictions of change. Similar to the "cyberhype" that Pearl noticed in 1995, people a century earlier had forecast that the telephone would connect the world: people would resolve their differences, barriers of class would fade, even local accents would disappear.[11] It was rather optimistic to speak of peace just then—and yet, it wasn't all hype. With mass communications and increased mobility, local accents *are* fading—albeit over centuries, not years. And the telephone probably did help to knit ordinary Americans into the middle class, even if the common factory worker cannot exactly dial up Donald Trump.

Where the hype was furthest from the mark was in assuming that revolutionary changes in *society* would produce a parallel success for shareholders. Having few facts at hand (who knew anything about the future of railroad profits in 1870?), investors tended to ascribe to the individual economic units—to the companies—the power of the technology. And the railroad was powerful. But it happens that it is far more difficult to predict whether a specific railroad will succeed, or even survive, than to observe in a general sense the vast societal changes wrought by speedier transportation.

Innovations from the cotton gin to, indeed, the Internet, have made society more productive, but the link between such general advances and specific (that is, corporate) profitability is fuzzy. In fact, increases in productivity can even *dampen* profitability. Most new technologies tend to smooth the furrows and the imperfections in the marketplace; they level the playing field. In so doing, they also obliterate the crevices and market niches in which companies can earn a superior profit.

If you think about it, most of the major new technologies have either shrunk the country physically, by improving transportation, or shrunk it mentally, with improved communications. Either way, they have whittled away the advantages of geography and information that enable companies to protect their margins. To take one long-lived example, the telephone let Sears, Roebuck contact suppliers more efficiently, the automobile allowed Sears to sell in stores as well as by catalog, and the radio enabled Sears to advertise nationwide. Yet as these innovations were also adopted by competitors, Sears's advantage over time was greatly diminished.

The Internet was the ultimate information dispenser. It was designed, much as Gilder hypothesized, to empower individual consumers—to level disparities in knowledge. It enabled people to investigate the furrows in the market and thus to insist on the lowest prices. It opened a channel for sales, but it opened it broadly and indiscriminately. Its effect, in the main, was not to enhance profitability but to trim it.

It is amazing that Wall Street could overlook such a truism, but it was blinded by a combination of childlike euphoria and not so innocent greed. The euphoria, at least in the beginning, was genuine. In the late 1980s, futurists had begun to buzz over a looming upheaval in communications. No one was sure exactly what it would look like (people spoke of an ambiguous information highway), but a group of young bankers and venture men on the West Coast thought it could be very, very big. Frank Quattrone, a young banker with Morgan Stanley, was intrigued by the small companies working on connecting computers and office networks that still functioned as unattached islands of automation. In 1989, Quattrone recommended an IPO for Cisco Systems, which sold a novel router—a device for connecting networks. Quattrone was amazed to learn that, despite the lack of a sales force, Cisco was achieving sales growth of 60 percent a quarter. He asked John Morgridge, the chief executive, "Where will you get the salespeople to support your growth?"

Morgridge replied in his distinctive Wisconsin twang, "Well, to date, we haven't found the *need* to have a sales force because people are ordering these things like hotcakes over the *Internet*."[12] If Quattrone had heard the word before, he had thought of the Internet as a government-sponsored network used mainly by scientists for exchanging information. Now, in one transcendent moment, its commercial possibilities were revealed.

An entire generation seemed to have the same epiphany. Jeff Bezos quit his job on Wall Street, borrowed a Chevy Blazer from his dad in Fort Worth, and drove to Seattle, where he founded Amazon.[13] Then, in 1995, Netscape went public, awakening ordinary investors to the World Wide Web. Business school students thumbed their noses at Fortune 500 companies and headed for Silicon Valley. The whole country seemed to be tilting West. On a sweltering August morning in 1997, a Harvard Business School graduate named David Perry stuffed his belongings in his ten-year-old Maxima and started for California. Perry wore out the shock absorbers on the first day, then the radio quit on him. By the time he reached Nevada the Maxima was overheating, but Perry

drove as if possessed. He was doing eighty miles per hour north of Lake
Tahoe when both rear tires blew. Perry got a tow, bought a couple of
used tires, and sputtered onto Sand Hill Road in Silicon Valley—the
heart of the venture industry—where, mission accomplished, the Maxima stopped forever.[14] For Perry and thousands of would-be entrepreneurs like him, seeking venture money had become a calling, their
generation's equivalent to writing a novel. Venture firms were del-
uged—business plans were arriving at the rate of one an hour.[15]

The entrepreneurs descended on the Valley in waves. One month
they were pitching Web sites for gardening companies, the next it
was online department stores. They were passionate and smart; they
held degrees from the finest schools. But they were unprepared to talk
about sales ratios and inventory turns and margins—the flour from
which a business is baked. A married couple, from Tennessee, was pushing a site for sporting goods. They called it a killer category. Jim Breyer,
a venture man who retained a degree of skepticism, pointed out that
many, many sports retailers failed; why would online sports be different? The couple said if Breyer's firm, Accel Partners, invested, then
Amazon would. And if Amazon did, their dot-com would be first to
market, which was said to guarantee success.

The first-to-market cliché was accepted on faith; it had to be, for the
historical evidence did not support it. Many early innovators in the
past—the first manufacturers of automobiles, the first personal computer companies, and so on—had long since disappeared. But the Internet fostered delusions of omnipotence. Companies that established a
tenuous niche in one market thought nothing of broadly diversifying,
for a mastery of Internet technology was thought to override the need
for other expertise. Young Perry, having resettled on the West Coast,

organized an online market for biochemical supplies to connect whole-salers with drug companies. The project did not get off the ground, but rather than focusing on making it better, Perry branched out and began to develop so-called business-to-business markets in a half-dozen other industries as well.

Then there was Webvan, an Internet supermarket with a Niagara-sized plan to expand into books, electronics, dry cleaning, garden sup-plies, kitchen appliances, computers—virtually everything. Its founder, Louis Borders, who had cofounded the Borders book chain in the '70s and revolutionized bookselling by placing a punch card in every book, was not even interested in groceries; they were simply a product to move through Webvan's exquisite technology. A shy, aloof mathemati-cian, he hired more than one hundred engineers, as though Webvan were a secret bomb project instead of a supermarket. The engineers built unfathomably complex software so that Webvan could take orders, schedule pickups, and operate giant warehouses with cutting-edge au-tomation. When Mrs. Smith went online and ordered radishes, a light flashed next to the appropriate bin, the radishes were dropped into a plastic tote, and the tote would cruise along four miles of conveyors collecting whatever else Mrs. Smith might desire. Then the tote was weighed, checked against her order, and delivered at the requested hour. Borders insisted on every amenity; if Mrs. Smith wanted fresh lobsters she was to have them. Nothing was beyond the power of technology, or such was Borders's conviction. Not long after Webvan opened for busi-ness, Borders tried to scrap the system in which he had invested millions and replace it with laser-guided go-carts to collect the food instead.[16]

Webvan had the support of two of the most prominent venture firms in the Valley, Benchmark Capital and Sequoia Capital, and each was adamant that Webvan build not one warehouse but twenty-six, virtually simultaneously, around the country. The expense, the overcommitment of capital before the system was tried and the bugs worked out, was stupendous. But the venture firms, which prided themselves on their intellect, their cool detachment, had contracted a case of gold rush fever.

The venture industry had grown up in Boston after World War II as a sort of commercial adjunct to the area's universities. It relied for funds on a handful of wealthy families, who committed capital for long durations. An early success story was Digital Equipment, which became a computer giant thanks to a $70,000 investment in 1957 by American Research and Development.[17] In the '70s, as the avocado farms in Silicon Valley were being plowed under for, well, silicon, the industry's center of gravity shifted to the environs of Stanford. The venture firms of that era liked to nurture both their companies and the entrepreneurs who ran them. They were slow to invest, but once they did, they tended to hang on to their stakes for years.

In the '90s, however, their pulse quickened. Sensing that Internet winners would pay phenomenal dividends, venture firms began to charge into companies that were little more than concepts. The total of investment surged from $3 billion in 1990 to $60 billion in 1999, implying that venture firms were becoming more confident but also less discriminating.[18]

The typical venture man worked in an office with glass walls, tasteful art, and plants. Formerly, he had merely supplied capital to start-up businesses; now he aspired to something loftier. He not only funded businesses, he conceived them. He endeavored to conceptualize businesses that might, as it were, fill some gaping hole, visible perhaps only to him, in society as presently constituted. He spoke softly but stridently, often with a hint of condescension. He wore khaki trousers and open collars and affected a leisurely knowingness of the future.

But his patience was increasingly a fiction. Rather than nurture, he hurried his start-ups to a public offering. He encouraged his charges to spend (Webvan invested more than $1 billion) because the bigger the enterprise, the faster it could get to an IPO. And since venture firms invested at only a tenth (or even less) of the share price ultimately paid by the public, they had little at risk. Their name became a misnomer, for they ventured nothing. They invested in Internet start-ups almost irrespective of their prospects for success, for it was apparent that, with the help of Wall Street, they could readily sell at a higher price.

IPOs had not always been so easy. Wall Street underwriters had traditionally insisted that start-ups prove their substance by showing a year or two of profitability before going public. The person who enforced such standards was the security analyst. But with investors so eager to invest, bankers put increasing pressure on analysts to lower their standards. Analysts were commonly used to help market their firms' deals, and they were graded and paid according to their contribution to banking revenues. In truth, many of the analysts would have lowered their standards anyway; they were drinking the same intoxicating spirits as everyone else. Internet analysts such as Morgan Stanley's Mary Meeker exhorted investors to buy up stocks at whatever the price. The rising market had become their, and her, only logic, and to the possibility that she was pushing investors over a cliff, Meeker became remarkably cavalier. Thus, she wrote of Amazon: "We have one general response to the word 'valuation' these days: 'Bull market.'"[19]

The bankers later argued, not unlike a bartender with a thirsty patron, that they were not responsible; they were merely pouring the drinks their customers wanted. But Morgan Stanley is not a saloon; it has an obligation to know the customer and to deal with him fairly. The bank's imprimatur was on the cover of its underwritings supposedly to certify that the stock was a worthy, if not a guaranteed, investment. Moreover, the banks were anything but disinterested parties.

Underwriters collected 7 percent of every offering, a fixed rate impervious to time or competition. If the toll seems high, one must understand that IPOs were not free-market transactions in the normal sense; they were highly staged affairs and rife with favoritism every step of the way. In Silicon Valley, the bankers and venture men were as cozy as sparrows; it was not uncommon for a banker at Goldman Sachs or Credit Suisse to personally invest in a venture firm and then turn around and take one of the firm's young companies public.

When an underwriter approved an issue for an IPO the bankers typically ladled out a few percent of the coveted shares for friends, family members, prospective clients, and, indeed, venture capitalists. This was the most time-honored of scandals. In the 1930s, the public had been shocked to learn that the Morgan bank had rewarded leading public figures, ranging from the Stock Exchange's Richard Whitney to Charles Lindbergh, with allocations of shares. However, the payoffs then and since had been relatively small. In the 1980s, IPOs rose an average of 6 percent on the first day of trading; even in the '90s, up through 1998, the average gain was only 14 percent.[20]

But when IPOs began to double and triple, investment banks were in a position to dish out serious favors. The banks naturally allocated shares to investors who rewarded them with business. At Credit Suisse, the system of rewards was so openly routinized that recipients of shares were dubbed to be Friends of Frank—after Frank Quattrone, the former Morgan Stanley banker who had risen to be the head of Credit Suisse's high-flying technology department. On one IPO, of a hot software company called VA Linux Systems, Credit Suisse allocated 50,000 shares to Technology Crossover Ventures, a West Coast venture firm with close ties to Quattrone. When Linux soared 698 percent on its first day, Quattrone's favored client made a first-day paper profit of $10.5 million.[21] Such bonanzas exposed a blatant conflict between Wall Street and its ordinary customers, who bought into the deals at far higher, and far riskier, prices. And they were the ones holding the bag when, before too long, shares of VA Linux fell to under $1.

Quattrone had eliminated any potential gatekeeper problem by securing complete control over his (supposedly independent) analysts. Credit Suisse broke the mold in other ways; its salesmen elicited a kickback from certain hedge funds that it favored with IPOs.[22] But the underlying corruption was as true of other firms as it was of Credit Suisse. Banks ignored the Internet companies' patent lack of profits; they ignored the history of numerous other inventions (such as the railroad) that had led to speculative booms and busts. They, and their venture friends in Silicon Valley, simply sold stock with abandon.

Doerr, Amazon's and also Netscape's venture investor, was a singularly effective promoter. A former Intel salesman and now a partner at Kleiner Perkins Caufield & Byers, Doerr projected an image of the Valley as a benign, almost civic-minded enterprise, all the while it was selling to the public astonishingly overpriced shares. He repeated again and again that the Valley was spawning the "largest legal wealth creation in history." The phrase struck a popular chord. If Doerr, who had a history of success with earlier technology companies, such as Compaq and Lotus, was plugging the Web, it seemed safe for everyone else. In fact, he told *The New Yorker,* two years after the Netscape IPO, the Web might well be "*under*hyped."[23]

Doerr was also a vigorous partisan for the high-tech industry's political interests. As we have seen, he helped to quash the proposal to require an expense for stock options, and he led the Valley's campaign to protect corporations, and his many friends on corporate boards, from shareholder lawsuits. But Doerr and his allies would not have described themselves as traditional lobbyists; they argued, rather, that the old rules did not apply, or should not apply, to the new economy.

Internet companies were used to living outside the rules, and this applied, in particular, to their accounting. Companies such as Amazon simply ignored FASB (except in required filings) and published a pro forma earnings number that excluded whatever costs they pleased. Companies such as AOL took exceptional license in how they reported revenue. Once, when FASB was in the midst of reforming the rules on accounting for mergers, Doerr and John Chambers, the CEO of Cisco, visited Arthur Levitt and warned him not to let the change go ahead. Three times, Chambers declared that he had "lots of friends in this city."[24]

Having grown up in close quarters, people in the Valley did not recognize the clannish, inbred nature of the industry. They fancied themselves above regulation, though given the web of ties that knitted high-tech companies, banks, and venture firms, they were more in need of it than most.

Cisco, for instance, acquired start-up companies that had been funded by a venture firm—Sequoia Capital—one of whose principal partners was the vice chairman of Cisco's board.[25] And much or most of the money that Cisco invested in such companies was squandered. In 2001, Cisco wrote down more than $2 billion of its inventory, and its stock plunged from $80 to under $20. While Chambers was threatening the head of the SEC over merger accounting, he was running a conflict-ridden enterprise in which private allegiances overcame both good business judgment and ethics.

This is not to say that venture capitalists and bankers had to twist the public's arms. Main Street got Internet fever earlier than did many on Wall Street; it was a truly democratic bubble. People were using the Internet in their private lives, and that aroused their interest in the stocks. This had also been true, one supposes, when people had begun to ride the rails. But the Internet introduced a new, collective quality to investing. People were exposed online to all manner of market news, rumor, and opinion; this liquid mixture could not help but stimulate. Everywhere, one heard of promising young men or women who were making a killing on Internet stocks. In the Valley, even a bible study group experienced, as it were, a conversion, giving up their King Jameses and forming a weekly stock-picking club.[26]

Previously, investing in America had been mostly a private act. The cloak of privacy had begun to fray in the '90s, with the spread of financial-news broadcasts that were seen in offices, bars and virtually everywhere. With the Web, this evolution took a great leap forward. Investors in chat rooms could embrace each other like fans at an open-air concert. They formed, in effect, a crowd, which is the essential precondition for mass hysteria. If one thinks for a moment of the first people to ride the rails, chugging through what had been untamed wilderness, the conversation must have surely turned to the fortune to be made by investing in such a wondrous new mode of transport. And the more they talked, one imagines, the more eager were the passengers to purchase shares. Internet users were, in a sense, passengers in a giant rail car.

The financial media might have tried to deflate the bubble, but it chose, in large part, to join the parade. CNBC pioneered a breathless sportscaster's version of financial reporting that kept its audience at a fever pitch, beginning with the countdown to morning trading. Throughout the day, anchors passed along a confection of news, tips, and trivia that could only nurture in its audience a yearning to speculate. One might have expected more from print journalists, but they, too, were increasingly narcoticized. *Forbes* described Jay Walker, the promotional founder of Priceline, a money-losing reseller, as a possible "New Age Edison."[27] *The Wall Street Journal* went further, offering in 1999 to "rethink" for its readers the "quaint idea" of profits. The newspaper of financial record observed that Internet companies beset by losses had "some distinctive financial strong points." And what were these? The ability to finance themselves with "wondrous ease."[28] The *Journal* appeared not to grasp the inherent circularity, for the vaunted ability of dot-coms to obtain fresh financing was of course dependent on the continued willingness of investors to overlook their mounting losses.

Mutual funds that piled into Internet stocks were widely touted in the press, as had been the go-go funds of the '60s and, indeed, the junk bond funds of the '80s. Their managers were treated as heroes. "So what is [Ryan] Jacob's secret?" wondered *USA Today.* "He says he has developed a proven method of Net investing."[29] The article was timed so that readers could invest in the twenty-nine-year-old's new fund, Jacob Internet, which over the subsequent two years lost precisely 91 percent of its capital.

The more pervasive flaw was the tendency of journalists to endorse, rather than to seriously challenge, the tenets of the new economy. The cliché that knowledge was now a company's most valuable asset and the assumption that more powerful computers inevitably boosted productivity were often repeated but hardly ever examined. A preposterous forecast that the Internet economy would soon account for half of the U.S.'s electricity consumption (3 percent was closer to the mark) was widely reported.[30]

Yahoo was the most popular Internet stock. As a portal, or doorway, to the Web, Yahoo was a proxy for one of the bubble's most alluring fantasies. Portals such as Yahoo or AOL were supposedly new-age networks, with theoretically unlimited appeal to advertisers. There were two problems with the theory. First, the supply of advertising space on the Web was also unlimited. Second, people use the Internet to do things so they tend to be unreceptive to the distraction of ads. But Yahoo attracted more viewers—more eyeballs, in the jargon of the era—than anyone, and according to Wall Street, eyeballs were as good as gold. When Yahoo's stock was added to the Standard & Poor's 500—a step that did not add a penny to its sales—the stock surged 64 percent in a week, and before long, Yahoo reached a market value of $100 billion. Dot-coms from Yahoo to iVillage were not, in fact, overly concerned with the effectiveness of online advertising, because they had discovered a target market that was similarly blasé—other dot-coms. What a virtuous circle—the public invested, which dollars provided money for advertising, which boosted revenue, which in turn attracted investment. The loop was closed.

The advertising delirium reached a peak of sorts early in 1999, when the venture firm Idealab launched Free-PC.com, which *gave away* Compaq PCs to consumers who would, in turn, watch ads on the Internet. "We believe in the long term this model will provide cost savings to a full range of PC offerings," said Bill Gross, the CEO of Idealab.[31] In the logic of 1999, distributing free computers was a business model. A few months later, a group of Stanford business school students hatched AllAdvantage.com, which proposed to pay Internet surfers fifty cents an hour for the privilege of beaming ads to a viewbar at the bottom of the user's screen. Millions of new "members," many of them college students, signed up to collect checks.

The magical rise of such profitless companies distorted the scales of traditional business, now derisively referred to as the old economy. By 1999, Priceline, which resold airline tickets but owned neither gates nor planes, was worth almost as much as the entire, tangible airline industry; eToys, a tiny but well-publicized retailer, went public with a value three times that of Toys "R" Us. It is worth reflecting on just how lopsided such a ratio was: eToys had revenue of $25 million; Toys "R" Us, $11 billion.

The bizarre yet inescapable conclusion was that according to the mathematics extant at the turn of the millennium, a dot-com stock was worth more than an actual, cash-generating business. To Wall Street, the

1,400 stores of Toys "R" Us were not an asset but an albatross, an anchor on its steadily sinking stock price. Anything touched by new technology soared; all else was tainted. The Dow Jones average ended 1999 at 11,497, up 25 percent for the year. However, the *median* stock was flat, meaning that half of all stocks were falling or failing to rise. And those, of course, were the half in the old economy.

One might have thought that traditional companies would redouble their efforts to earn higher profits, the better to distinguish their genuine enterprises from the sudsy effluvium of Silicon Valley, but their instincts were otherwise. Companies in the old economy hastened to become, or at least to appear, like those in the new; that is, companies with profits, reputations, and histories tried, as much as possible, to transform themselves into companies that were businesses only in name.

Their executives, too, wanted a dot-com stock; they wanted the currency, the cheap capital—and they wanted the options and the personal riches that went with it. The executives were counseled by consultants who were fluent with Web technology and, in particular, with its fashionable argot, according to which the old economy companies ran the risk of being Amazoned, disintermediated, and generally rendered extinct by a dot-com hatching in some garage perhaps at that very instant—unless, that is, they hired the consultant to digitize its operations and, to some extent, its soul. Douglas Mellinger, a consultant, pointedly warned an audience at Baruch College, "There is a dot-com bullet awaiting every large corporation."[32] And though these consultants were younger, often much younger, than the executives they counseled, they were hard to dismiss, especially as they were echoed by the press and, most especially, by the brash young dot-commers themselves, many of whom became overnight billionaires. Josh Harris, the founder of Pseudo.com, which he fancied to be the first Web TV station, blandly told a reporter for *60 Minutes*, "Our business is to take you guys out . . . to take CBS out of business.[33] That's why we're going to make the big bucks." It mattered little that Pseudo.com was a compilation of deviant sex, rap music, and video gaming—*Harris was going after CBS*. Wall Street mindlessly endorsed such notions: Ralph Acampora, an analyst with Prudential Securities who specialized in divining the meaning of price charts, allowed to *USA Today*, "Norfolk Southern or Cisco Systems: Where do you want to be in the future?" as though the superiority of Cisco's stock to that of a mere railroad hardly required explanation. (During the following year, though, Norfolk Southern's stock rose 33 percent, while Cisco's shares, vastly inflated by dot-com euphoria, fell 65 percent.[34])

And the executives believed: they were too dazzled, too tempted, not to believe. George Shaheen, the head of Andersen Consulting, gave up a lucrative retirement for the top job (and 15 million options) at Webvan. His banker, Hank Paulsen, the CEO of Goldman Sachs, was worried that Goldman, a century-old firm, would be rendered irrelevant by another broker. After touring the Webvan warehouse, Paulsen stood up at a dinner in Silicon Valley and vowed that Goldman would not become the Safeway of Wall Street, as if it were foregone that Safeway, with its 1,600 supermarkets, was a dinosaur, that Webvan was to blanket the country. A Goldman rival, Chase Manhattan Bank, was so eager to participate in the new age of banking that it spent $1.2 billion (at the market top) for a West Coast investment bank.[35]

Many old economy companies set up Web sites; some incubated their own dot-coms. A few sought something deeper, a more soulful transformation. Jack Welch, the most admired CEO in America, held that adapting corporate functions to the Web would occasion a spiritual renaissance. His program for reinventing General Electric was dubbed, in earnestness, destroyyourbusiness.com,[36] meaning *GE's* old business— the way GE had done business for a hundred years. It was an article of faith that not only was the digital economy bestowing miracles of progress but also that everything older was merely a hindrance; it had nothing to teach. *Destroy it.*

John Reed, the idealistic chairman of Citicorp, thus looked to re-create his entire bank in cyberspace. Reed picked a dreamy technologist—not a banker—from Viacom to run e-Citi and deliberately walled it off from the rest of the bank, signaling that technology took precedence over making loans and trading currencies. Reed thought people on the ground would stop going to branch banks altogether, just as Louis Borders figured they would give up going to supermarkets. Edward Horowitz, the guru in charge of e-Citi, spoke casually of "blowing away the terrestrial world," by which he meant blowing away the physical branches that were the cornerstones of his own institution.[37] *Destroy it.*

Horowitz sent Citi's top two hundred executives a copy of *The Innovator's Dilemma: When New Technologies Cause Great Firms to Fail,* a dense tome that became a must-read for Fortune 500 executives anxious to mend (or discard) their tired ways.[38] The only way to cope with looming revolution, according to the book, which was written by Clayton Christensen, a Harvard Business School professor and consultant, was to set up an autonomous suborganization of presumably more free-thinking innovators than the drones who were otherwise running the company (meaning, at Citi, the working bankers who were making the money). *Innovators* was unabashedly subversive of the old order; it advised, even, that paying attention to one's customers could be a fatal mistake—for who was more locked into the old familiar ways of doing business than one's customers? *Destroy it.*

A bubble has something of the momentum of a passionate affair. It has no stable state—it must become ever more manic and voracious. In previous bubbles, the public had often progressed from owning direct shares to a second stage—to funds or pools proffering speculation of a higher order. And though these funds were merely derivative instruments, the public's ardor for them was, in fact, greater than for the underlying securities that were the ostensible basis of its enthusiasm. Thus, in 1929, the investment trust sponsored by Goldman Sachs, known as Shenandoah, which invested in the most speculative and over-priced of New Era securities, itself rose to a fabulous premium.[39] The fantasy reached a second degree—for if the public unashamedly clam-ored for stocks, how much more would they clamor for stocks that only a Goldman could choose? A similar dynamic propelled the shares of conglomerates, such as International Telephone & Telegraph, in the 1960s, and of holding companies through the ages.

The Internet equivalent was the incubator. Incubators were in the business of forming new dot-coms; as such, they subscribed to the par-ticular conceit that corporations could be systematically engineered, from the laboratory. The most prominent was David Wetherell, a for-mer programmer who took over an old-style New England marketer, CMGI, and developed a Web browser, analogous to Netscape's. In the mid '90s, CMGI sold the browser to AOL for what, then, was a tidy for-tune. Wetherell presciently recycled the profits into a collection of In-ternet start-ups. One, a search engine named Lycos, went public at a spectacular price, after which CMGI began to draw notice. As an incu-bator, it was a stock of stocks, for it allowed the little guy to participate in start-ups before they went public and thus to reap the rewards of IPOs.[40] In this sense, it was a proxy for the entire period.

Wetherell had an instinct for mass psychology, a kind of tropism that steered him toward whatever would please the market. He had little in-terest in the details of his companies but was obsessed with generating a favorable image on Wall Street. He would head off dissension by par-roting slogans and made certain that CMGI spewed out an unending torrent of bullish "news." Whenever the head of one of CMGI's units reached a milestone, no matter how trivial, Wetherell would inevitably lean forward and exclaim, "That sounds like a press release!"

An avid bird-watcher, he became fascinated by the splendid variety of dot-coms; the World Wide Web was his rain forest. Wetherell liked nothing better than to explore a new site. Once, when he discovered a financial chat room begun by a trio of college students, he invited one of them to his home in North Andover, Massachusetts, bought him a pizza, and acquired his business.[41] He used CMGI stock for every deal he made, and though he acquired companies pretty much on a whim, each (well-publicized) deal further raised his stock. This was the game that Kozlowski at Tyco and many others were playing, but Wetherell's stock was far more virile. Over the five years from its IPO to early 1999, CMGI's stock rose 140 times, giving it a market value of more than $6 billion.

None of CMGI's various businesses were close to making money.[42] But the parent generated cash by periodically selling a piece of one of its start-ups in an IPO. What Wetherell had really built was an IPO farm—the quintessential Internet business. Moreover, though his assets were highly disparate—they included an ad broker, a company that targeted commercials to Web sites, an entertainment company, and so on—they were linked by the grand theme of Internet advertising.

If one did not look too closely, the big picture seemed to be of an emerging media titan. According to *Business Week*, Wetherell was becoming "a major force on the Web."[43] Microsoft and Intel each acquired a minority stake. The rising stock and the appearance of so much activity suggested an enterprise of substance. Wetherell was known in private as The Internet's Warren Buffett, although his chief financial officer simply referred to him as the The IG (The Internet God).

Just as a person in the throes of love does not—cannot—see the world as he did before, the vision of those in a bubble is altered. Their frame of reference, their yardstick, is different, and the new scale necessarily invalidates the old. This was the inescapable background for an encounter between Wetherell and Barry Diller, the entertainment mogul.

Diller was also building an online business, and early in 1999 he proposed to merge certain of his assets with Lycos, the public company of which CMGI owned 20 percent and of which Wetherell was a director. Though initially a search engine, Lycos now was more of a portal, one of those coveted doorways to the Web. Nonetheless, Lycos generated only $100 million in revenue and operated at a loss.

Diller, who ran USA Networks, was offering to contribute assets with revenue of $1 *billion* and—dare one say it?—profits of $300 million. Unlike Lycos, Diller's Internet business concentrated on selling mail-order goods and ticket reservations, not advertising. However, Diller figured that by merging he could expand his market to the millions of people who entered the Web by Lycos. And Lycos, for its part, would be getting real, cash-earning assets. It would be exchanging some of the immense future hopes that were reflected in its sky-high stock for dollars that were tangible now. When the deal was presented to the Lycos board, Wetherell stood up and applauded.

But when the deal was announced, Lycos's stock plummeted 26 percent. CMGI's stock also fell. People who owned Internet stocks did not like the deal. Why would an Internet company want to merge with somebody that sold kitchen appliances or costume jewelry over the telephone? Why cash out an Internet dream for mere *profits?* The press, with the notable exception of James Surowiecki writing in *Fortune,* regarded the merger as a Hollywood-Internet wedding.[44] James Cramer, writing in the *TheStreet.com,* said Lycos had been dazzled by Diller's glitz. The spin was that an old media mogul was going after a new economy gem, although, in fact, the deal had nothing to do with media. It was about selling goods to viewers, not about marketing eyeballs to sponsors. Nonetheless, Wetherell, who spent significant time in market chat rooms, deduced that investors hated the deal. The cash flow standard of Diller simply could not coexist with the airier standards of the new economy. Wetherell backed away from the merger.

Diller, hoping to save the deal, visited Wetherell in North Andover. The Internet God said calmly, "I have to protect my stock." Diller dryly suggested that an opinion poll was not an adequate cause for terminating a deal that Wetherell himself had applauded.[45] But the merger was dead. "Net bulls should rejoice," Cramer observed. "Frankly, this [deal] frightened the heck out of me."[46]

Wetherell's choice—stock price over real cash flow—epitomized the bubble as nothing else. It snapped the slender threads that still bound the market to a faint sense of reason. Once the specter of the merger had been put to rest, the dot-com market went into a fever, where it remained for fully twelve months, until the spring of 2000. Now, investors discarded every yardstick and disowned all proportion. They were free perhaps as the mad are free. Scores of stocks went public at fantastic valuations. Priceline went public at $16 and ended the day at $69. iVillage, a women's site without a remote possibility of profit, went out at $24 and soared to $80. Late in '99, when the mania for consumer sites gave way to a frenzy for business sites, Ventro, the brainchild of David Perry (and a favorite of Mary Meeker's) climbed from $15 to $240. FreeMarkets, which had a site for selling industrial supplies, went public, in December 1999, at $48; the first *trade* was at $250. Glen Meakem, the chief executive, who had traveled to New York with his wife and two of his children to witness the carnival firsthand, was so overcome by the tension that he spent the morning of his IPO puking in his hotel, across from the World Trade Center.

The top-performing IPO of 1999 was Internet Capital, an incubator of business Web sites similar in structure to Wetherell's CMGI. It had gone public in August at $6. It closed on December 31 at $170. The assets of Internet Capital cast a cold light on the arithmetic of the day. The company was valued at $46 billion. After netting out its cash, the market was implicitly assuming that Internet Capital's other assets, which consisted of investments in 47 start-up ventures, were worth, on average, an implausible 120 times the money invested.

CMGI, in the year after its flirtation with Diller, multiplied an amazing seven times. By March 2000 the stock stood at $145, an 870-fold increase in six years. It was then worth just over $40 billion, and Wetherell, a former programmer for the Boston & Maine Railroad, had a fortune of $5 billion. By then, the price-earnings ratio of the average technology stock was well over two hundred. Nasdaq, which had been under 2,000 only sixteen months earlier, broke 5,000. By the peak of the bubble, the first quarter of 2000, a technology company was going public and doubling every other day—a speculative orgy without precedent in public markets.[47]

From 1998–2000, investment banks earned $3.9 billion in fees for technology deals. Credit Suisse alone earned $785 million, and Quattrone personally earned more than $100 million, most of it for brokering companies not remotely close to earning a profit.[48]

One of Quattrone's clients was AllAdvantage, the improbable dotcom that had recruited millions of members, each of whom it paid to surf the Net. AllAdvantage funded this immense expense by selling shares to venture capitalists—who, in turn, were counting on selling their ownership to the public. If this seems to bear at least a passing resemblance to a pyramid scheme, one must add that the founders earnestly believed that AllAdvantage would be able to leverage its members' eyeballs into advertising dollars. In the spring of 2000, everyone believed.

The very week the Nasdaq hit 5,000, the AllAdvantage founders—three recent Stanford graduates and an older entrepreneur—were further introduced to the working world by Credit Suisse, which whisked them by private jet to Aspen for a weekend of traveling by helicopter to remote ski slopes, visits to a spa, and a conference hosted by Quattrone. Three weeks later, when the Democratic Party staged a fund-raiser in the Valley, it chose the home of the senior founder, where not only Quattrone but also President Clinton paid AllAdvantage tribute as a paragon of new economy inventiveness. The only ones who seemed, as yet, unconvinced, were advertisers, who were distressed by the low response rate of AllAdvantage's members—a passivity that was not so surprising in that, as it developed, the majority of clicks received from members' computers in fact represented members only in appearance. As an investigation by an AllAdvantage customer had determined, and as had been communicated to a small group within the company, the clicks came mostly from robots that were programmed to look like actual surfers and to whom AllAdvantage was, unwittingly, sending monthly checks.[49] Credit Suisse was apparently unaware that its client was, in large measure, a fraud, although it knew that advertising revenue, only $9 million a quarter, was pitifully small, and the underwriter was pressing ahead with a billion-dollar IPO.

SEVEN

Enron

If a single corporation could represent the corruption of shareholder value, it would be one in which the executives were riveted, minute by minute, on the stock price. The desire for a higher stock would dictate every facet of the company: its disclosures would be scripted, its accounting would be rigged, its strategies and even its lines of business would be chosen with buy/sell orders in mind.

The executives would be consumed with their company's appearance, and they would doubtless enlist a network of well-paid professionals—accountants, analysts, and even lawyers—to buttress the corporate image. Though praised as exemplars of shareholder value, these executives would in fact be single-mindedly obsessed with their own enrichment. They would be at first indifferent and, later, with the confidence wrought by success, arrogant about their disregard for legal and ethical norms.

Whatever its industry, our company would stress the mobile, streamlined character of its operations. It would endeavor to shift assets and related liabilities off the balance sheet and away from prying eyes, and the need for such would nurture in our company a virtuosity in finance. It would hire the brightest of MBAs, seek out the most fashionable of consultants, adopt the most modern of management theories. Ever in step with the prevailing winds, our '90s archetype would loudly proclaim the virtues of deregulation while, privately, it would cultivate the coziest of ties to government. It would champion free and open markets, but its financial wizards and their hired auditors would labor overtime to obfuscate its true condition. The board of directors would come to see, at the very least, that the managers were cutting corners. But then, even the directors would be mollified by the appearance of success, by the inertia that settles onto boards, and by their own escalating fees.

And by the new millennium our company would have joined the information age. To outward appearance it would have refashioned itself into a child of the new economy, and, assuredly, it would have a glorious stock chart to show for it. As it happens, this is almost a perfect profile of an improbable energy trader, the Houston-based Enron.

1. Profile

Enron's modern history begins when the culture was taking root, during the 1980s merger wave. The reader will recall that energy companies were at the heart of the takeover craze, and an Omaha-based pipeline, InterNorth, had been put into play by Irwin Jacobs, a much-feared corporate raider. Desperate to stay out of Jacobs's clutches, InterNorth in 1985 acquired Houston Natural Gas, which was run by a benevolent-seeming executive who was much occupied with civic and fund-raising activities that were making him a player in political circles, Kenneth Lay.

Lay, who became CEO of the new company, was an ardent deregulationist, a cause he had preached as a government economist and, later, as undersecretary of the Interior. At Enron, as the new combination was called, Lay hoped to exploit the evolving market in natural gas, which was emerging from government controls. But Enron bore the stain of its birth—$5 billion of debt from the merger.[1] As a trading company's credit is its most important asset, the stain was particularly unwelcome. Thus, from the very first, Lay was anxious to clean up Enron's balance sheet.

Lay's background—he was the son of a Baptist minister who also sold farm equipment—was modest. Nonetheless, he had a genteel manner, as if born to privilege, and a taste, perhaps acquired in his Washington years, for money and for moneyed friends. Only a year after Enron was created, Lay became the fifth-highest paid of CEOs,[2] which owed less to his then-modest achievements than to a certain *droit du seigneur*. Lower-ranking employees regarded him as a sort of grandfatherly patron. Lay was indifferent to the gritty detail of management, and his desire for wealth, combined with his aversion to unpleasantness, gave rise to a significant flaw—a permissiveness toward underlings who did do the dirty work. As a result, the controls at Enron never matched the growing complexity of its operations. In 1987, Lay was apprised of some dishonest bookkeeping in Enron's lucrative oil-trading division. He decided not to sack the culprits, reckoning that Enron needed their specially tailored profits.[3] However, the improprieties could not be contained. Enron ultimately lost $150 million (a large sum for it then), and two traders were convicted of fraud. Perhaps most alarming, Enron never explained the episode to shareholders in subsequent annual reports.[4] Even then, Lay had a kind of fetish about his stock price and thus with guarding Enron's image.

In refashioning Enron, Lay leaned heavily on Jeffrey Skilling, a consultant then in the Houston office of McKinsey and a fellow crusader for free markets. A Harvard MBA, only thirty-two in 1986, when he began to work with Enron, Skilling was disdainful of the traditional pipeline business; in fact, he oozed disdain for *any* traditional business. Skilling sensed, with precocious intuition, that physical assets would increasingly be viewed by Wall Street as passé. His aspiration was toward something fleeter—to occupy the lighter space in between the lumbering giants who actually owned plant and equipment.

An episode early in his career suggests that Skilling was always more adapter than innovator—a trait that harmonized perfectly with the lemminglike instincts of Wall Street. With the gas industry deregulating, Skilling was drawn toward trading, and in 1989, he suggested that Enron establish a gas bank—a studied, hip way of saying that Enron, like a bank, would pool the resources of producers and supply them to industrial consumers. The idea for the gas bank actually had sprung from the man in charge of Enron's intrastate pipelines, but Skilling took the credit for it.[5] He had the consultant's knack for framing strategies so as to sound modern; he didn't coin ideas, he marketed them. Short and slight, he was awkward socially and uncomfortable speaking off-the-cuff.[6] In such settings, he could be surprisingly shallow. But on scripted occasions, Skilling shone. McKinsey considered him a rising star, which endeared him to Lay, who liked the company of stars. In 1990, possessed by the fantasy that this deep thinker could reinvent the company, he hired Skilling to take charge of Enron's trading.

Trading requires capital, and capital wants for credit. As Enron grew, it was forever in need of both. To remedy this need, in 1991, it concocted a series of special-purpose vehicles.[7] As noted, these vehicles were mostly financed with credit, but to legitimize them outsiders did put up a 3 percent sliver of equity. This enabled Enron to declare that, for instance, certain of its gas assets were no longer under its control and to remove the offending assets from its balance sheet. That, in turn, enabled it to borrow more.

The architect of such fine footwork was Andrew Fastow, a young financial whiz, formerly with Continental Bank in Chicago and Skilling's protégé. Skilling himself engineered a cosmetic alteration that allowed Enron to boost its reported earnings. In the early '90s, he convinced regulators to let Enron adopt the mark-to-market method of accounting. This method is used by brokerage firms to record the value of securities at the close of market every day. But the application was different—far more subjective—in the case of a pipeline. The value of a thousand shares of IBM is known with precision; the value of a long-term gas contract is not. Consequently, Enron began to book earnings that were, in fact, merely the projected profits from many years after. A few years later, *Forbes,* citing Enron's aggressive accounting, warned that the stock posed "hidden risks" for investors.[8] In 1995, Lay was warned of such risks in private. He responded with his characteristic calm and certainly did not restrain his protégé.[9] The truth is that Lay was dazzled by Skilling.

Skilling launched a new plan, a new business, virtually every year, an approach calculated perfectly to appeal to Wall Street. One year it might be gas distribution in Brazil; the next year, Canadian paper mills. Such diverse ventures reflected his view that expertise was less critical than talent, which is to say, Skilling believed that Enron could fearlessly enter terrain in which it had little or no experience. Enron thus became something of an open laboratory. With its legions of consultants and freshly minted MBAs, the company made a fetish of its talent, as though it were not an energy company but a vast, roving McKinsey project. A book by three McKinsey consultants, which boasted of the rejuvenation wrought at Enron, observed that employee value was "the holistic sum of everything people experience. . . ." and that successful companies would encourage workers to try the challenges associated with "jumping from one rock face to another," as if Enron were merely an exercise in personal discovery, more yoga than business.[10]

Skilling's playbook embraced the full panoply of new economy chic: the seamless corporation, the free-form career path, the stock option.

Supervision was exceptionally loose, as though the operational controls that were routine elsewhere were too constricting for the innovators at Enron. Skilling paid no attention to the expense line, arguing that what really mattered was entrepreneurial spirit.[11] Of course, *real* entrepreneurs (think Sam Walton) are obsessed with costs. What Skilling embraced was not the spirit of entrepreneurs but the spirit of the stock market.

An odd conceit of Enron's was to affect a market-based scheme for employee assignments. If more employees asked to work in wind power, so the thinking went, they must have eyed lucrative prospects there; thus it would pay for Enron to let the workers move—and to invest in windmills. If, on the other hand, employees voted with their feet for pipelines, so be it. According to Skilling, this market would help Enron allocate its capital, just as the stock market did. In practice, it suffered from the very same defect; it didn't correct management's prejudices, it reinforced them. Knowing which industry was Skilling's latest pet, employees simply asked to work in the flavor of the day—a phrase coined by Lay.[12]

Though Enron was a trend-conscious place, its outer face was decisive and macho. Skilling affected a haughty arrogance; he was forever demeaning those that he deemed less smart than he. He exuded contempt for bureaucracy—for the normal rules that bound others. He embarked on daring adventures, skydiving or trekking in the Australian outback, and, as if guided by some McKinsey leadership manual, goaded his employees to join him. His bravado was imitated by many on Enron's staff (judging from the parking lot, Ferraris and Porsches were practically the company car). But the image of daring was, in an important sense, false. Skilling refused to tolerate genuine disagreement; he gave latitude to those in his favor, but he was curtly dismissive to those who doubted him. When challenged, he would simply growl that the offending employee didn't get it. This pattern of responding either in black or white, with nary a shade of gray, reflected Skilling's lack of comfort with detail—his consultant's utter lack of hands-on experience.[13] And it nurtured a corporate culture that, for all of Enron's supposed individuality, was surprisingly sycophantic.

Skilling was able to project a very different image to the world. In the annual *Fortune* survey, Enron was voted the most innovative company six years in a row. Outsiders saw Enron as a band of creative entrepreneurs who had grafted the new finance, especially derivatives, to energy. The heady notion (trumpeted by financial scholars) that any commodity could be reduced to a financial quotient, to a subparticle of tradable risk, was tailor-made for Enron—which thus spread its wings from gas markets to oil to paper and so forth. The *Journal of Applied Corporate Finance* applauded its "genius" for transforming energy markets. "Enron's business model," the *Journal* intoned after interviewing the trinity of Lay, Skilling, and Fastow, "differs in a very critical way from that of other energy companies, that traditionally invest heavily in fixed assets. Enron instead focuses on leveraging its investments in *human* capital."[14]

The notion that Enron was not pursuing hard assets was among the larger fictions surrounding it. In the early to mid-'90s, it invested in—to cite only a few—power plants in the United Kingdom and India, a pipeline in South America, a utility in Oregon, a wind-power company in California, and mining in Panama. Its strategy was to acquire assets in each field to get a foothold in trading—where its grandest ambitions lay. By such a capital-intensive process, its trading operation evolved to include electricity, paper, metals, plastics—even derivatives tied to the weather. Enron was really a projection of the country's faith that markets were ever the optimum engine for allocating resources.

With Enron growing so swiftly, Lay began to harbor grand and, seemingly, improbable ambitions. In 1996, when its revenues were barely one-ninth those of Exxon, Lay declared that his goal was nothing less than to become the "world's greatest energy company."[15] The detached CEO seemed scarcely aware that many of Enron's acquisitions were ill-timed and, indeed, unprofitable. (Despite its sophisticated image, when it came to acquiring assets Enron was something of a green-horn.) Its acquisitions left it perpetually starved for cash, and its credit rating, BBB+, was uncomfortably close to junk-bond level, a reminder of its uneasy birth. This debt was an iron manacle on its growth, and the entire experiment would surely have gone aground but for Fastow's increasing dexterity in whisking assets, and debt, off the balance sheet. This is not to say the assets no longer existed, only that Wall Street could now ignore them—a testimony to the profound power of appearance in the culture of shareholder value.

Then, at the end of 1996, Skilling was promoted to president of Enron, replacing a more traditional manager. He and Fastow, now the thirty-four-year-old senior vice president for finance, were thus freer to pursue their strategies. Fastow had already concocted scores of partnerships; he had turned Enron's finance department into (his own words) "a capital raising machine."[16] Like many corporations, Enron increasingly used special-purpose vehicles to finance projects, borrow money, and so forth. But these vehicles were frustrating to Fastow, for the simple reason that outsiders controlled them. Outsiders *had* to control them, for that was the sole justification for permitting Enron to report its assets as separate from theirs.

Fastow's new solution bordered on the diabolical: to create a vehicle that was separate and yet not separate, that was independent of Enron and yet controlled by Fastow personally. In short: a personal fief within the public company. This demand was so counter to the proper spirit of the public corporation as to testify to the unhappy debasement generally of managerial culture—to the long years of executive profiteering. Indeed, Fastow seems to have felt that profiteering was nothing less than his due. Vinson & Elkins, Enron's outside law firm, said the obvious conflict of interest would require a public disclosure—which Skilling wanted to avoid. (Skilling evaluated every proposal according to its effect on Enron's image.) Fastow petulantly replied that since investment bankers were allowed to invest in *their* company's deals, why wasn't he?[17]

The question speaks volumes about the evolution of corporate finance. Once, as noted, finance merely supported the primary business. It had slowly been elevated to a profit center, and at Enron, it had become *the* business, much as at a bank. Indeed, Enron conceived of itself as a bank, and Fastow, who had assembled a crew of a hundred-odd junior wizards, must have thought of his operation as a bank within a bank—as the heart of the genius that was transforming Enron.

Unwilling to hear no, he next proposed that the partnership, which was to be known as Chewco, after a character in *Star Wars*, be run not by Fastow but by Michael Kopper, a protégé of Fastow who worked for him in finance. Since Kopper was a lower-ranking employee, his involvement would not trigger a disclosure requirement. But Kopper, a virtual creation of Fastow, was sorely conflicted nonetheless; he reported to Fastow at Enron, he was an investor in Chewco, and he also managed Chewco.

Conflicts of interest are typically—and rightly—rejected because of the mere possibility of corruption. It is enough to know that City Hall does business with the mayor's brother; we need not know the precise terms in order to cry foul. Enron was the rare case in which not only the conflict but also the corruption were blatant. Fastow seems to have totally forgotten where his obligations lay. He bullied Enron's negotiators, with the superciliousness that only a young and intelligent man can muster, to give Chewco, and Kopper, a sweeter deal than they would have otherwise and to accept a less-sweet deal for Enron. (As a result of such cronyism, Kopper, his protégé, made $10 million on an investment of $125,000.[18])

The purpose of Chewco was unabashedly cosmetic. Created in 1997, it immediately bought a half-interest in a portfolio of Enron investments, thereby keeping hundreds of millions of dollars off Enron's books.

Its financing—and this was key—was to include a smidgeon of equity (that 3 percent sliver) from outside institutions. But Fastow merely reported to the executive committee of the board that Chewco was an unaffiliated vehicle with outside and unrelated investors. Astonishingly, he did not mention Kopper's role. One can only guess where Fastow gained the boldness to mislead his board; did he suppose that investment bankers did that, too, or was he merely so intent on having his way?

Vinson & Elkins, the law firm, whose biggest client was Enron, took care of the paperwork in a mere forty-eight hours.[19] Such eagerness was not atypical of lawyers, who had, in the '90s, come to identify quite closely with their executive clients. In a way, it was hardly surprising. Lawyers spent many hours with executives; they knew them, often fraternized with them, and of course were paid by them. The shareholders were a mere abstraction. Yet it was to that group that the lawyers were ultimately responsible—it was *their* money that paid the bills. Had the distinguished Vinson & Elkins recalled that Enron's owners were its true clients, it would not have been so quick to sign off. Perhaps, then, it would have discovered the truly troubling facts regarding Chewco.

In fact, the outside equity did not exist. Fastow had been unable to find investors for even the 3 percent of equity required for Chewco to be considered independent.[20] The entire purchase price of nearly $400 million (other than Kopper's investment) was borrowed from banks, and Enron guaranteed both the loans and the portion of the capital that was supposedly equity.[21] To summarize, then, Enron sold a half-interest in an energy portfolio to a paper shell managed by its own employee, and—in violation of every accounting standard—kept hundreds of millions of dollars of unprofitable assets off its balance sheet. The fiction that Chewco was an independent entity permitted Enron, in 1997, to report an additional $28 million of net income—a significant contribution to its total of $105 million.[22]

2. Stepchild of Silicon Valley

Nineteen ninety-eight was the year of eBay and Amazon, and Enron wanted in on the party. It wanted to exploit the Web and, just as importantly, to exploit the stock market's love of the Web. Skilling had seen a stock chart put together by Credit Suisse in which new economy stocks were clustered at the top, with high multiples, and all of the rest were far below. It made an enduring impression on him. He told a friend he wanted to move Enron to the other group, where the dot-coms were.[23] Thus, having moved from distribution to trading to finance, Enron was to be reborn again. EnronOnline would trade energy products—that much was predictable—but Enron would also trade broadband, that is, capacity on the fiber-optic networks that were crisscrossing the country to carry Internet traffic. More improbably, Enron invested in a fiber network itself, acquiring and building a patchwork system that stretched for 18,000 miles.[24]

Skilling figured that online trading—it could have been online anything—would get Enron's stock moving.[25] The stock was ever his prime consideration. It had doubled in the early '90s, but from 1993 to the end of 1997 it noticeably slowed, rising from $14½ to only $20¾, hardly a stellar performance.

Sensing that he had a good story, Skilling began to promote Enron's new economy credentials with gusto. Stock traders might suppose that this is the proper job of executives—to promote their stock. In the late '90s, many if not most chief executives agreed. But a CEO who is properly focused on building long-term value for *ongoing* owners should be interested only that the stock, over time, approximate the value of the underlying business—not that it soar to unsustainable peaks. He has no business playing pitchman. Enron's executives, who could track their share price minute by minute at television monitors strewn about their headquarters, differed from others of the era only in the degree to which they violated this maxim.[26] Its executives and other employees received 15 million stock options in 1998 and 35 million the following year—an amount equal to 5 percent of the outstanding stock, a percentage that, before the era of shareholder value, would have been unthinkable.[27] Enron's executives thus perceived that promoting the stock was a matter of urgent self-interest.

Not surprisingly, they viewed securities analysts as a tool for priming the stock. When John Olson, a Merrill analyst in Houston, refused to issue more than a lukewarm recommendation, Lay and Skilling complained—and then served notice by yanking Enron's considerable banking business away from Merrill. They soon got results. In April 1998, Olson's boss flew down from New York and greeted him with three words: "Enron, Enron, Enron." Olson took early retirement.[28] In the Wall Street of the day, professionals that failed to heed the god of shareholder value did so at their peril.

The import of Enron's Internet aspirations became clear in 1999. Enron had made a tiny investment in Rhythms NetConnections, a start-up company that connected businesses to the Internet using digital subscriber lines. In April, Rhythms went public. It was a vintage IPO. Rhythms, which had minuscule revenues and, of course, no earnings, went public at $21 and closed after a day at $69. Enron's investment soared overnight to $370 million. However, it was restricted from selling the stock before the end of the year. This presented the sort of problem that was mostly unknown before the heady enthusiasms of the Internet.

Fastow, recognizing that the stock could easily lose much of its value, concocted another of his trademark partnerships to hedge Enron's investment. But while active markets existed for investors to protect their investments in, say, IBM, none existed for Rhythms NetConnections. It was simply too risky. Therefore, Fastow offered to guarantee the value of the partnership with—Enron's own stock! It was a bit like offering to indemnify one's own insurer.

Moreover, Fastow, who had been promoted to chief financial officer and who must have been chafing over the windfall he had arranged for Kopper, insisted that this time he, Fastow, be able to invest in, and control, the partnership, known as LJM, and also a sister partnership, LJM2, formed a few months after. The LJMs were at the heart of Fastow's abstruse manipulations. They, like others of his creations, were employed to conceal large losses from the market, inflate earnings, keep debt off the balance sheet. As we have seen, shoddy accounting leads to a lack of candor, and while Enron did disclose that an unnamed officer was general partner of the LJMs, it in no way communicated the substance of the matter. Shareholders could scarcely guess that its chief financial officer, the person most responsible for the fiscal integrity of the corporation, had used Enron's resources to fashion a private empire, a series of accounting halls of mirrors, and that he would sit across the table from Enron in more than twenty transactions that would allow him personally to harvest tens of millions of dollars in profits.

Moreover, the LJMs were on their face fraudulent. It may help to recall the legitimate functions for which special-purpose vehicles are used every day. For instance, banks routinely sell credit card receivables to institutional investors, thus allowing the banks to take such assets off their books. The key point is that the outside investors are truly outside. They *want* to buy the receivables because, at the right price, they will turn a profit on them. Enron's vehicles were of another color, for the LJMs were used to transact deals that Enron could not, or would not, do with unrelated parties. They were artificial constructs—vehicles ostensibly owned by a third party but in which, in fact, only Enron had a meaningful economic stake. In essence, it was selling assets to, or buying protection from, itself.[29]

Skilling asked Vincent Kaminski, Enron's head of risk assessment, to evaluate the Rhythms hedge. Kaminski reported back that he thought it fatally flawed. Despite the pretensions of new finance, some risks cannot be hedged. They can be borne, or they can be transferred to other parties. The Rhythms risk looped all the way back to Enron. To Kaminski, the convoluted partnership resembled a perpetual motion machine in which Enron stock supported the LJMs, which in turn benefited Enron's stock. But Skilling's priorities were, indeed, to defend the stock. It now stood at $32—a 60 percent rise in little more than a year. If Wall Street was laboring under the impression that Enron was a new economy stock, Skilling would not disabuse it. Kaminski soon heard from an intermediary that the hedge had "too much momentum" to be stopped. Shortly after, Kaminski, who had been such a bother to Skilling, was transferred.[30]

Final approval for the LJMs fell to Enron's board. Fastow, as CFO, was required to seek a waiver of the company's conflict-of-interest policy. For the board to grant it was a major step. However, the board's review of the LJMs was extremely perfunctory. The audit and finance committees devoted at most ten to fifteen minutes to the LJMs, relying on the cumulative assurances of Lay, Skilling, Arthur Andersen, and various employees (who reported to Fastow!) that the LJMs were structured properly and that any deals they struck with Enron would be reviewed by objective parties. The word cumulative is key, for no one party took responsibility—or as a special committee of the board later reported, "no one was minding the store."[31]

This failure cannot be called accidental, for it stemmed from the long-noted cronyism in America's boardrooms, which neither the New

Dealers of the 1930s nor the reformers of the '70s nor Levitt in the '90s had licked. Lay, who held the title of both CEO and chairman, was a prototypical imperial executive—one who, indeed, was not above using Enron for private gain. A sister of Lay's operated a travel agency, and Enron employees were strongly encouraged to patronize it.[32] That Lay was a political and civic force in Houston, not to mention a close ally of the Bush family, heightened his sway among directors. Indeed, five so-called independent directors had serious conflicts of interest.[33] Enron made large contributions to the University of Texas's M. D. Anderson Cancer Center, whose president, John Mendelsohn, served on Enron's audit committee. Enron employed another director as a consultant. And Wendy Gramm, the former commodities regulator whose husband, Senator Phil Gramm, was the second-largest recipient of Enron contri- butions, was unlikely to be a problem.[34]

Enron steadily increased the value of directors' compensation, which in 1999 reached $200,000. As this translates to something on the order of $2,000 per hour, it is fair to ask, just what did management think (if not loyalty) it was buying? Beyond *that,* Lay and Skilling attended the meet- ings of the important, ostensibly independent board committees.[35] Thus, even the possibility of objective oversight was effectively foreclosed.

The board seems to have imagined that the LJMs would function as merely another bidder for Enron's assets and thus would strengthen the corporation's hand.[36] This was incredibly naïve. Fastow was hardly just another bidder. He was in a position to exert considerable influence over what Enron offered to the LJMs. He knew what Enron needed to sell, whether it had competing bids, and so forth. Indeed, he bragged to in- stitutional investors, "It's very hard for me *not* to see competing bids."[37]

Many companies at least attempt to separate conflicting activities by erecting a Chinese wall. Not Enron. Fastow performed his LJM work right alongside the ordinary Enron people, many of whom he super- vised. In fact, he brazenly marketed LJM2 as an opportunity to leverage his personal inside dope. He boasted that LJM would have access to opportunities unavailable to others, and the papers he sent to investors revealed that Enron controlled 50 percent more in assets than had been disclosed to the public—including the public shareholders for whom Fastow was a fiduciary.[38]

One is reminded of John Dean, the Nixon aide who found the corruption in the Oval Office so pervasive, so insinuated in every consideration of the Nixon gang as to resemble a cancer growing on the presidency. This cancer may have been particular to Enron, but the virus that triggered it stemmed from corporate America's long pursuit of private (over shareholder) gain, its increasing evasion of responsibility, its escalating tendency to shade the truth. Enron was but the full manifestation, the malignancy in its most potent form. Indeed, the investors in LJM2 included the cream of corporate America—Merrill Lynch, J. P. Morgan, GE Capital, and Citicorp[39]—and while they had no obligation to Enron's shareholders, it is notable that none felt put off by Fastow's obvious intention to use the partnership to exploit his own shareholders.

O nce he had the uncommon license of the LJMs, Fastow became even more brazen. Indeed, he began to concoct deals that can best be described as outright theft. The LJMs would acquire (always from Enron) interests in a score of assets ranging from power plants in Brazil and Poland to a gas-gathering system in the Gulf of Mexico—assets that it frequently resold to Enron and always at a profit to the LJMs, even when their value appeared to have declined. Indeed, most of the assets performed poorly. That the LJMs nonetheless turned a profit was no mere accident. Fastow had a secret (and, according to his later indictment, illegal) guarantee from Enron that the LJMs wouldn't lose money in any of their joint transactions. But as the deals ridded Enron of poorly performing assets and thus improved its reported results, they kept Fastow's masters happy.[40]

Indeed, management was getting just what it had sought from Fastow. The company's risk-management manual openly stated that Enron's risk strategies were "directed at accounting rather than economic performance"—a remarkable admission that Enron concentrated on the form rather than the substance.[41] This open embrace of financial cosmetics was a sort of milestone for devotees of shareholder value. Previously, companies such as Lucent and Xerox had stumbled into managing their earnings through weakness or desperation; at Enron, prettification was policy.

In one case, Enron was avidly trying to sell three barges that were generating power off the coast of Nigeria in order to boost its earnings for the 1999 fourth quarter. But no one wanted them. In desperation, Enron contacted Merrill Lynch; it also refused. So Enron promised—orally—that if Merrill did the deal, Enron would later unwind it at a profit to Merrill.

It is hard to think of anything more suggestive of the general state of corruption than Enron's under-the-table proposition—except for Merrill Lynch's willingness to implement it. In the final days of December, with no due diligence, Merrill suddenly acquired the barges, with Enron providing financing. Six months later, LJM2 reacquired Merrill's stake at a price that netted Merrill, as promised, a 15 percent annualized return. Enron had to pay LJM2 a hefty fee, but as far as the public was concerned, Enron got to record a profit.[42] Of course, the people who bought Enron's shares on the basis of its reported earnings had not the remotest idea of the deception that lay behind them.

The rub for Enron was that each deal simply raised the bar for more earnings, more deals. The only plausible escape was to convince Wall Street to love the stock irrespective of its earnings—that is, to become, truly, a new economy darling. This was easier than one might have guessed. At the beginning of 2000, investors were in a heat to find companies that got the Web. It is doubtful that Alfred Harrison, an Alliance Capital mutual fund manager who made a huge bet on Enron, understood the vagaries of its derivative business, but it is probable that he was impressed by Ken Lay's assertion that Enron could become the world's "preferred platform" for e-commerce.[43] No one questioned, nor even blinked, at such Caesar-like aspirations. Journalists, now well accustomed to the newspeak of Silicon Valley, found it natural that Enron, which was such a master of metamorphosis, would again transform itself, this time more beautifully than ever. Even the usually skeptical *Economist* soon was lavishing praise on Enron's "spectacularly successful [albeit not yet moneymaking] Internet effort."[44]

Skilling was even more charged over Enron's broadband business than he was over Internet trading. Broadband, the high-speed lines that conveyed millions of e-mails and other data without which modern man would be unable to function, was the shovel to the Internet's gold. Enron had entered the business when it acquired Portland General, the utility, which owned a modest fiber-optic ring around Portland, Oregon. (The businesses were a natural fit, because fiber-optic lines were laid alongside gas pipelines.[45]) Skilling characteristically decided that fiber-optic capacity could be *traded*. As it happened, bandwidth capacity was in huge oversupply; in terms of its scarcity value, one might as well have traded air. No matter—Enron, as usual, invested in a capital asset so as to gain entrée as a trader, which in this case meant that it strung together a national fiber network. It was poorly conceived and poorly integrated, but no matter that, either.[46] Kenneth Rice, the head of Enron's broadband unit, declared publicly that the broadband trading platform would, within a few years, be worth precisely $22 billion—a prophesy that presumably did little to hurt Enron's stock price.[47] On Wall Street, the notion that Enron had discovered a new commodity to trade—one linked to the Internet; the very *fiber* of the Internet—stirred ripples of interest in its stock. In 1999 the stock had risen smartly, from $28½ to $44; in the first *three weeks* of 2000, as word of its broadband plans leaked, it surged another 20 percent, to $53.

That is where it stood on the morning of January 20, 2000, when Enron hosted a conference in the Four Seasons Hotel in Houston. The purpose was to introduce its telecom profile to Wall Street. It was a magical day—the very height of the excitement over the new economy. Lay, Skilling, and various underlings waxed poetic about people's insatiable demand for content, such as movies, games, and entertainment. And what was the promise of the Internet, if not to break down barriers, to liberate data—content, that is—from the chains of time and place? People would want to download every movie, every game, anything that had formerly been shown on a strip of celluloid or been shipped on a magnetized disk, every day, every second, wherever they were and whatever they were doing. And soon, Enron would be transmitting *Snow White* and *American Beauty* and such to people's TV screens, their cell phones, their automobiles, their PalmPilots, their beepers perhaps, and almost every other contraption short of their electric toothbrushes.

Then, the executives talked of their other business—of the yawning need for the fiber to serve this demand. How would a telecommunications company, an Internet access provider, and so forth be able to procure just the capacity it needed, just the fibers to complement its network? How would so many burgeoning fiber networks fill in all of their gaps? And here, the executives smiled knowingly. This was the kind of problem Enron had solved before. A *market* could solve this problem—Enron's market. Lay actually predicted—or rather, it appears that he simply divined—that Enron's business in trading broadband would "dwarf" its volume in electric power and gas.[48]

And then, the executives trotted out Scott McNealy, the chairman of Sun Microsystems, from which Enron was buying thousands of computer servers. And McNealy obliged his host, who was also, of course, his customer. McNealy said, "We think Enron does have some secret sauce here." McNealy didn't identify the sauce, but according to the Enron executives, it was not a pipedream but was ready now, right that moment in Houston. And as the Enron executives talked, Enron's stock price rose by the hour. Stock analysts who didn't know broadband from baseball kept breaking from the meeting to phone their clients, urging them to buy more Enron. It almost seemed that the entire chorus of the new economy, the entire priesthood of shareholder value, was squeezed into one hotel room. And Enron's stock rose that day to $67. It rose fourteen points—25 percent—in a single day.[49]

The press reported Enron's optimism without a blush—without even the nominal degree of skepticism that it applied to dot-coms. *Fortune,* in a particularly credulous moment, declared that Enron had dispelled "any doubt" about its telecom venture—dispelled it, that is, before it was even off the ground.[50] Not surprisingly, the stock continued rising.

That summer, Enron announced a joint venture with Blockbuster video to supply movies to people's homes. It might have been observed that the American consumer suffered no lack of access to the cinema, at home or otherwise. But it is in the nature of a bubble that, in some unconscious realm, investors understand they are grossly speculating on unsubstantiated hope—thus they grasp at any morsel of fact, no matter how inconsequential. The Blockbuster news was received as dramatic confirmation. Enron now had the shimmer of Hollywood, and its stock vaulted to $90, a new high. It was now worth a total of $70 billion.

We can hardly understand this heady inflation without looking more closely at the telecom boom of which, briefly, Enron was a beneficiary. The telecom bubble was less widely chronicled than the dot-com mania, but in terms of the promises made, the dollars invested, the capital em-

ployed, and the risks to the economy engendered, it was by far the
greater of the two.

3. The Other Bubble

The emergence of the Internet spawned unprecedented optimism in
telecommunications. In the '90s, it was widely said that as a result of
burgeoning Internet use, traffic was doubling every hundred days. This
is a fantastic growth rate, more than ten times per year. (By an illustra-
tion close to home, if the population of suburban and bucolic Westfield,
New Jersey, were to expand at such a pace, within four years it would
equal that of the rest of the United States.) Internet traffic grew that
quickly when the Web was taking off, but by 1997 at the latest, growth
had cooled to a still impressive but far tamer two times per year.[51] However, the notion of tenfold growth refused to die. It passed from executive to analyst, was picked up by the press and even by the federal
government. As late as September 2000, an executive at WorldCom's Internet unit told *The Washington Post*, in terms that did not leave room
for doubt, that Internet traffic had been doubling every three months
"over the past five years."[52]

   The propagation of this myth is, in some sense, the story of any bubble. There is always a germ of truth, a half-fact or momentary fact that,
taken to hyperbole, can justify the most fantastic projections. In 1844, to
gauge demand for the Manchester & Southington Railroad, a traffic
taker counted the number of sheep on a fair day, doubled it to account
for projected development, and thus arrived at an estimate of daily average freight.[53] Counting sheep on the Internet was not altogether different. What made the calculations tricky is that the volume of data
transversing a network varies every second. The problem greatly occupied the executives at UUNet Technologies, a Virginia start-up that, in

the late '80s, was one of the first companies to begin connecting businesses to the Internet.

The person at UUNet who calculated traffic was an engineer in his midthirties named Tom Stluka. Stluka would use his estimates to build a model of UUNet's projected demand and, therefore, its need to develop infrastructure. Then he would send the numbers to Kevin Boyne, the chief operating officer. Boyne would inevitably respond that Stluka's numbers were too low.

After a while, Stluka realized that Boyne already had a number in mind. Boyne insisted, despite all evidence, that traffic was doubling every hundred days. Boyne had a reason for inflating growth. Just as it would be in General Motors' interest for its suppliers to produce a surplus of tires, UUNet wanted to make sure that its suppliers made plenty of fiber circuits. At least as Stluka understood it, the idea that Internet traffic was doubling every hundred days began as a marketing ruse.

Then, in 1996, UUNet was acquired by WorldCom, an unheralded but fast-growing carrier. Executives at WorldCom, including Bernard Ebbers, the chief executive, began to parrot the doubling idea. Stluka duly informed his superiors that traffic was not growing nearly that fast. He would say, If traffic is growing at 2X why are we increasing capacity at 10X? By now, though, people were using "10X" to justify their budgets. They didn't want to hear carping from the guy who had built the model. Pretty soon, Michael Armstrong, the chairman of AT&T, who must have figured that Ebbers couldn't be wrong, started using the statistic, even though AT&T's own traffic wasn't growing nearly that fast and even though Andrew Odlyzko, an AT&T researcher, had published a stark refutation of it. In April 1998, a Commerce Department report (relying only on WorldCom as a source) said Internet traffic "doubles every hundred days." Having gained this official imprimatur, doubling became a staple of every banker, consultant, Wall Street analyst, and plain old promoter of the telecom industry.[54]

. . .

The context for this promotion was the dramatic improvement in fiber technology. In the early '80s, a glass fiber could transmit only a single wavelength. By the early '90s it could carry two signals simultaneously; soon the figure rose to *eighty* signals.[55] Moreover, each wavelength could handle more data, thus resulting in a geometric increase in capacity. As the new fibers, each as thin as a human hair, were not much more expensive than the old ones, the cost of transmitting a single call plunged. The local Bell systems, with their copper networks, were suddenly seen by George Gilder and such as easy prey for a new generation of fiber carriers.[56]

Congress, hoping to release the latent power of the technology, passed a bill to deregulate telecom in 1996. Long-distance service had been competitive for some time, but the law created an expectation that revolutionary change was afoot. A wave of start-ups were formed, predicated on the supposedly insatiable demand for bandwidth. But their optimism ran counter to the grain of history. Multiple networks have typically led to consolidation and failure. There were fifty telegraph companies in 1851, of which only Western Union survived. The telephone industry traversed the same ground, with literally thousands of small competitors succumbing to the Bell system.[57]

The fact that telecom costs were plunging merely enhanced the Darwinian danger. As we have seen in the dot-com episode, innovations that cut costs inevitably lead to lower prices, thinner margins, and commoditylike returns. Just as airlines resembled flying utilities, the new telecoms were akin to underground airlines, poised to bleed each other to the last drop of their equity.

Why, then, were telecoms (and their financiers) so reckless? First, the notion of limitless growth blinded them. Companies from World-Com to Enron dug up the nation's thoroughfares and dove to the ocean floor to lay millions of miles of fiber that, for the most part, would remain dark. Executives were so swept up in the talk of galloping demand that they didn't think about galloping *capacity*. In 1998, an executive with IXC Communications tried to reassure a journalist that his network would be able to handle all that future traffic, observing, "I'd say that we are using, at most, one-fiftieth of our domestic backbone capacity." The executive, Michael Vent, did not venture a guess as to when IXC would begin to use the other forty-nine fiftieths of its capacity, nor did this surplus seem to trouble anyone on Wall Street.[58] The tremendous redundancy—the fact that seventeen almost identical long-distance networks were cropping up to compete in a market once shared by three—was, remarkably, ignored.[59]

The cumulative investment marked the greatest binge in the history of private finance. In the half-decade after deregulation, telecom companies borrowed $1.6 *trillion* from banks and enlisted Wall Street to sell $600 billion in bonds.[60] They raised billions more in stock sales. Most of this money was spent on woefully redundant networks.

A second explanation is that the twisted ethic of shareholder value, which naturally found currency in high-growth sectors, permeated telecom as no other industry. We have seen that stock options can distort the personal risk/reward calculus of executives, and option grants in telecom were probably the highest of any. Executives who had none of their own capital at risk had every incentive to pour the shareholders' capital into high-risk projects, and their bankers—who should have known better—egged them on. Wall Street's fees for selling telecom stocks and bonds totaled more than $20 billion, vastly more than the bankers' take on the much-ballyhooed dot-coms.[61]

The leading player in the boom was WorldCom. The company's origins were improbably humble. After the antitrust-inspired breakup of AT&T in 1983, would-be entrepreneurs around the country started to look for ways to break into the telephone business. One of them was

Bernie Ebbers, a former high school basketball coach in Mississippi who owned a chain of budget hotels. Ebbers was an early investor in Long Distance Discount Services (LDDS), an upstart founded to serve small companies in Mississippi, and he became its CEO in 1985. Annual revenues started at around $1 million.

Ebbers's formula for growth consisted of merging with the biggest available fish, then to merge again. Under his aegis, LDDS was always in deal mode, making more than sixty acquisitions in fifteen years.[62] It rarely paused to integrate the old before it proceeded to the new; rather, it assembled an empire ad hoc and thus it achieved its growth not from whatever benefits could issue from a true integration but from the steady rise in its shares and the familiar alchemy of merger accounting.

Indeed, rarely, if ever, has that alchemy worked so swiftly. By 1992, LDDS was one of the country's larger regional carriers, with revenue of roughly $1 billion. By 1995 it had gone international and, consequently, rechristened itself WorldCom. Its acquisition, the next year, of MFS Communications, which had just acquired UUNet, gave WorldCom a collection of local telephone networks as well as a piece of the Internet. It was that acquisition, for a then-staggering $12 billion, that started the land rush in telecom. Of course, the trouble with using mergers to increase earnings (as we saw with Tyco) is that one can never stop. Moreover, each deal must be progressively larger to achieve the same effect.[63] The next year, WorldCom bid for a prize some three times as large, MCI Communications, which catapulted the former Mississippi reseller to a giant with close to $40 billion in revenues. Surveying WorldCom's state-of-the-art fiber networks, its local telephony, its Internet assets, George Gilder offered a remarkably premature toast, declaring, in 1997: "It's all over. Bernard Ebbers of WorldCom has won."[64]

Such heady acclaim for Ebbers was heard more and more often. Known as a pool-playing, beer-drinking executive, a habitué of Jackson steak houses who had put up in a trailer on his soybean farm while getting a divorce, Ebbers seemed charmingly ordinary. And he managed, long after he had begun to indulge his prodigious appetite for stock options, to cultivate a reputation for down-home thriftiness. *Fortune* magazine saluted his "frugality."[65] Because he was so foreign to Wall Street, the blond, boyish Ebbers was perceived as the genuine article—telecom's Huck Finn, as it were—come to reinvigorate an industry dominated by bureaucratic Bells. But Ebbers was not a day-to-day manager. Like Skilling, he was essentially a promoter, relentlessly focused on his stock price.

A serial acquirer like WorldCom needed a regular investment bank, a need exploited by an analyst with a perfect ear for the times, Salomon Smith Barney's Jack Grubman. Grubman and Salomon financed dozens of telecom companies, and the public was so revved up that, now, all a telecom had to do was announce it was ripping out its old network and installing—at huge cost—the next generation of fiber and its stock would soar. The investors, who would meet the executives and their bankers at road shows, were strikingly nonchalant; in general, they demanded fewer details than would buyers at a good antique show. James Q. Crowe, founder of the upstart Level 3 Communications, would charm his audiences with talk of "Silicon economics,"[66] as though the economics of Adam Smith were inapplicable to broadband. His banker—it was Grubman—asserted that "no matter how much bandwidth is available, it will get used."[67] For some bond issues, underwriters dispensed with road shows altogether. They simply staged drive-bys; the broker would telephone appropriate fund managers and announce that a financing would close at noon—wire money.[68]

Grubman became so close to Ebbers, in particular, that he attended selected WorldCom board meetings to advise on deals, including the MCI deal. This rare insider's role did not restrain Grubman from issuing unfailingly positive reports on the stock, which he alternately described as a must-own for investors and as one for which investors should "load up the truck." Touting the stock hugely benefited Ebbers, who—it warrants repeating—received a succession of extravagant option grants. Grubman was repaid in kind—indeed, it was a feature of the late '90s that, as the saying on the Street went, "Everyone gets paid." Thus, Grubman's firm reaped by far the biggest share of WorldCom's business, and Grubman personally earned on the order of $20 million a year.[69]

Ebbers and Grubman represented the warped symbiosis of corporate executive and Wall Street analyst as did no other pair. So intent was Grubman on helping Ebbers to choreograph the stock that Grubman would prepare WorldCom officials in advance of analyst conference calls by suggesting answers to likely questions, lest the executives be forced to render spontaneous and, presumably, less varnished replies.[70]

Nor was this Salomon Smith Barney's only favor to Ebbers. From 1996 to 2000, Salomon allocated shares in twenty-one of its hottest public offerings to Ebbers. The IPO allocations, on which Ebbers made a total of $11 million, can best be understood as an indirect kickback for the $107 million that WorldCom paid in banking fees to Salomon. To rephrase in the language of the future bankruptcy examiner, the allocations created an appearance that "valuable corporate business opportunities were being traded for personal gain."[71]

The stain of self-dealing permeated the industry. Gary Winnick, the architect of Global Crossing, a transoceanic fiber developer, was the most brazen of the bandwidth barons and, indeed, operated on a grand scale reminiscent of the original robber barons. Winnick had started in furniture sales and progressed to bonds, in which he was lucky, or unlucky, according to one's ethics, to have been tutored by Michael Milken. He was part of Milken's original team of traders. After Milken was indicted, Winnick received immunity from prosecution for agreeing to testify against his boss, although ultimately he didn't testify.[72]

Winnick's ambition at Global was nothing less than to circle the globe with fiber-optic cable. He also spun a web of political connections, which he used to lobby the federal government to block a rival's application for an undersea license. He contributed heavily to both political parties and enlisted investors such as the former president Bush and Terry McAuliffe, who was a top Clinton fundraiser in the 1996 campaign.[73]

Working from an opulent Beverly Hills headquarters, whose inner sanctum was modestly designed to resemble the Oval Office, Winnick borrowed billions with a facility that did Milken honor. He also treated Global as his private bank. Its lavish offices were rented from a company owned by Winnick, netting him millions in real estate income; what's more, Global paid Winnick and three other Global directors a fee of $7.2 million for arranging financing of an undersea cable—that is, for doing their jobs. Most remarkably, in return for Winnick's presumably nonpareil advice, Global agreed to pay 2 percent of its revenues to Winnick's private holding company. In 1998, when the arrangement was canceled, Winnick and his confreres collected an astounding termination fee of $135 million in stock.[74] It is noteworthy that Winnick seized this plunder before any part of his undersea network was operational. In other words, he rewarded himself well before his backers could be assured of any reward at all. Indeed, public investors were only then putting their money *in*.

A distinct feature of the corruption of the late '90s was that it tainted the entire financial community. The junk-bond bubble, in which Winnick cut his teeth, and other such episodes were relatively contained. But in the late '90s the money flowed so freely and the abandonment of standards was so complete as to taint analyst as well as banker, executive as well as auditor, brokers, and lawyers, too.

The telecom episode added to this dispiriting group the commercial banker. The telecoms had a prodigious appetite for loans; moreover, the boom coincided with the repeal of Glass-Steagall, which had separated underwriting from banking. Banks such as Chase Manhattan (soon to be J. P. Morgan Chase) were now thirsting to move into underwriting. With telecoms equally thirsting for cash, banks used loans as bait to get the inside track on underwriting assignments, the precise abuse that Glass-Steagall had been intended to prevent. As Julie Creswell later revealed in *Fortune*, Chase was a notorious offender.[75] It not only cut its fees to worm its way into banking deals; it courted Winnick, who had a weakness for being seen with important people, which he generally defined as exceptionally wealthy people, by introducing him to David Rockefeller, Chase's former chairman. One wonders if the octogenarian Rockefeller, who had spent a lifetime cultivating a reputation for modesty and rectitude, was aware of Winnick's penchant for self-enrichment or his lavish taste (reportedly, he spent $90 million for a home in Bel Air, California).[76] In any case, Rockefeller escorted Winnick, a Long Island native whose father had run a restaurant-supply business, on a private tour of the Museum of Modern Art. By such means, Chase became Global's banker and, indeed, the telecom industry's commercial banker of choice. There is no evidence that the bank of David Rockefeller was overly concerned with whether demand for bandwidth was truly insatiable or—in the event it was not—with how its loans would be repaid. For Global's income statement painted a picture that, to the financial eye at least, was less appealing, if more germane, than the impressive de Koonings and Picassos at the MOMA. In 1999, Global showed earnings of $10 million—*before*, that is, Global's interest expense of $92 million. No banker—no genuine banker—would lend on the basis of such numbers, suggesting mightily that Chase and the rest were scrambling after fees—were, that is, risking their shareholders' capital in order to book short-term profits, the very definition of shareholder value run riot.

EIGHT

Bankrupt

It was in January 2000, at the very dawn of the millennium, that AOL, the preeminent Internet company, struck a merger with Time Warner, perhaps the preeminent old media company in America. Commentators scored it as a coup for Time Warner, which agreed to relinquish control of its storied magazines and its cable television assets for a chance to participate in the new economy. Actually, it was AOL, whose contributions to the marriage consisted largely, as it would develop, of air, that was the more desperate suitor, so much that it inflated its financial results both before and after the deal was consummated. In retrospect, this unhappy marriage spelled the end of the dot-com bubble. But few people realized it at the time. There was no outward signal—no obvious trigger. The public appetite for dot-coms was, merely, exhausted by the unceasing parade of IPOs. In the middle of March, two months after the merger had been announced, Internet stocks cracked, and when they did, investors, not unlike the familiar cartoon character, saw that they had been running on air. Stripped of the element of belief, dot-coms had nothing to sustain them. In a mere month, Yahoo was cut in half, Wetherell's CMGI surrendered two-thirds of its once-stupendous valuation, and Ventro, the brainchild of David Perry, who had driven West in such a haste, was reduced, with similar dispatch, from $239 to $26, or almost 90 percent. Henry Blodget, ever a reader of trends, gave up the ghost and declared that exuberance was dead. In mid-April 2000, the Nasdaq plunged 10 percent in a single day.

Larry Summers, the Treasury secretary, appeared on CNN and in the tradition of the office appealed for calm.[1] But this time, there was no rebound. An investor who bought on the dip, as the soothsayers of the '90s had so unceasingly urged, over the ensuing twelve months saw technology issues cut in half yet again. By early 2001, the Nasdaq had plunged from 5,000 to under 2,000, and the value of Amazon had shrunk from a peak of $37 billion to under $5 billion. Webvan, the extravagant grocery of Louis Borders, gave up its dream and liquidated; lesser dot-coms folded by the dozen. The IPO market shut down, dooming such hopefuls as AllAdvantage. Disillusioned Webbies, many of them now jobless, bought return tickets East. To the suddenly impoverished dot-commers, new economy became a term of bitter irony.

The collapse augured a changing of the seasons—a grim foreboding not just for Internet issues but for a culture of optimism that had defined a decade. The culture had spread its rays like a golden sunshine; Internet stocks had been merely the most exotic flower in the hothouse—the last to bloom, the first to expire. It was simply realistic to think that others would expire, too. First the cool of evenings, then the killer frost.

But Wall Street was not quite ready for realism. The habit of speculation was too entrenched, the Indian summer too delicious. It is human to write off the dream that has died and yet to hold ever more tightly to the one that remains. It is human to rationalize. Internet stocks had

always been a fantasy—so investors now reckoned. If they had lost
money on Yahoo or on Amazon, perhaps they had themselves to blame.

Telecoms were another matter. The investment in telecoms was at
least twenty times greater than in dot-coms.[2] People thought of their
WorldCom shares—even their Global Crossing shares—as safer, less
adolescent, than the plunging dot-com stocks. They were more integral
to the general economy. In the spring of 2000, investors remained wildly
optimistic about the prospect for telecommunications growth. The collapse of the dot-coms did not for a moment interrupt the feverish work
of laying fiber, whose total already was vastly greater than what users of
the Internet, and even of the telephone, could hope to need. Indeed, the
pace of new investment actually accelerated.

There was a precedent: in the early 1980s, the world was said to be on
the brink of a calamitous oil shortage, though in fact oil was in surplus.
Refineries could not sell their product; service stations were everywhere
closing. But the belief in imminent scarcity was so ingrained that oil
company stocks were buoyant. Drilling rigs rose over the Gulf of Mexico, and oil bankers were said to pour whiskey out of their cowboy
boots. Then all realized there was too much oil, not too little, and the
stocks and the drillers and various banks went bust.

Just so, in 2000, new money poured into fiber optics, and for the financial literati—for mutual funds and for the man with a dollop of current, if conventional, Wall Street wisdom—telecom stocks remained a
must-own. The stock market value of Global Crossing reached a peak in
March of $45 billion, equal to General Motors. WorldCom was valued at
well over $100 billion. And yet the businesses were inarguably deterio-
rating. Bandwidth prices were in free fall, and long-distance carriers
were embroiled in rate wars. The man on the street, besieged by offers
of cheaper telephone service, might have wondered why the industry
needed ever more investment dollars—why it needed *his* dollars. In the

industry, there was a fear that a day of reckoning was near. If tenfold growth turned out to be a myth, there could be little hope for companies such as Global.

1. Salmon Upstream

In June 2000, Leo Hindery Jr., the chief executive of Global Crossing, sent a desperate memo to Winnick, Global's chairman. Hindery said Global, which had invested in a network of 100,000 miles of fiber and had accumulated liabilities of $8 billion, was doomed, and he wrote with the eloquence of the condemned: "Like the resplendently colored salmon going up river to spawn, at the end of our journey our niche is going to die rather than live and prosper." In a phrase that could have stood for the age, Hindery added, "The stock market can be fooled, but not forever."[3]

Global's executives could have alerted their shareholders, but they chose, to the contrary, to maintain an appearance—a false appearance—of prosperity for as long as possible. This pattern was pervasive in the industry.

The vehicle for the masquerade was the capacity swap. Carriers had long exchanged leases on pieces of each other's networks without the exchange of cash or any accounting effect. In the latter half of 2000—that is, at the very time their performance was souring—the game significantly changed. Carriers began to swap broadband leases for large, identical sums of cash. The money was simply round-tripped; checks were sent in both directions to no net effect. Nonetheless, each carrier booked its side of the swap as revenue. Some twenty public companies, telecoms and also energy companies, including Qwest Communications International, 360networks, AOL Time Warner, and Enron, resorted to swaps. In all, they padded their revenues by an estimated $15 billion.[4] Global took the deception one step further, according to a lawsuit filed by a former executive, and booked the totals into cash flow. The alleged sham was so blatant, the ruse so obvious, as to seem comical. No cash was added; the corporate accounts only made it seem so.[5] But telecom executives were evidently past the point of subtlety. The hour was too late for a fine shading of the truth; only a big lie would do.

In public filings, Global alluded to capacity swaps as routine deals to enhance its network: "These transactions were implemented in order to acquire cost-effective local network expansions; to provide for . . . alternatives to new construction in certain markets . . . and to provide additional levels of physical diversity in the network as Global Crossing implements its global mesh architecture."[6] This was baldly misleading. In fact, Global was swapping willy-nilly, often with no business purpose, and much of the bandwidth obtained was never used. In one round-trip, with Qwest, Global traded away valuable pieces of its network in Asia and South America in exchange for capacity in North America it didn't need.[7] There was a total disconnect between Global's engineers, who were incensed at the pointless shuffling, and the sales force, now a virtual arm of the finance department. In the final two days of 2001's second quarter, Global made no fewer than eleven swaps with nine different carriers, attesting to a frenetic atmosphere in which sales people cut any and every deal to boost reported revenues. These swaps accounted for more than 20 percent of Global's revenue in the first half of 2001 and virtually all of its cash flow.[8]

Telecom execs insisted on a fig leaf of legitimacy, and, here, the execs were extremely lucky to have the services of Arthur Andersen, which audited many of the major fiber networks. Andersen not only sanctioned swaps; it promoted them. It was a feature of the '90s that investors focused obsessively on what the reported numbers were while ignoring what they meant.[9] Andersen's practice seemed perfectly designed to exploit this intellectual lacuna. Its exquisitely numeric, ethically deficient auditors labored over a white paper that detailed just how to structure swaps so as to achieve "a significant effect on . . . financial reporting."[10] The white paper, available by late 2000, became a must-read in telecom circles; a cookbook for companies that wanted to sift from a recipe of technicalities and legalisms a clean-looking and "successful" quarterly report.[11]

The cynicism of the late '90s was so pervasive that whenever a company transgressed, auditors such as Andersen and also lawyers and other professional hand-holders were sure to be found busily dotting the i's. They were less professionals than mercenaries, who rationalized that their counsel, in each of its particulars, was legal. This conveniently overlooked that, in its totality, their handiwork was designed to deceive the owners of the business: their true clients. But to a large extent, they had forgotten who their clients were. The long hours these professionals for hire spent with executives, and also the professionals' more-than-ample fees, forged an identity of interest, a society of mutual co-conspiracy.

At companies such as Global, the society was thick. Roy Olofson, a vice president of finance, actually did raise his hand to protest the use of swaps. The reception to Olofson amply demonstrated the low state of professionalism. Joseph Perrone, the first person to whom Olofson complained, was a senior finance executive at Global. Until shortly before, Perrone had worked at Andersen—indeed, he had been the Andersen partner in charge of the Global account, where he had written a memo detailing just how to ensure that capacity swaps would pass muster with auditors. Such facile transfers between auditor and client had often, at other companies, dulled the effectiveness of the gatekeepers. And upon hearing of Olofson's unhappiness, Perrone duly informed him that his status at Global was in jeopardy. Olofson then wrote to Global's ethics officer, who promised to investigate, but once again, the inside man had strings to the outside. The ethics officer was a former partner at Global's prestigious counsel, the New York firm Simpson Thacher & Bartlett. And Simpson Thacher had conflicts of its own, for some of Global's swaps had been hatched in its elegant, East Side offices, and some of the law partners personally owned Global's stock. In light of these entanglements, it is perhaps not a surprise that neither anyone at Global nor at Simpson Thacher bothered to respond to the substance of the letter, nor (before Global's subsequent collapse) did any of them take the letter to the board. As for Olofson, the only reply he received, other than an education in the ways of corporate America and in its pinstriped mercenaries, was his swift termination from Global.[12]

Global's public face, meanwhile, was that of unadorned optimism. As late as January 2001—nearly a year after Hindery's memo—Global was insisting that its outlook couldn't be better; indeed, the CFO was promising cash-flow growth of 40 percent.[13] Largely thanks to such deceptions, the stock remained tolerably high; thus Winnick sold $735 million of personally owned shares, including $261 million in April 2000, two months before he received the notorious salmon upstream warning, and a further $123 million in May 2001, a year after the warning. Other directors and executives sold a total of $582 million worth. Favored political insiders profited, too; Bush Senior pocketed $4.5 million on his investment, and McAuliffe, who was later elected chairman of the Democratic National Committee, reportedly made several times that amount.[14] Considering that the ordinary shareholders eventually lost every penny of their capital, the insiders' $1.3 billion in profits ranks as one of the more extravagant stings in the history of public securities.

Industrywide, insider selling was epidemic, particularly as telecom shares peaked. In 2000 and 2001, insiders at Global, Qwest, and others sold more than $8 billion worth of stock.[15] Such opportunism was relatively unknown to dot-com executives, many of whom were either idealistic, deluded, or both. Executives at eToys, Webvan, and many others never sold a share; they believed their own stories. Telecom executives were not so naïve. Criminal insider trading is difficult to prove, and the executives, later, would protest they had been as unaware as anyone. But the pattern of massive selling, unwarranted optimism, and often-deceptive disclosure suggests otherwise. The corporate elite in America had too long embraced a Gordon Gekkian notion of stewardship; the telecom executives simply embraced it on a colossal scale.

WorldCom was a distinct case. Immediately after its absorption of MCI, Ebbers, in his practiced style, hatched plans for yet a bigger merger, with Sprint Communications. However, in June 2000, as the outlook for telecom was turning gloomy, the Sprint merger was derailed by the Department of Justice. Mergers having been the indispensable key to WorldCom's earnings growth, its executives then knew—even if no one else did—that the game was done. There now ensued a broad effort to manipulate results through a variety of tactics.[16] One of these bears mention. WorldCom, like other telecoms, paid hefty fees to gain access to other companies' networks. These so-called line costs were a significant expense, especially as the revenues that WorldCom gained from using these networks were shrinking. To mask this deteriorating picture, Scott Sullivan, the chief financial officer, began to capitalize—rather than expense—the company's line costs.

It is an old principle of accounting that ordinary expenses (unlike capital goods) must be deducted from income in the period in which they are incurred. By a homely analogy, a teenager with a paper route would deduct the cost of gasoline in figuring his weekly profits but would spread out the cost of a new transmission over a much longer period. If, however, he were also to account for his gasoline as a long-term cost, it would inflate his apparent profits. In the corporate world, capi-

talizing expenses is considered a blatant fraud—not a borderline fudging but a criminal violation. This is precisely what is alleged of Sullivan.[17] The amounts were not trivial. For the first quarter of 2001
WorldCom reported pretax profits of $988 million, of which only $217
million was legitimate.[18] This pattern was to continue.

We do not know what role, if any, was played by Ebbers; only that he
had inculcated the culture of shareholder value, with its overriding emphasis on quarterly profits, in WorldCom's fiber. Moreover, at the time
of Sullivan's machinations, Ebbers had a particular interest in propping
up the stock. Ebbers, who owned roughly 20 million shares of World-
Com, had pledged more than $1 billion of his stock as collateral for
loans, much of which he had used for personal businesses.[19] Indeed, he
seems to have regarded WorldCom as his personal business. And the
stock was drifting downward. From late '99 to mid '00 it fell from $60 to
the mid-40s. Thereafter, it sank like a stone. By the end of 2000, World-
Com had plummeted to $14, and Ebbers was getting margin calls.

We should note that Ebbers's financial troubles did not arise from
any parsimony on the part of the compensation committee, which
awarded him $45 million in cash pay over the period 1997–2000 in addi-
tion to his millions of stock options. Nonetheless, what he owed was
more than what he had. Now, Ebbers began to exhibit a certain desperation. In the fall of 2000, he procured a loan from WorldCom of approximately $50 million. Board approval for the loan had not, in fact, been
reduced to writing at the time that Ebbers pocketed the money, which
suggests that, properly speaking, it was not a loan at all. Nonetheless,
approval was forthcoming (and was conveniently backdated).[20]

Such charity, far from humbling Ebbers, seemed to embolden him, as
may happen when a riverboat gambler, seemingly out of luck, discovers
a hidden billfold. Rather than liquidate his timber company, his ranch, or
his assorted other interests, Ebbers continued to borrow from World-
Com, whose board, making him a further gift of shareholder assets,

charged him a below-market interest rate of only 2.32 percent. The directors rationalized that by lending money to Ebbers, and thereby averting his need to sell stock, they would defend WorldCom's share price.[21] Nonetheless, they did not trouble to interpret this design too strictly. For Ebbers borrowed from WorldCom, a company he was in the process of wrecking, a grand total of $408 million, including not only cash for margined WorldCom shares but also $27 million for purposes that were wholly unrelated to WorldCom, including the construction of Ebbers's new home, an allowance for an Ebbers relative, loans by Ebbers to family and friends, and $22.8 million for his personal businesses—in all, a staggering and unprecedented taking of corporate funds.[22]

2. Blanket over Houston

The crash of broadband put Enron, too, on a downward spiral. But at the dawn of 2001, few people outside of Enron seemed to know it.[23] The stock, at $83, was near its high. Wall Street analysts were bullish. *Fortune*, citing Enron's "reinvention skills," had recently tapped it as one of ten stocks to own for the *decade*—in other words, as a sure thing. The magazine's breezy assurance that Enron's broadband unit "should turn profitable in a few years" typified the tendency of investment writers (to a much greater degree than business writers generally) to echo the chorus on Wall Street—especially in the ubiquitous ten best lists that magazines and newspapers trumpeted to hype their sales. On average, the ten stocks in *Fortune*'s list—patently a compendium of technology, media, and financial favorites—would ultimately fall by an average of 80 percent.[24]

It was easy for supporters of Enron's stock to claim, later, that they had been mislead by Enron's various charades. But we should not acquit the investment community so easily. The collusion on Wall Street, the conspiracy to push share prices ever higher, was abetted by investors (even though investors were, of course, the ultimate victims). The danger signs were there; investors simply chose not to see them. In Enron's disclosures specifically, the references to Fastow's partnerships were so obscure, so confusing, that to the few investors of an inquisitive mind, the lack of transparency clearly spelled trouble. The accounting, even to those not in the know, was aggressive; indeed, it was patently deficient. Kim Schnabel, an analyst at TIAA-CREF, which manages pension money for teachers, actually called Enron's department of investor relations to complain. An employee spat back, "We're Enron; we don't need to have good accounting."* *Why* didn't Enron need good accounting? Enron had observed that analysts such as Schnabel were rare. Skilling and Lay had correctly reckoned that most investors wouldn't read its reports; they would give Enron a pass.

Even if one accepted Enron's accounting, its results were not of a caliber to justify its soaring stock. Quite simply, over the four years that followed Skilling's 1996 elevation to president, Enron's net income, as reported by the company, rose from $1.08 a share to precisely $1.12.[25] That is growth of less than 1 percent per annum. Enron impressed upon analysts that they should focus on other, more favorable yardsticks, which did not include various onetime events—such as, in 2000, a disastrous markdown of Enron's Argentine waterworks. And of course, they projected stupendous growth in the future. But its net income, the actual record, was in black and white for all to see. The supposed growth that made Enron a Wall Street darling, that led to a quadrupling of its stock price, simply did not exist.

What drove Enron's stock wasn't its results but the perception of its results—of its image as a new economy changeling. Put differently, the Enron bubble was as much a public relations phenomenon as it was an

---

*Schnabel courageously recommended that TIAA-CREF's portfolio managers sell their Enron shares. TIAA-CREF was one of the few major fund organizations not to get burned.

accounting phenomenon. In this sense, Enron was the lineal descendent of a generation of share-price promoters—of Lucent, Tyco, and the Internet kingpin CMGI. Enron was simply slicker. Skilling made a priority of Siliconizing Enron's image, in part through p.r. stunts (to promote the notion that Enron operated on Internet time, he ordered elevators removed so that employees could bound the stairs and not lose "momentum"[26]) and by hammering away at the theme of Enron's digital rebirth.

Tellingly, Enron wrote, in its annual report for 2000: "We have metamorphosed from an asset-based pipeline and power generating company to a market and logistics company whose biggest assets are its well-established business approach and its innovative people. Our performance and capability cannot be compared to a traditional energy peer group." If this passage means anything, it means that by shifting its emphasis from energy assets to "logistics," its value was now derived more from its people than from its pipelines and that it consequently should be valued more highly than a traditional energy company. The report carried no indication that Enron was involved in risky energy trades; indeed, it portrayed the company as a beacon of calm amidst volatile markets.[27]

In this and other respects, Enron's image at the turn of 2001 appears to be a gross case of mistaken identity. The company had not only not forsaken assets; it was sinking under their weight. Its roster of white elephants included a costly power plant in India that had become ensnared in a political dispute, the Portland utility, a water company in England with a scheme to capitalize on global deregulation, a fledgling venture to sell energy services to corporations, a Bolivia-to-Brazil gas pipeline, a failed IPO for an electricity retailer (the New Power Company), and so on. Its cash flow was turning negative, and its margins were plummeting. Though *Fortune* ranked Enron as America's seventh-largest company, this, too, was misleading—for Enron included in its $100 billion of revenues its massive online business, in which it brokered energy and other commodity products. As the dollars from this business essentially passed from buyer to seller, they were not, in a meaningful sense, revenues to Enron. Put differently, Enron encountered the same difficulty on the Web as did everyone else—huge traffic, little or no profit.

The real Enron had an extremely profitable—but also an extremely volatile—business in energy and derivatives trading. Contrary to repeated management assertions that Enron was essentially a middleman, the company was in fact making highly speculative bets on the direction of energy markets.[28] In 2000, Enron earned more than $1 billion by speculating on prices in California, which was then suffering intermittent blackouts and a serious power shortage.[29]

Politicians in Sacramento suspected Enron of manipulating its energy prices, but Enron had another reason for playing down its involvement in the state. Since trading is inherently volatile, the stocks of trading companies generally trade at a low multiple of earnings. For a Goldman Sachs, for instance, a price-to-earnings ratio of twelve would not be uncommon. As Enron's stock had soared to *seventy-five* times earnings, Lay and Skilling did everything to distinguish Enron from the Goldmans of the world. Ultimately, Enron's every deception was tied to the desire to promote the stock.

When Enron met with securities analysts, in January 2001, Skilling was the very picture of bluster; his optimism was proportionate to the company's underlying troubles. To a stock promoter, compromise can never be a virtue. Just as a dictator's slightest concession to reform can incite a revolution, so, for a company in a bubble, the most trifling admission of weakness can trigger a collapse. And Skilling had the intuition of a great promoter. He declared that Enron was significantly *under*-valued—indeed, he said, it was worth no less than $126 a share. He upbraided the analysts for not giving Enron's broadband operation, in particular, a higher valuation—*$30 billion*, to be precise. As Enron had lost $60 million in broadband in the just-completed year, and as the entire broadband *industry* was in a state of collapse, one marvels at his cheek; perhaps he figured it was all or nothing.

The analyst meeting, again in Houston, was a tour de force. One hundred and seventy analysts and professional investors attended. They sat through a day of elaborate presentations, detailed forecasts, Power-Point graphics—all the props of shareholder value. One effect of such a carnival was to diminish the likelihood of intelligent appraisal. Ronald Barone, an analyst with UBS Warburg, afterward confessed to feeling "brain-drained." This did not keep him from raising his forecast. Another, Curt Launer, of Credit Suisse, diligently reported, "Trends in all of our modeling inputs point to earnings of $2.20 in 2002."[30] To judge from Launer's stilted phraseology, he wasn't thinking critically, as is required of an analyst; he was modeling inputs that the company had dropped in his lap. The truth is that the analysts, and also their lemminglike clients, *wanted* to be led by Enron; they wanted, in a sense, to be misled. As the analysts knew, Enron was making its numbers only by selling assets. Quarter by quarter, it sold the requisite total to make up the deficit from normal operations and thus paint a happy picture of consistency. That the picture was false hardly mattered; what mattered was Enron's commitment to the ritual and the Street's collective willingness to applaud it.[31] Enron was really the Street's creation—the creation of its faith. It was the creation of a decade of lesser Enrons, of General Electric and Amazon—of companies that had conditioned the investment community to act on faith. Donato Eassey, the new analyst at Merrill Lynch, which had discharged the unlucky Olson, the analyst found by Enron to be insufficiently bullish, opined that Enron was "uniquely positioned to be the General Electric of the new economy."[32] At the zenith of shareholder value, this was a kind of a code; it meant investors need not worry about Enron's numbers nor about its accounting. All would be set right.

Enron's distortions spawned vast opportunities for its executives. This twisting of incentives was always the problem with conventional stock option plans—with shareholder value. Enron, like its spiritual brethren in telecom, simply turned personal enrichment into an art form. In the last quarter of 2000 and the first quarter of 2001—that is, just before and during the Houston meeting in which Skilling said the stock was significantly undervalued—Skilling sold $26 million of it. Enron's officers and directors as a group sold $125 million in the same period. What's more, early in 2001, numerous executives collected cash bonuses that were conditioned, in part, on the performance of the stock. Lay got $10 million, Skilling $7.5 million, Fastow, $3 million.[33] Even forgetting just how the executives had gotten the stock to rise, the system was conceptually flawed. No stock will remain at an unwarranted peak, but the bonuses were forever.

Over a longer time frame, the executives' sales clearly dovetailed with the period of headiest promotion. In 1999–2001, as Enron shares were peaking, officers and directors sold approximately $1.2 billion—an awesome total. Even allowing for the rise in the stock's price, this represented a drastically quickened pace of selling. In the three preceding years they sold less than two million shares. In 1999–2001, during the period of most intense hype, the executives sold *20* million shares.[34]

The insider selling does not suggest that Skilling, who succeeded Lay as chief executive early in 2001, or anyone else, knew that the end was near. Life is rarely that clean. What it shows, rather, is that the executives were increasingly eager to unload the stock just as Enron was reporting increasingly bogus numbers. Skilling, in particular, sold less than $3 million worth before the beginning of 1999, $68 million after it.

Lay, who received by far the biggest option awards and who remained chairman after Skilling's promotion, cashed in $10 million in '98, $30 million in '99, and *$145 million* in 2000–2001. Like WorldCom's Bernie Ebbers, Lay had borrowed from his company against his stock, and some of his sales were forced by margin calls. Lay's defenders have put forth a not implausible defense that he believed in Enron till the end. With the election of Bush, Lay had a friend in the White House (he had also been close to the elder Bush), and politics increasingly distracted him from business. Having been among the biggest donors to Bush over the length of his career, Lay was invited to advise on energy policy at the most senior level of government (all while Enron's hired hands were lobbying Congress, during 2001, on seventy distinct pieces of legislation).[35] As his distractions increased, Lay became even more detached from the day to day at Enron, though one senses his hand in some of its more profligate gestures, such as erecting a palatial new tower in downtown Houston, from which the top executives could overlook a vast electronic trading pit, and putting Enron's name on the local baseball stadium.[36] But Lay's distractions do not explain how he could accept such lordly compensation ($31 million plus millions of options from 1998 through 2000) and yet remain, at best, so uninformed. More difficult, still, except by the curiously forgiving standard of shareholder value, is to reconcile Lay's income with his furious borrowing. Like Ebbers, he adopted an ATM approach to the corporate treasury, helping himself to $77 million (far above what the board had authorized) in return for which he pledged his shares.[37] This was exceeding reckless.

The other sign that the executives were operating under duress is that Enron's deal-making became increasingly suspect. Enron disclosed in 2001 that it had managed to sell some of its surplus fiber-optic network (known as dark fiber, because it was not yet operational) to a "related party" for a $67 million profit. What was not disclosed was that the related party was LJM2, the Fastow partnership, and that, as Enron had promised to make LJM2 whole, the entire sale was bogus. Still, one marvels at Enron's misdirected cleverness. While all the world was sinking under the weight of excess fiber, Enron—and only Enron—managed to sell some of its inventory, for an apparent 200 percent profit.[38]

More desperate, still, were Enron's efforts to raise cash without owning up to borrowing. Beneath its drivel about having metamorphosed, Enron in its essentials was the same company—asset-heavy, cash-poor and debt-ridden—as the one that had emerged from the original 1980s merger. Its hollow claim to being asset-light was suggestive of one of the unspoken myths of the new economy—that the country could run wholly on circuits, absent any plant or equipment.

Enron concealed its old economy burden by persuading banks to make what in substance were loans but in a form that enabled Enron to book the money as cash flow. This was done by dressing the loans as investments in energy assets and cycling the money through special-purpose vehicles, creating a chimera of distance. In its simplest form, banks lent money to partnerships, which went through the motions of purchasing assets from Enron. The net effect was that the bank loans passed through to Enron.[39]

In a series of deals with Morgan, money flowed simultaneously from Morgan to a Channel Islands partnership known as Mahonia and from Mahonia to Enron. The money was ostensibly a hedge against the price of gas and was booked by Enron as a trading profit. However, Enron agreed to purchase an equivalent gas hedge from Morgan six months later, at a slightly higher price. The gas deals netted out to zero; gas had nothing to do with it. The only net effect was that Enron collected $350 million and bore an obligation to repay Morgan a slightly higher sum. This is normally known as borrowing.[40]

Morgan's role reminds us that Enron was not the work of only a few bad apples in Houston. Morgan had the highest pedigree of any institution on Wall Street; its name stood for "first-class business, and that in a first-class way," which was the standard sworn to by J. P. (Jack) Morgan Jr. during Congress's hearings into the causes of the Great Crash. Long after J. P. had left the scene, Morgan standards remained a cut above. It was not till the age of shareholder value that Morgan executives so fully abandoned their birthright. Eager to convince investors of their own transmutation into New Age bankers, Morgan and its merger partner Chase acquired a dot-com bank, then shoveled money at telecoms, now did sham trades with Enron—the great triad of *fin de siècle* excesses.

As we have seen, with the repeal of Glass-Steagall bankers could dream that loans would lead to underwriting assignments. This annulled a principle of J. Pierpont Morgan (Jack's father) that the prime consideration in lending should be the character of the borrower. The bank's modern-day rival, Citigroup, was if anything more susceptible to temptation than Morgan. Citigroup had been formed by the merger of Travelers, an insurance and investment banking giant, and Citibank for the purpose of cross-selling Wall Street products to depositors. The architect of the deal, Sandy Weill, had spent a lifetime trying to build a financial supermarket. The Citigroup merger, announced in 1998, was his crowning achievement; as noted, it was predicated on Glass-Steagall's repeal, and it induced Congress to finish the job of tearing down the ancient regulatory barrier.

It was not until Enron, though, that Weill's minions reaped the full harvest of repeal. In 2000, Citigroup invested in an off-the-books partnership—this one was named Bacchus, after the god of wine—to which Enron transferred pulp-and-paper assets. However, as Citigroup had received an oral promise from Enron of "support" (i.e., repayment), the investment was in fact a loan. That Citigroup had secretly extended a favor to Enron, for which the bank expected repayment, was clear from an e-mail, written by a Citigroup banker, at the end of the year: "We made a lot of exceptions to our standard policies . . . let's remember to collect this IOU when it really counts."[41]

Not everyone at Citi was happy about it. When Enron, in 2001, proposed another such deal, Dave Bushnell, Citigroup's chief risk officer, argued that Citigroup was already too exposed to Enron. Trying to quash the second partnership, he pointed out that Citigroup could face embarrassing questions if the details ever became public. However, bankers who saw Enron as a limitless fount of business kept pushing. "One side of the house is trying to be strict, while the other is committing capital to" Enron, Bushnell wrote in a memorandum. That single sentence devastated the post–Glass-Steagall pretext that an informal, so-called Chinese wall would immunize banks from conflict. The deal was approved.[42]

None of these deals could have gone forward without the sanitizing varnish provided by Enron's outside auditor, Arthur Andersen. Andersen was implicated in Enron's every pore, and if we wish to understand Enron's climatic undoing, the Andersen relationship is central. The first point is that it *was* a relationship: Andersen did not merely audit Enron's books; it was involved in the company on a daily, ongoing basis. As many as a hundred Andersen employees worked on Enron—they worked *at* Enron, on a full-time basis at its headquarters, providing not only auditing but consulting services, an arrangement that had come a cropper at another Andersen client, Waste Management. The timing is important. Andersen's lead partner on the Enron account, David Duncan, first expressed his unease with Enron at a meeting of the board's audit committee in Houston, early in 1999, when he declared that Enron was "pushing the limits" of acceptable accounting. Not long before, a group of senior partners had issued a memorandum warning that Andersen had to toughen its audits. The firm's audit of Waste Management was under an intense microscope at the SEC, and Levitt was starting to demand an end to all such auditor/consulting arrangements.[43] The partners knew that if the Enron audit were ever found to be faulty, it would look very bad if the auditor were also the consultant.

But the firm's brass had become obsessed with increasing consulting revenue, for reasons general to the industry but also specific to Arthur Andersen's history. The two sides of Andersen (consulting and auditing) had become impossibly divided, and by 1999, the firm was in the process of a bitter divorce (the original consulting wing would be renamed Accenture). The traditional auditing partners, who were facing the loss of their lucrative consulting unit, were thus particularly eager to stoke their own practice.[44]

In this context, Enron seemed to hold special promise. Andersen not only prepared the Enron audit; it prepared the numbers that were the *basis* of the audit—a job normally handled by internal corporate staff. In effect, Andersen was auditing itself. This seamless meshing of internal and external functions appealed to Skilling, because it diluted the auditor's independence—diluted its gatekeeper role. It also appealed to Andersen, which was hoping that such integrated audits would curry favor with a wider clientele. Andersen even produced a videotape, for marketing purposes, in which an Andersen auditor, boasting of her closeness to Enron, remarked "Out here, we don't call audit audit."[45] It is a commentary on the state of public accounting in America that an auditor could have expressed such a humiliating obeisance to a client as though it were a virtue.

In 2000, Enron asked Andersen to help structure four special vehicles that Skilling felt were crucial to Enron's future. The particulars suggested that Enron was, again, pushing the limits. Carl Bass, a member of Andersen's professional standards group in Houston, tartly protested. But his partners were either too greedy or too weak to stop it. The firm was like the timid accomplice, half hoping his partner will stage another bank heist, half hoping he will call it a day. Abject agreement was the only response of which the ever more implicated Andersen was capable.[46]

The four new partnerships—dubbed, with the usual lurid nomenclature, Raptor—were to provide Enron with a hedge against a decline in the value of various of its merchant investments. In other words, if the value of the investments declined, Raptor would make up the difference. It was a standard derivative contract, except that Raptor had no independent source of equity. LJM2, the Fastow partnership, invested $30 million in each of the four vehicles, but the money was (by prior arrangement) quickly returned with a substantial profit to LJM2 and, indeed, to Fastow.[47]

Raptor's primary asset was Enron stock. The details were madly complex, and one suspects that Fastow thrilled to their complexity, not just because it served him to keep the arrangement obscure but because he was one of those bright, hyperattenuated executives who took pleasure in devising Rubik's Cubes beyond the powers of ordinary mortals. It would serve no purpose here to penetrate this Fastowian maze, but we can describe its essentials plainly: as Raptor's ability to pay Enron depended on Enron's stock remaining strong and even on Enron's stock increasing, Enron did not have an independent and genuine hedge.* Indeed, the arrangement violated a basic principle under which companies may not recognize on the income statement gains resulting from the increase in the value of their stock.[48]

Andersen showed extraordinary license in permitting such a structure, as did Enron's board. The corporate secretary observed, at a meeting of the finance committee, that Raptor "does not transfer economic risk but transfers P&L volatility."[49] The sentence speaks for the age, for it confirms that directors knowingly approved a structure to shore up Enron's appearance—that is, the empty ciphers on its profit and loss statement—while doing nothing for the substance of its business.

During the latter half of 2000, Enron's merchant investments deteriorated, but—as planned—its reported income was inoculated by Raptor.

---

*The third Raptor was intended to hedge Enron's investment in the New Power Company. It held stock in New Power—the very asset it was intended to hedge and thus had a similar conflict to the rest.

To outward appearance, Enron's results were bright but only because, over that span, it had reported some $500 million more in profit than it would have absent Raptor's hedge.[50] Since Raptor had thus become the fulcrum on which Enron's public profile depended, maintaining Enron's stock price now became a matter of the first priority.

Skilling's insistence, early in 2001, that Enron was worth an extraordinary $126 a share can be understood only in this light: not as a candid reflection of enthusiasm but as a desperate plea to bolster an increasingly imperiled operation. By February, the value of Enron's portfolio had sunk further, and Raptor's obligation to Enron had grown to troublesome proportions. Skilling, now, was pressing for a way to fix Raptor's credit. He tended to think of every problem as a public relations problem—as a challenge to Enron's image.[51] True to form, Enron proposed a fix for Raptor that was merely cosmetic, a financial face-lift. Otherwise, at the end of the March quarter, Enron would be forced to take a $500 million charge.[52]

But would Andersen approve the fix? Bass, the firm's standards officer, argued against it. A refusal could mean the loss of Enron as a client, an option the partners actively debated. But that would mean forgoing Enron's lofty fees—a bountiful $52 million in 2000. Moreover, Andersen was no longer quite capable of deciding the matter on its own; it had become infiltrated by Enron people—by Enron's mind-set. Every time Bass raised a concern to his partners it was leaked to Enron—perhaps by Duncan, who was a golfing partner of Richard Causey, Enron's senior accounting officer. Private deliberations at Andersen were no longer private; the firm had become an arm of its client. At the urging of Causey, for whom one diligent auditor was evidently one too many, Bass was taken off the account; in March, Andersen approved the fix. Skilling was so overjoyed by the accountants' cleverness that he personally called one to thank him. Remarkably, neither he nor anyone informed the board that Enron had narrowly, and quite dubiously, avoided taking a massive charge.[53]

Such reticence should not surprise us, for burying the whistle-blower was one of Enron's identifying traits. It emanated from Lay as well as Skilling, and though the two had different styles, the net effect was remarkably effective, as though a blanket had been draped over Houston. Various employees had raised concerns about the partnerships to Skilling; his reflexive response had been to muffle the complainer.[54] Some of their unease percolated up to Lay, in a more informal and sporadic manner. *The Washington Post* reported a telltale instance: in the spring of 2000, Alberto Gude, an Enron vice president who had known Lay since 1977, felt moved to warn the chairman about the character of Skilling and certain of his associates. "I really believe you are in trouble," Gude reportedly said.[55] Lay responded cordially; he was never as confrontational as Skilling. The problem was his tendency to do nothing—to procrastinate. He depended so heavily on underlings that he was unwilling to ever undermine them. That was the case with Lay and the oil traders in 1987, and it was true of Lay's relationship with Skilling and Fastow now.

Death of the Raptor

A year after Gude's warning, the gods abandoned Enron. In March 2001, Bethany McLean, a young journalist at *Fortune*, wrote a probing, critical piece that asked a question overlooked by others: How, exactly, did Enron make money? Enron replied that the details were "proprietary."[56] For a company with public shareholders this was remarkably unforthcoming. It showed a certain touchiness; Enron had been nicked. Soon, investors began to ask it similar questions. In April, Enron dis-

closed its results for the previous quarter. It didn't *formally* file these results with the SEC (it did that four weeks later)—rather, it "disclosed"
that portion of its results that it wished to publicize, by a conference call
with the usual Wall Street professionals. As Enron reported that its income
had risen sharply, the investors on the call were effusive, even congratu-
latory. They were not alarmed by the fact that Enron's cash flow—the
actual dollars generated by operations—were deeply negative—for the
simple reason that Enron had not yet disclosed its cash flow.

However, one investor asked how Enron was managing its trading
risks, particularly in California. The question seemed to hit a nerve.
Skilling went into a harangue, the substance of which was that Enron
managed its risks with a state-of-the-art, proprietary system that cali-
brated its exposures every day.

Now, a hedge-fund investor from Boston named Richard Grubman,
who had been selling Enron short, asked to know Enron's trading exposures. Grubman was particularly curious about an entry on Enron's balance sheet denoted "accumulated other comprehensive income." It
referred to the net fluctuation in investment assets that didn't hit the income statement. At the end of 2000, Enron's accumulated other comprehensive income was negative $1 billion. Grubman wondered whether
the deficit had widened; indeed, he thought Enron might be using the
balance sheet to hide its losses.

Skilling said the numbers weren't available; they would be filed with
the SEC within forty-five days of the end of the quarter, as required by
law. Grubman said that was odd: Enron was the only major financial institution to his knowledge that couldn't produce a balance sheet at the
end of the quarter. Then, Skilling lost it. He said, "Thank you very
much, asshole."

The comment stunned his many listeners. It exposed a truth that
Wall Street, previously, had failed to see: when not provided with a

smooth script, Skilling was defensive and inarticulate. Behind the promotional veil, the Oz-like mists, Skilling did not have answers.

Wall Street can be fooled, as the memo writer for Global observed,
but not forever. When investors catch a scent of weakness, they
will turn with surprising haste. All former affection is forgotten; now
they want only to sell. And so it was with Enron. Month after month the
stock declined—$80 at the end of January, $68 at the end of February,
then $58, $62, and $52 at the end of May. The investors, most of them,
did not know exactly why Enron was falling (nor had they understood
its rise). Enron, it is true, was absorbing a string of blows—the loss of
the only customer for its Indian power plant, the early termination of its
video project with Blockbuster, the collapse of an agreement to sell the
Portland utility. Investors weren't necessarily aware of the details—
only that the sheen was gone. Perhaps it was as simple as the protester in
San Francisco, where Skilling spoke on the state's electricity crisis—and
where he was hit in the ear with a blueberry tofu cream pie. When Wall
Street is nervous, blueberry tofu is all the reason it needs.

In any case, the Street was nervous. By the end of July, the stock was
$45. Because of Raptor's dependence on the stock, its credit deficiencies
were mounting—in fact, they were becoming intolerable. And the stock
was a problem Skilling couldn't fix. He had always resorted to image-
making, but Enron's image was beyond repair—the sinking stock was a
reflection of its image. And so, Skilling committed the quintessential act
of a man who has lost his script—he exited the stage. In the middle of
August, he quit.

Enron attributed the CEO's resignation to a "personal decision." Lay,
who reassumed Skilling's duties, tried to reassure the public by comment-
ing that Enron did not have "accounting issues"—that it was, indeed,

"in the strongest shape it's ever been in."[57] The remark did not fool any-one (the stock kept sliding) except, possibly, Lay himself. There are cer-tain men who say, and perhaps even believe, what others wish to hear.

But the next day, Lay received an anonymous letter—apparently from an employee—that depicted a more troubled Enron. Lay had known whistle-blowers before, but this one was different—utterly alarmed and disturbingly informed. What Lay read now was not the whispered allusion of wrongdoing but the bald charge—not vague as-sertions but detailed facts.

Sherron Watkins, who promptly identified herself as the author, was an executive in finance. She was neither a moralist nor an ethicist; in-deed, the first paragraph of her letter could have been written by a younger Andy Fastow:

> Dear Mr. Lay:
> Has Enron become a risky place to work? For those of us who didn't get rich over the last few years, can we afford to stay?

Watkins made several points. The accounting for Raptor and other SPVs was deceptive, quite possibly fraudulent. Raptor and LJM (and hence, Fastow) had been protected by "a veil of secrecy." But now, given the attention focused on Enron by Skilling's "shocking depar-ture," investigative journalists, investors and others would surely be poring over Enron's disclosures. They would see that its filings, its foot-notes, and its amplifications did not explain its manifold transactions. They would ask more questions. In short, Enron was about to be ex-posed.

> I am incredibly nervous that we will implode in a wave of accounting scandals. My 8 years of Enron work history will be worth nothing on my resume, the business world will consider the past successes as

nothing but an elaborate accounting hoax. Skilling is resigning now for "personal reasons" but I think he wasn't having fun, looked down the road and knew this stuff was unfixable and would rather abandon ship now than resign in shame in 2 years.

Ever the pragmatist, Watkins laid out two possible courses of action. First, if Lay felt "the probability of discovery" was low enough, Enron could try to quietly unwind the partnership deals, reverse the accounting, and take the necessary charges. Otherwise, it should publicly disclose the problem and do its best to contain the damage.[58]

A week after receiving the letter, Lay met Watkins in his office, for approximately an hour. He was both impressed and concerned and promised to investigate the issues raised in the letter. Watkins recommended that Lay hire a major accounting firm—obviously, not Arthur Andersen—and a law firm other than Vinson & Elkins, the company's regular counsel, to investigate. Lay, who was hoping for a quick resolution, did neither. Instead, he passed the letter to the very same Vinson & Elkins, whose partners took it straight to Duncan, the Andersen partner who oversaw the Enron account. Duncan assured the lawyers that the accounting, however questionable it might appear, "satisfies the technical requirements." This is the trouble with finely written rules—they are a prescription for what is permissible as well as what is not. Had Vinson & Elkins checked with any other auditor they would have heard that, in fact, the accounting for Raptor satisfied virtually no one. But the lawyers, who had helped to create the very structures they were now investigating, decided to accept the "treatment provided by AA" on its face. That meant its inquiry would not be an inquiry at all. Vinson & Elkins duly reported that no further investigation was warranted.[59]

This was faintly comic, for even "AA" had come to realize that Raptor wouldn't hold. The Watkins letter had scared the Andersen partners, and they were—finally—pushing Enron to act. At the end of September, Lay ordered his lieutenants to terminate Raptor and take a charge to earnings.

However, Lay was not yet willing to own up to the consequences. Late in September and early in October, he met with his two most loyal constituent groups: Enron's employees and the outside directors. The employee meeting took the form of an Internet chat: an electronic pep rally. Many of Enron's workers had invested their savings in the stock, which in the aftermath of the September 11 terrorist attacks had plunged to $25. Lay urged them to keep the faith—even to buy more. In fact, he said *he* was buying it. This was remarkably dishonest. Actually, over the past month, Lay had *sold* $20 million worth, with which he had repaid advances from the company.

Two weeks later, Enron's executives met with the board. Lay glossed over Raptor's troubles and made only a vague reference to an employee's having questioned the company's accounting. Incredibly, the directors left thinking that Enron was in good shape. Thus, in a fortnight, Lay had managed to deceive the two groups that were his most steadfast supporters.[60]

In mid-October, Enron did disclose a $710 million pretax charge resulting from the termination of Raptor.* A subsequent investigation concluded that over five quarters, Raptor had manufactured 70 percent of Enron's reported earnings.[61] Enron also admitted to huge losses in its water company and in broadband. However, Enron did not identify Raptor by name, nor did it own up to Fastow's role. Indeed, its press release was a triumph of spin. It downplayed its losses as onetime occurrences, aside from which, the company asserted, its "core" results had been "very strong." This was also the theme struck by Lay in the customary conference call. Instinctively and probably unconsciously, Lay

---

*The figure equals the excess of Raptor's liabilities over its assets plus a $35 million payment that Raptor made to LJM2 in September.

had blended Sherron Watkins's two suggested responses into the most publicly palliative strategy—"we find a way to quietly and quickly reverse, unwind, write down these positions" and "develop damage containment plans and disclose."

But nobody bought it. Of the write-offs, an analyst from Goldman Sachs asked simply, How do we know there won't be more?

There is little so dispiriting as trying to support a stock that has run out of believers. Ultimately, one stops believing it oneself. A couple of days after the conference call, Enron met with investors in Boston, at the Four Seasons Hotel. One of the first people to arrive was Grubman, the hedge-fund manager who had been insulted by Skilling six months earlier. This time, the Enron people were solicitous. They complimented Grubman, who they knew had been betting against Enron's stock, for having asked such intelligent questions. Then, Lay came by and apologized for Skilling's outburst. Abruptly, he added, "Can I join you for lunch?"

The two of them, the short seller and the teetering tycoon, sat together, nearly alone. Lay tried to reach out—he noted he was only six months shy of sixty, and, as he told it, he had been nearly retired, his wife had been planning a round-the-world-trip, his guys had made a mess of it all, and Lay had been stuck trying to fix it. He did not seem to grasp that his guys had merely been following his own implicit instructions—to build a stock price, to generate reportable earnings, to do the things that had brought a congenial preacher's son to the inner circles of the White House.

Grubman felt awkward—not inclined to ask questions. He said, "Ken, this must really be tough."

Lay seemed to know how it would end. He asked about the hedge-fund business—Grubman's work. When Grubman finished, Lay leaned back with an air of resignation. "Well, you must be some pretty bright guys," Lay said, "'cause you been making a bundle while I been losing one."[62]

There was no stopping the dominoes, now. *The Wall Street Journal* was on to the story of Fastow's special vehicles and the millions he had earned (later estimated at $50 million) on illicit deals that had seemingly wrecked the company.[63] Then, the SEC launched an investigation into the partnerships. Lay briefly defended Fastow; then, he fired him. By the end of October, Enron was preparing to admit, retroactively, that Chewco, the first of the troublesome SPVs, had never had sufficient outside equity and thus should have been consolidated in Enron's results all along. This would result in a massive restatement of its earnings and a sharp revision of its debt over a full five years.

Virtually all of the gatekeepers that had once conspired to shelter Enron—the purported GE of the new economy—now abandoned it. The press and the regulators were digging up scandalous details by the day. The auditors were forcing a restatement. The directors, finally, had recruited a competent outsider, the dean of the University of Texas law school, to join the board and conduct an investigation. Analysts were jumping ship. The only gatekeeper not completely lost to Enron was the one that was most important: the credit-rating agencies. Enron had always been a credit story, ever since the takeover era and the merger that saddled it with debt. Fastow's trickery—the debt he didn't call debt, the equity that wasn't equity, the hedge that was nothing more than Enron stock—had always been aimed at preserving Enron's credit. Without credit it was nothing.

The rating agencies had been as derelict as anyone in scrutinizing Enron, but by the end of October, they had awoken. Lay, with his formidable political connections, called Alan Greenspan and two cabinet officials to see if someone—anyone—could persuade the agencies not to downgrade.[64] This was Enron's usual modus operandi—to arm-wrestle a gatekeeper. The officials refused. In the first week of November, Fitch Ratings downgraded Enron to just one notch above junk-bond level. Its stock was now in the single digits. As the market knew, a trader, specifically, cannot survive the loss of credit. Enron's trading partners were demanding collateral, and Enron was, indeed, hemorrhaging cash. At this late hour, Morgan and Citigroup agreed to provide $1 billion of liquidity, a remarkable show of allegiance. But they could not restore Enron's credit, which is an intangible that derives not merely from the borrower's balance sheet but from the market's trust. A year earlier, no company had been accorded more faith than Enron; by late November, none was trusted less. And so, a gasping gurgle, a desperate SOS: Enron, the emblem of free markets, the champion of deregulation, reached into its depleted treasury and forked over $100,000 to each of the major political parties' campaign war chests.[65] Then, it shuttered its online trading unit—its erstwhile gem. On November 28, Standard & Poor's downgraded Enron to junk-bond level—which triggered provisions in Enron's debt requiring it to immediately repay billions of its obligations. This it could not do. Its stock was seventy cents and falling, and, now, no gatekeepers and no credit remained. Accordingly, in the first week of December, Enron, the archetype of shareholder value, availed itself of the time-honored protection for those who have lost their credit: bankruptcy.

NINE

Year of the Locusts

From the moment Enron admitted to having misstated its books, Wall Street and also a considerable stretch of corporate America were never the same. They suffered the shock of recognition—as if an attic trapdoor had been flung open exposing the family's supposedly demented aunt, and all of her cousins, nieces, and nephews had seen a ghostly reflection of themselves. The main components of the scandal—the unvarnished greed, the conspiratorial neglect by gatekeepers, the hysterical attention to share price—were simply too common to think that Enron was unique.

Its seamier revelations turned the public's stomach. The news that Enron had locked down its 401(k) program to prevent rank-and-file employees from selling stock—even as executives whose own pensions were protected were bailing out—presented a revoltingly greedy picture of the corporate suite. The revelation that Enron had paid $55 million in retention bonuses in the month before the bankruptcy seemed too shocking to believe. Just as painful was the retrospective discovery that

Chung Hu, a Houston stockbroker who warned his clients in August to get out of the stock and thereby demonstrated the integrity lacking in almost every other watchdog, had been summarily fired by UBS PaineWebber for the crime of upsetting the senior executives of Enron.[1]

In every way, the deck had been stacked against the average investor. Alfred Harrison, the mutual fund manager who had blown hundreds of millions of his shareholders' dollars on Enron, pocketed a personal reward of $2 million, confirming that the interests of fund managers were not aligned with those of their shareholders.[2]

Worse, it was soon learned that Arthur Andersen, Enron's primary gatekeeper, had undertaken a concerted effort to hide the truth by shredding trunk loads of papers. The appearance of criminality at Andersen, formerly the gold seal of trust, heightened the public's impression that Enron was the result of a systemic, as distinct from a singular, breakdown. The bull market had already cracked, and after Enron/Andersen it seemed not just over but invalidated—as though it had been based on shoddy premises all along. The bubble now seemed to have been not merely doomed but foredoomed.

Many small investors returned to the older, cynical view of the market that the fat cats would always, ultimately, trump the little guy. The fact that Enron's executives had pocketed millions while its workers had lost more than a billion in savings was deeply offensive. For the first time in a decade, average investors pulled money out of equity mutual funds and rediscovered bonds. The love affair was over.

It is impossible to separate the effect of Enron from that of the other, practically concurrent disaster—the terrorist attacks of September 11. Throughout the '90s and until September 11, Americans had lived in a post–cold war world, one symbolized by the collapse of the Berlin Wall. The people who had toppled the Wall (for it didn't merely collapse; it was stormed) were understood to want freedom in all its guises—including economic freedom. The Wall's toppling had symbolized not only America's defeat of Russia but the victory of capitalism over communism, of markets over collectivism. The indelible image of the Wall had imparted to market societies a moral license. September 11 redefined the world with an image even more bracing than Berlin. When the towers fell, America became, instantly and enduringly, a more fearful place. An era of caution commenced, and caution is by nature hostile to enterprise. So much more, the extreme giddiness of the late '90s was wholly out of place in a world of firefighter's funerals, security checks, and all the rest.

The attacks forced President Bush, a political heir with no apparent interest in the potential of government, to become a more activist executive than he had intended. Bush had campaigned on a platform of reducing taxes and generally liberating Americans from Washington. His primary message had been negative—it was about what government should *not* do. The attacks did not alter his fundamental conservatism, but they forced him to redefine his conception of the job—to lead the government rather than merely shrink it. Once the Pentagon had been torched by a hijacked airliner, it became unseemly—even unpatriotic— to demean Washington, D.C., as a sinkhole of bureaucracy, waste, and so forth. Bush himself was soon proposing a new cabinet department and a vastly increased budget.

Ordinary Americans reverted to their traditional wartime reverence for Washington. The U.S. Government was, again, seen as the country's defender rather than (as conservatives had seen it) a usurper of individual freedom. The reemergence of a federal deficit—formerly a political no-no—underscored that the business of government now was too important to be tailored to the whim of the bond market. No one could think, in the aftermath of September 11, that government didn't matter, nor could one believe that markets were the best or the only forum for resolving every conceivable problem. There was an attitudinal shift, greatly enhanced by the market's failures. In California, the tortured experiment in competition in electricity supply had prompted a backlash; other states were tabling plans for a similar deregulation.[3] It is not too strong to say that after two decades of swinging toward freer markets, the pendulum had begun to swing back. The collapse of Enron and the disastrous results in the newly deregulated telecom industry suggested that the mania for deregulation had been pressed too far. The fervor for free markets had upset the social balance. The rich had become increasingly brazen about employing patent and abusive shelters to duck their taxes; now, in state after state, budgets were falling into crisis.

Christmas 2001 was especially somber. For the first time in eleven years, the economy was in recession. This was a significant market failure; it refuted the new economy chestnut that economic cycles had become outmoded and snapped yet another fantasy of the boom. Though the recession had begun before September, there was no doubt that terrorism, as well as Enron, had accentuated the slowdown. In the financial world, the two catastrophes were metaphorical twin towers. The reckless optimism of the '90s had been doubly extinguished, leaving in its wake a tentativeness, a mistrust of the highest institutions of finance.

By January 2002, Global Crossing, the doomed salmon that had spawned so many eggs for its insiders, had followed Enron into bankruptcy. By March, prices in wireless were plummeting, and WorldCom and Qwest had disclosed that their accounting was under investigation. Arthur Andersen was indicted for obstructing justice; the firm's survival was now in grave doubt. Then, Adelphia Communications, a publicly owned Pennsylvania cable operator, revealed that it had secretly guaranteed $2 billion of loans to the Rigas family, which controlled it. Adelphia had all the earmarks of the failed corporate governance that brought Enron low. Its four highest-paid officers consisted of John C. Rigas, the chairman, and three of his sons. Coincidentally, no doubt, five of Adelphia's nine board members were also Rigas family members.[4] This was the sort of utter cronyism qua corruption typical of 1902, perhaps, that was thought to be impossible in 2002. The crisis was widening.

It is an American tradition that financial scandals bring investigations in Congress. They serve, at least, a theatric function. Lawmakers will do their best to exhume the most outrageous of Wall Street's corpses and promise worthy reforms. Generally, once the public outrage dies, so does the legislative effort. However, in 2002, the breadth of the wrongdoing, and the high level of public awareness, forced the Congress not only to hold hearings but to consider substantive changes. Its early deliberations naturally focused on Enron. Representative Billy Tauzin solemnly declared to *Business Week,* "We're finding out that there are real problems endemic in the structure of Corporate America that we need to deal with. Enron is just the worst example."[5] Readers may recall that Representative Tauzin, who received $57,000 in contributions from Arthur Andersen, had been so enraged by the SEC's earlier attempt to bar auditors such as Andersen from providing consulting to auditing clients that he had threatened to quash the SEC's authority. This too is part of our political tradition; ex post facto, lawmakers frequently discover a latent (and expedient) sense of outrage.

When the Senate commenced hearings into Enron, early in 2002, the members, significantly, focused on the systemic nature of the debacle. Carl Levin, a Michigan senator who had fought unsuccessfully for accountability in stock options, observed, acutely: "It may be that Enron and Andersen broke laws, or it may be that the principal scandal is what passes for *legal* conduct in today's marketplace." This raised the question of the need for substantive change in securities laws.

The first witness was Arthur Levitt Jr., the former SEC chairman, who succinctly declared, "Enron's collapse did not occur in a vacuum.

Its backdrop is an obsessive zeal by too many American companies to project greater earnings from year to year."[6] The senators treated Levitt as a returning sage, obsequiously praising efforts that many of them, a short while before, had blocked when he was in power. Their flattery for the former chairman was a backhand way of expressing concern over the new head of the SEC, the man most crucial to the administration's Wall Street agenda, Harvey Pitt.

Pitt was a Wall Street lawyer with close ties to, among others, each of the big accounting firms. He had represented the accountants in their successful fight against Levitt over auditing, and his nomination had been worrisome even before the outbreak of the Enron scandal. It is true that two of the most stalwart SEC chairmen—Kennedy and, of course, Levitt—had hailed from Wall Street. However, Pitt differed from such predecessors. He was argumentative where they were political—ideological as opposed to pragmatic. Moreover, whereas Levitt's experience as a broker had seemingly disabused him of any illusions as to Wall Street's character, Pitt's long tenure as an advocate had merely hardened his sense of self-righteousness.

In October 2001—that is, when Enron was very publicly in its death throes—Pitt gave an address to accountants in Miami Beach in which he lamented that the SEC had not, previous to his reign, been a "kinder and gentler place for accountants."[7] The industry heard this remark to mean that the chairman of the SEC would continue to be their man. His agenda was indeed the exact opposite of one prepared to roll back, or at least to closely examine, the excesses of a decade of shareholder value.

Before long, Pitt was on a hot seat. One of the first proposals from Congress was to separate auditing from consulting. The accounting industry lobbied stridently against it. (To paraphrase Charlie Munger, the vice chairman of Berkshire Hathaway, it is an unfortunate and dishonorable trait of American lobbyists that they respond to any grave harm done to society by their members not by offering a public apology but by redoubling their efforts to protect their industry's ability to do further harm.)[8] Pitt reflexively took the side of his former clients, defiantly asserting, "Auditor independence is not the cause of the problems that we are witnessing."[9] This was naïve and also dangerously out of step with the evolving public sentiment. Even the editors of the deeply conservative *Wall Street Journal* called for Pitt's removal. "Financial markets," the *Journal* intoned, "are looking for more honesty in business bookkeeping. . . . [Pitt has] gone too easy on his old friends in the accounting trade, especially in protecting the industry's lucrative consulting business."[10] The country was eager for stronger regulation; its chief securities regulator was not. Nor was the head of state.

Bush was almost wholly occupied with America's efforts to combat terror, and corporate malfeasance was not an issue likely to ring his bell. The Bush cabinet was famously a government of former CEOs; however, as James Surowiecki pointed out in *The New Yorker*, the businesses that most of the Bush CEOs had run depended on political connections and lobbying of one sort or another—assistance on tariffs, government contracts, subsidies, deals with foreign states, and so forth.[11] Virtually none of the cabinet CEOs had been an entrepreneur; their careers had advanced in closed rooms, not open markets. The two most prominent examples were Bush himself, who had parlayed his name into a seat on the board of Harken Energy and a lucrative stake in the Texas Rangers baseball team, and Vice President Dick Cheney, who had landed the top job at Halliburton, an oil-service contractor, almost wholly because of his own political connections. The Bush team was less apt to be offended by conflicts and crony capitalism because many had been crony capitalists themselves.

Bush's service at Harken had been marred by a questionable sale of 212,000 shares of company stock—two-thirds of his holdings—for $4 a share, in June 1990. Curiously, he did not report the sale until some thirty-four weeks after the law required him to do so. Moreover, the company had been in a financial bind. It subsequently restated its results, and after Bush's sale the stock plunged to $1. The SEC (which, of course, reported to Bush's father) investigated the son for trading on inside knowledge of Harken's troubles—a charge the younger Bush has always denied. It also looked into a deal in 1989 (when Bush served on the audit committee) in which, more curiously still, Harken loaned money to a group of insiders who purchased control of a Harken subsidiary— thereby enabling Harken to shield millions of dollars of its debt.

In October 1993, by which time Clinton was in office, the SEC decided to terminate the investigation and to take no action. The most convincing thesis is that a president's son with a history of recklessness cut a questionable corner and that, having made him suffer through an official investigation, neither his father's government nor its successor (each for its own reasons) wished to carry the matter further.[12] This was hardly the background of a man disposed to reform. Indeed, the Harken episode, small as it may have been, touched on most of the major elements—faulty disclosure, hidden debt, inside sales, boardroom laxness, and even the coincidence of its being a politically connected Houston energy company—that made such headlines at Enron.

The corporate scandals obtained new piquancy in the spring of 2002, when the stock market began a steep slide. This roused the public to the long-simmering issue of executive compensation. For as long as stocks had been rising, investors, save for a few familiar gadflies, had paid little attention to CEOs' exorbitant pay. Institutional shareholders had been especially, even abjectly, silent. This year was different. The Dow, well above 10,000 at the beginning of March, began to plummet just in time for the annual proxy disclosures. The juxtaposition of market losses with huge bonuses for CEOs made clear what should have long been obvious: CEOs were vastly overpaid. Indeed, their poor performance *contributed* to their excessive pay, for many took advantage of their slumping shares to grab fresh boodles of low-price stock options.

John Chambers, the CEO of Cisco, celebrated the end of the high-tech boom, as well as the collapse of his stock, by taking options on 4 million shares. Another CEO, William Harrison, the CEO of J. P. Morgan Chase, which in 2001 had seen its stock fall, its net income plunge, and its reputation stained by its links to Enron—ultimately resulting in a $1.3 billion charge against the bank—nonetheless claimed an 80 percent raise in pay, to $17 million.[13] But it was Christos Cotsakos, the chairman of E*Trade and an entrepreneur synonymous with the online bubble who, now that his industry was in ruins, violated every standard of decency.

Cotsakos received a rather astounding package of $80 million. The figure was disclosed at the end of April, at which point E*Trade stock had fallen from a high of $60 to precisely $7½. A nasty tempest ensued. "What did he do, get the stock to go from $6 to $7?" a wag asked rhetorically of *The Wall Street Journal*. Patrick McGurn, a vice president with Institutional Shareholder Services, told the *San Jose Mercury News*, the hometown paper in the Valley, that Cotsakos's compensation "is a microcosm of everything that's wrong with corporate pay packages today." This was truer than he suspected: the chairman of E*Trade's compensation committee was David Hayden, the founder of Critical Path, a struggling software company of which E*Trade was a customer, and thus a highly conflicted arbiter.

Such conflicts were not new—only the public agitation. Institutional holders began to dump the stock, which promptly fell by a quarter. One institution threatened to withhold its proxy—the boardroom equivalent to storming the Bastille. Cotsakos now attempted to quell the furor, but his Antoinette-like gesture to give up a fraction of his compensation, leaving him, still, with $60 million—merely underlined the wholly excessive nature of his pay. The further details of his eight-figure retirement package, of the first-class air travel that was guaranteed to Cotsakos family members, of the tuition for Cotsakos to complete a Ph.D in London, soured his once-enthusiastic following. Months later, Cotsakos resigned.[14]

Belatedly, observers began to see that the pay problem and the auditing scandals were linked. One of the first to grasp the twisted circle of option incentives and accounting distortions was Michael Jensen, the academic champion (circa 1989) of stock options. As early as April 2001—six months before Enron imploded—Jensen, now a Harvard professor emeritus, declared his apostasy in a paper pointedly entitled, "How Stock Options Reward Managers for Destroying Value." Few Frankensteins have turned so fully on their creations. Jensen did not rule out all incentives, but he recommended that "a company never again issue another standard stock option." Later that year, Jensen completed the loop by calling on corporations to abandon the whole business of kowtowing to Wall Street, in particular by setting growth targets or by forecasting earnings. (This paper, with Jensen's characteristic rhetorical flourish, was entitled "Just Say No to Wall Street.") Jensen elaborated, after Enron's collapse, that he had not, previous to the bubble, realized the harm that comes from an *overpriced* stock. "It's like managerial heroin," he remarked. "It feels good but it's absolutely destructive."[15] Managers with the wrong incentives strain to get a high stock and push their organizations to bend or manufacture results to justify it. Something like Enron is the result.

In May, as criticism of pay plans mounted, the New York Stock Exchange floated a simple and sensible idea: why not require listed companies to get their shareholders' approval before approving option plans? Unaccountably, the plan was opposed and, indeed, was met with righteous indignation from the Business Roundtable, a lobbying group for chief executives.[16] Such indignation followed form. Nary a month went by in 2002 without fresh details of corporate malfeasance, yet it was the unhappy pattern of executives and also of auditors and lawyers to deny any suggestion of wrongdoing and to resist, to their utmost, even the merest wisp of reform, no matter how blatant the abuse. A proposal to force companies to expense stock options (the well-trod battleground of the '90s) was rejected by business and by President Bush. Such intransigence would have likely forestalled any corrective whatsoever but for a singular fact: the scandals continued to deepen. Just when it seemed the public had heard the worst imaginable, there came to light some fresh and more offensive tale of executive wrongdoing. And with each new episode the market fell lower. As John Kenneth Galbraith had written, in *The Great Crash*, of 1929: "The worst continued to worsen."[17]

In June, Arthur Andersen was convicted. (David Duncan, the former head of the Enron account, had already copped a plea.) The firm was promptly dissolved. In the same month, three current or recent CEOs were charged with felonies. Dennis Kozlowski, the Tyco executive and, as it developed, connoisseur of Renoir and Monet, was charged with evading more than $1 million in sales taxes on six paintings purchased with $13 million that he borrowed from the company treasury.

Little more than a week later, four FBI agents appeared at an apartment house in SoHo, in downtown New York, at 6 A.M. and arrested Samuel Waksal, the founder of Imclone Systems, dragging him away in handcuffs. Waksal was charged with trying to sell his stock and tipping off family members after learning (but before disclosing) that regulators were about to reject the application for a promising cancer drug. The investigation quickly broadened to include the celebrity home-décor promoter, Martha Stewart, a friend of Waksal's who had sold Imclone stock a day before the regulators' decision was announced. Stewart was also a

director of the New York Stock Exchange and one of the most prominent executives to fall under scrutiny.

Barely a week after that, Martin Grass, the former CEO of Rite Aid,
was charged with a massive books-cooking conspiracy on counts that
included fraud, fabricating board minutes, secretly funneling money to
personally controlled entities, and witness tampering. The fraud was exposed after Joe Speaker, a newly promoted CFO, reported evidence of
serious errors to the audit directors who—unlike those at Enron—
pushed for an investigation. The sarcastic and perhaps excessively cocky
Grass had bragged to a wired employee that the government would not
get hold of certain incriminating evidence "unless they use a Trident
submarine."[18]

This litany of corporate disaster, almost Homeric in its breadth, took
a steady toll on the market. On Friday, June 21, the day of the Grass indictment, the Dow fell 180 points to 9,250, an eight-month low. Wall
Street bankers repaired for the weekend, the first of summer, to watering
holes in the Hamptons, no doubt praying for a respite from further scandal. On Monday, June 24, markets were quiet and grand juries were in-
active. However, the audit committee of the board of WorldCom was
meeting in urgent session. In recent months, the company had suffered
widespread layoffs, the resignation of its previously ebullient CEO,
Bernard Ebbers, the loss of its former auditor, Arthur Andersen, the
downgrading of its credit to junk status, and the further erosion of its
stock, to ninety cents.

Moreover, some intrepid employees in WorldCom's internal audit
department had taken it upon themselves to investigate the company's
singular practice of capitalizing line costs. After several weeks, Cynthia
Cooper, a thirty-seven-year-old auditor and vice president who had
grown up in Clinton, Mississippi, near WorldCom's headquarters, and
who had worked at the company since the mid-1990s, alerted the chairman of the audit committee to the appearance of improprieties. The

board sought an explanation from Scott Sullivan, the chief financial officer, who submitted a white paper in defense of his policies. However, neither Andersen, still supplying vestigial counsel, nor KPMG, World-Com's new audit firm, agreed with his rationale.[19]

After its meeting on the twenty-fourth, the audit committee ordered Sullivan to resign. The following day, WorldCom announced it would restate its results for 2001 and 2002—wiping out an eye-popping $3.8 billion of its previously reported earnings. It filed for bankruptcy the following month.

WorldCom staggered the public. Although Enron was the more egregious scandal, WorldCom had been the bigger and, to the average American, more familiar company. (Its restatement was also bigger.) The notion that the entirety of its value, which had been so loudly trumpeted by Wall Street, could have simply evaporated, seemed inconceivable. To see Ebbers defrocked was especially painful. The folksy CEO had been a favorite of journalists, analysts, and investors. He was better known than Skilling and better liked. Miscast as a Horatio Alger, Ebbers turned out to have been another sort of American archetype: the flawed charmer.

The image of CEOs took a serious hit in the popular culture. Newspapers bewailed the fallen state of ethics in business, and pollsters reported that respect for executives had plunged.[20] *Law & Order,* a television show admired for its gritty realism, taped an episode about a CEO so determined to suppress the truth about his stock that he resorted to murder. Investors had genuinely looked up to CEOs during the boom; their disenchantment now was laced with bitterness. With share prices falling by the week, sincere outrage mingled with anger and hurt over lost profits.

Meanwhile, the scandals' ramifications were spreading. Job losses from Enron, Global Crossing, Lucent, and many others climbed into the tens of thousands. Employers, both public and private, were reeling from deep losses in their retirement funds. America's business scandals so alarmed European regulators that they backed away from plans to adopt America's system of financial reporting, long considered one of the country's singular strengths.[21]

The roster of accused felons did not begin to measure the damage to Wall Street's image. A more telling roster was the numbing list of earnings restatements. Jack Ehnes, the chief executive of the California State Teachers Retirement System, made the unremarkable but, in the current climate, apt demand: "Investors expect financial statements to be accurate." The scope and scale of corporate transgressions, *The Wall Street Journal* observed, exceeded anything the United States had witnessed since the Great Depression. The comparison to 1929 was increasingly invoked. Senator Paul Sarbanes, chairman of the Senate Banking Committee, quoted from Ben Graham's account of the shoddy state of American corporate reports (circa 1929) on the floor of the Senate. Joel Seligman, the historian of the SEC, commented on the amazing parallel to the '20s—when, too, "the worst abuses had occurred after a sustained bull market."[22]

The earlier abuses had provoked the Congress to enact the basic federal securities laws. The present Congress, aside from dramatizing the scandals in hearings, had done nothing. Senator Phil Gramm, who was, as noted, married to an Enron director, was busy plotting with corporate and accounting industry cronies on how to stymie legislation. The strategy was working. About a week before WorldCom dropped its bombshell, Senator Jon Corzine, a liberal and a former CEO of Goldman Sachs, publicly lamented, "It's becoming increasingly clear that we may not get real reform."[23]

The executive branch, despite its probusiness tilt, had at least responded with vigor to actual *instances* of corporate fraud. The Justice Department was developing cases against former executives at Enron and at other companies. The SEC, for all of Pitt's personal agonies, had opened a record number of financial-reporting cases.[24] What was missing from the SEC's agenda—indeed, what the Hooverish Pitt was actively resisting—was any broader effort to take stock of what had gone wrong and why and to propose substantive reforms. And this, in sum, was the general failing of the Administration. It did not realize—as it assuredly did on the issue of terrorism—that the landscape had changed. The time was ripe for a wholesale examination of securities laws, including the long-neglected arena of corporate governance.

The most zealous crusader, to date, was the New York State attorney general, Eliot Spitzer, who was using an old state law, on the books since the 1920s, to investigate Merrill Lynch and its now-resigned Internet analyst, Henry Blodget. By leaking some sensational e-mails, Spitzer, who was not without political ambition, was able to put considerable pressure on Merrill, as well as on other underwriters, and awaken the SEC to the long-evident problem of corrupt Wall Street research. Still, the sum of reform initiatives was hardly commensurate with the degree of abuse.

WorldCom completely altered the political calculus. "People"—in Washington no less than elsewhere—"were stunned," a Congressional insider noted. Speaking to the National Press Club, Hank Paulsen, the present Goldman CEO and a man little given to publicity, declared that the reputation of business leaders in his lifetime had never been so low.[25]

The sense of epidemic failure galvanized the Senate, where the Democrats enjoyed a majority of one. In a mere three weeks after WorldCom, the chamber passed a comprehensive reform, spearheaded by Sarbanes, a modest and, despite his five terms, little-known lawmaker from Maryland. The bill addressed (and augmented) the responsibilities of executives, board directors, outside auditors, corporate lawyers, and Wall Street analysts.

It was far stronger than anything endorsed by the White House, and the president was now on the defensive. Commentators were blaming Bush's tepid response to WorldCom for the market's continuing weakness. Appearing before the Senate Banking Committee in mid-July, Alan Greenspan cast a vote for reform. "Although we may not be able to change the character of corporate officers," he allowed, "we can change behavior through incentives and penalties. That, in my judgment, could dramatically improve the state of corporate governance." Otherwise, Greenspan warned, the aftereffects of scandal would continue to weigh on the economy.

In the month following the WorldCom disclosure, the Dow dropped below 8,000 and the broader Standard & Poor's 500 dropped an astonishing 20 percent. Democrats were calling on Pitt to resign. Tom Daschle, the Senate majority leader, pointedly asked the SEC to open its files from the ten-year-old Harken investigation. As a fresher source of embarrassment, the SEC was probing Halliburton for booking disputed (and uncollected) revenue during Cheney's tenure as CEO.[26] In short, the political heat of scandal was becoming too hot to ignore.

Four days after WorldCom's disclosure, Bush met with advisers and agreed to produce a more vigorous response. It is easy to speculate that their conversion was expedient; it is also beside the point. Few presidents act in a vacuum, and it is quite plausible that Bush was, ultimately, as shocked as anyone else. Perhaps he would just as soon prefer that the scandals had not come to light—but they *had* come to light and on his watch. Addressing a gathering on Wall Street in early July, Bush declared, "The business pages of American newspapers should not resemble a scandal sheet."[27] Significantly, the president ordered the creation of a prosecutorial task force to focus on corporate fraud.[28] He went on to endorse, among other reforms, shorter timetables for reporting executive stock sales (the very area where he had personally run afoul in 1990).

The Sarbanes-Oxley Act of 2002 (which incorporated and, indeed, toughened the Senate bill) was signed into law at the end of July.* It was the fullest and most significant tightening of securities laws since the Depression. The flagship provision called for a dose of executive truth serum: CEOs and CFOs were required to swear to the accuracy and fairness of their financial statements, with the threat of jail time in the event of material misstatement. What's more, executives could be made to disgorge any profits from selling stock before a misstatement was made public.

Sarbanes-Oxley appropriately zeroed in on accounting lapses as central to the crisis. Under the act:

- The audit committee of the board (not management) has responsibility for appointing the outside auditor and for overseeing the audit and resolving any conflicts between it and management. The auditor is required to inform the board of the policies followed in its audit and of any alternative accounting treatments discussed with management.

- Outside auditors are prohibited from providing certain (not all) consulting services. The lead auditor on an account must rotate every five years.

---

*Representative Michael Oxley, the House sponsor, had long been one of Wall Street's most loyal (and most generously underwritten) allies. Before WorldCom, the Ohio Republican had opposed virtually every proinvestor reform, including many that were included in the law bearing his name.

- The SEC was required to create a new board to oversee public accountants. The board would adopt rules relating to auditing, quality control, ethics, and independence and would have the power to investigate and discipline auditors.

Many of the other provisions were obviously drafted with Enron, WorldCom, Tyco, and such in mind.

- The SEC was required to formulate new requirements for corporate disclosure of off-balance-sheet partnerships and SPVs. In addition, the SEC, which would receive greatly increased funding, was required to review every public company at least every third year.

- Executives were required to report stock sales on a more timely basis—within two days of the sale. Also, corporate loans to executives (such as the one extended to Ebbers) were prohibited.

- Criminal penalties for various types of fraud were increased.

- Protection was extended to whistle-blowers.

- Corporate lawyers were now required to report evidence of unlawful conduct to the general counsel, the CEO, or the board.

- The SEC was ordered to effect a greater separation between research analysts and investment bankers.

Two days later, the New York Stock Exchange approved measures to tighten standards of corporate governance. On all listed companies:

- A majority of directors must be independent. Outsiders with material relationships with the company would not be considered independent.

- So as to heighten the board's oversight of management, independent directors were required to meet regularly *without* the presence of management.

- *All* directors serving on the audit, compensation, and nominating committees must be independent. At least one member of the audit committee must have significant accounting expertise.

- Stock-option plans must be subjected to shareholder vote, with a majority necessary for approval.

Even as the law was being adopted, the climate in boardrooms was changing. By common account, the level of directors' awareness and scrutiny was perceptibly rising. Most probably, this would have occurred with no new law. Whatever else they lack, directors do not lack for self-interest, and it was clear that the previous standards of governance were no longer acceptable. The question was how much of the change would stick as the sense of crisis faded.

But the crisis did not as yet fade. The wave of white-collar scandals and executive indictments continued. Indeed, there were days on which the newspapers read like a police blotter. John Rigas, the seventy-eight-year-old patriarch of Adelphia, was arrested and handcuffed. Martha Stewart was forced to resign from the stock exchange. She was subsequently indicted. WorldCom admitted to $3.3 billion *more* of "improperly reported" earnings. Scott Sullivan, the former WorldCom CFO, was indicted at the end of August. AOL, its stock already down by 85 percent, was revealed to be a target of SEC and Justice Department accounting probes. (Some months later, Steve Case, a cofounder of America Online and a seminal figure in the popularization of the Internet, resigned as AOL's chairman.)

Then a House committee turned on Salomon Smith Barney, which had so favored Bernie Ebbers with lucrative IPO allocations. Jack Grubman, Ebbers's ally at Salomon and a symbol of the pivotal role played by analysts in the '90s, was forced to resign. However, the revelations went far beyond a single firm. The committee soon disclosed that Goldman Sachs, too, had routinely awarded IPO allocations to the CEOs of its clients, including the chief executives of Ford, eBay, Starwood Hotels, and many more.[29] Such disclosures, even if they fell short of explicit illegalities, provoked a widespread dismay. The most dispiriting revelations of the 1930s had been the House of Morgan's admission that it had routinely lavished shares on the rich and powerful; now, as then, such favoritism undermined the public trust.

By September, some sixty telecom companies had failed, underwriting of new stocks had ceased, investment by American businesses had plunged, and consumer confidence was tumbling toward ten-year lows.[30] The stock market fell ever lower. Tyco's Kozlowski, once a paragon of shareholder value, was indicted on further, and more shocking, charges of looting the company for million-dollar homes, pricey art, foreign junkets, and jewelry. His $17,000 toiletries case, like his $15,000 antique umbrella stand, his $6,000 shower curtain and other perks, were of the scale of a Carnegie, save that the original robber barons had paid their own way. Evidently, the scale that boards had used to weigh rewards had terribly malfunctioned, or perhaps they had used no scale at all. Mark Swartz, Kozlowski's CFO and soon his fellow accused, had taken—with the approval of two directors and when he was already under a grand jury investigation—a severance of $45 million. Boesky had been proven wrong; greed in itself was proven neither healthy nor good.

Tyco added a new layer to the perception of the general sickness. One of the unhappier debasements of the '90s was the frequent transformation of the corporate lawyer into a well-spoken fixer. Wherever chief executives had managed the numbers or parsed the truth, lawyers had been backstage, soothing their consciences and sanctioning the deals. The lawyers had provided a cover—a gloss of legitimacy. Their culpability was increasingly felt but difficult to prove. However, Mark Belnick, Tyco's general counsel, was charged with falsifying records to conceal a $12 million bonus received from Kozlowski. The allegation against Belnick made vivid the broader unease concerning lawyers that had been gathering since Enron.[31]

The burning issue of executive greed gained a larger resonance with yet another revelation, this time about a far more admired chief executive. Details of Jack Welch's rich retirement package from General Electric were leaked from Welch's racy divorce proceedings. According to his estranged wife, Welch's lifetime perks included the use of a $15 million Manhattan apartment with complimentary wine, food, laundry services, newspapers, and toiletries; and access to a corporate jet, floor-level tickets to the New York Knicks, courtside seats at the U.S. Open, a box at the Metropolitan Opera, and a car and driver. This cushy arrangement raised two questions: Why had the details not been disclosed by GE, and what entitled Welch, who had a $350,000-a-month pension and, what's more, past earnings of more than $400 million, to live in splendor at his former employer's expense? The recently retired Welch quickly agreed to give up some of his perks; others, he claimed, had been exaggerated.[32]

No matter—his iconic stature was badly damaged. Welch was soon being lumped with such disgraced CEOs as Bernie Ebbers and Ken Lay. A cover of *The Economist* showed a bust of Welch knocked from its perch, the head split open. Though Welch had violated not the law but fairness—though clearly, he was *not* in Ken Lay's camp—his fall was in some sense more painful. The undoing of a villain titillates but doesn't sting; it is the fall of a role model that truly hurts. "General Electric's board, and Mr. Welch, should have known better," the editors of *The New York Times* intoned. This echoed the page's painful lament—"Why It Hurts"—in 1933, following the revelations of the Morgan favors. In both eras, the business leaders regarded as heroes had been proved unworthy. The sense that Welch had recognized no limit to his pay offended decency, just as Kozlowski had offended it. They were both guilty of hubris. And it now appeared that Welch's reward *had* been excessive. GE's decade-long string of increasing earnings was about to snap (its earnings fell in the fourth quarter). More importantly, critics were openly questioning whether GE, stripped of its accounting gloss, had performed as well as advertised even in its good years. The stock had fallen by half. Welch now looked like just another overpaid boss.[33]

The Welch nightmare returned attention to the general problem of excessive compensation—always close to the roots of the crisis. William McDonough, chairman of the New York Federal Reserve and the second-most prominent public banker in America, appeared at Wall Street's Trinity Church on the first anniversary of the terrorist attacks and symbolically linked September 11, which he was there to commemorate, with the crisis in corporate accountability. Citing a study that CEO pay had risen to four hundred times that of an average production worker (the ratio had been only forty-two times two decades earlier), he declared, "CEOs and their boards should simply reach the conclusion that executive pay is excessive and adjust it to more reasonable and justifiable levels."[34] He did not say that greed was good.

On October 1, Gary Winnick appeared before the House Energy and Commerce Committee. Unlike Ken Lay and Bernie Ebbers, each of whom had pleaded the Fifth Amendment rather than answer lawmakers' questions, Winnick testified that he had been unaware of his company's precarious position when he sold its stock.* His lawyer, Gary Naftalis, roundly declared, "What he did was totally and completely proper, and there isn't a shred of evidence that he did anything wrong in connection with his trading."[35] This was a commentary only on the debased meaning of right and wrong—even to a blue-chip New York lawyer—in the twilight of shareholder value. Throughout the year, as losses and evidence of impropriety mounted, the repeated protestations of innocence from bankers, lawyers, and executives; the exhortations that no laws had been broken; that the enablers hadn't known; that the decisions had been vetted by auditors, lawyers, and so forth provided a sickening backdrop. And it continued.

The day after Winnick testified, Andy Fastow was charged with conspiracy, money-laundering, and fraud. The *enfant terrible* of Enron was led into the federal courthouse in Houston in handcuffs—"repeating a drama," *The Wall Street Journal* observed, "that has become familiar in recent months."[36] (Within eighteen months, Fastow and seven other Enron executives, including Fastow's former assistant, Michael Kopper, would plead guilty, and many others would be indicted. Fastow would be sentenced to ten years in prison.) The stock market, by now, had been in a virtual free fall for six months. It had fallen 11 percent in September alone, then 5 percent more at the start of October. One week after the Fastow indictment, the S&P 500 closed at 776—exactly half of the peak it had reached in March 2000. The Dow, barely above 7,000, had fallen almost 40 percent. This was its steepest slide in thirty years. Some $7 trillion of the public's savings had evaporated. The Nasdaq, now close to 1,100, had fallen 78 percent, the largest slide by a major index since

---

*Winnick also offered $25 million to Global Crossing employees whose 401(k) retirement accounts had gone up in smoke. The offer represented only 3 percent of Winnick's trading profits, and Global employees were not sufficiently mollified as to drop their suits against the company.

the Great Depression. Of some 825 companies that had gone public in
1999 and 2000, 715 were below the offer price and 303, including David
Wetherell's CMGI and David Perry's Ventro, were trading under $1 or
had been delisted.[37]

And still, the chiseling of prominent busts continued. There was no
person on the Street more powerful, or more remarkable, than Sandy
Weill. Though not a financial genius, Weill was more driven than any
other banker, and this drive had taken him from a tiny brokerage to
the top of the largest financial company in the country. He had single-
handedly *built* the largest bank in the country. Weill was "nearing"
retirement—it had been said for years—and he wanted, naturally, to
leave on a high note. He had watched uneasily as the details of Citigroup's involvement with Enron had become public, and he had suffered through the defrocking of his telecom analyst, Jack Grubman. But
Weill had not been touched personally.

However, in October, the investigation of Grubman (pursued, vari-
ously, by Congress, New York State, and the SEC) turned to the analyst's
relationship with AT&T. In the late '90s, Grubman had been negative on
AT&T's stock; the phone giant, as a result, gave its choicest banking assignments to Salomon's rivals. Weill, who sat on AT&T's board, was eager for Grubman to revise his opinion. And late in 1999, Grubman, did,
indeed, raise his rating on the stock. This proved unlucky for investors,
as AT&T almost immediately went into a prolonged and steep swoon.

When the matter was reexplored, in 2002, Grubman did not try to
pretend that he had genuinely believed AT&T to be a good investment.
Why, then, the change? It developed that Weill had asked his star to take
a "fresh look" at the stock. Grubman, in turn, had wanted a favor of
Weill. The analyst who could move billions of dollars of stock was
nonetheless unsure of getting his twin two-year-olds into the nursery
school of his choice. Elite preschools in New York City are said to have
lower acceptance rates than Harvard and, according to an e-mail of

Grubman's that surfaced later, Grubman was willing to raise his rating on AT&T (and thus mislead thousands of investors) in return for Weill's undoubted influence in academe. After Grubman raised his opinion, Weill helpfully donated $1 million of Citigroup's money to the 92nd Street Y, and Grubman's two-year-olds, who remained blissfully ignorant of such details, were admitted. The Weill affair exposed the patent conflict at the core of Wall Street research, and it proved that the corruption extended to the highest levels.[38]

A more serious (though less-publicized) abuse, brought to light by Attorney General Spitzer, involved Morgan Stanley, which was found to have made under-the-table payments to rival firms who agreed to issue positive research about Morgan clients.[39] This and other of the Spitzer revelations left no doubt that Wall Street research was thoroughly corrupt.

As a result of the cases brought by New York State and the SEC, ten underwriting firms agreed to fines of $1.4 billion. The firms were required to insulate their analysts from investment banking pressures and to swear off the long-troublesome practice of allocating IPO shares to corporate executives and directors.[40] Analysts were barred from promoting their firms' IPOs. Moreover, the firms agreed to publish quarterly data on their analysts' stock-picking performance—which data, it was hoped, would motivate at least some analysts to call stocks on their merits.

Grubman, for his part, was permanently banned from the securities industry, as was Blodget, the Internet analyst who, despite his modest role, came to symbolize the profession's corruption. Frank Quattrone, the Credit Suisse banker who had hatched so many IPOs, was indicted for encouraging bankers to destroy files relevant to a federal grand jury investigation.

The cloud of scandal persisted still; it touched down in no predictable pattern, sometimes slowing, sometimes accelerating, but never fully lifting. It had claimed accountants and analysts, bankers and lawyers, and also CEOs. Perhaps it was preordained that before finally running its course it would topple a bust in Washington, too. It was there, in any case, where Harvey Pitt, the man charged with carrying out reforms, was unhappily wrestling with the various mandates of Sarbanes-Oxley. Of these, the most urgent was clearly the new board that was to oversee public accountants.

It was natural that accounting be the focus of reform: it had only been by twisting the rightful function of accountants that shareholder value had itself been twisted into such a caricature. The identity of the head of the new board, whose purpose was to prevent such trespasses in the future, was a matter of highest attention. It was widely hoped that Pitt would select a guardian of the stiffest character. Presumably, in the aftermath of so much scandal, there could be no question of "kinder, gentler," nor of some remote or—heaven forbid—lax overseer. This was an hour for a firm hand.

So it was, at first, with perplexity that observers greeted Pitt's choice of William Webster—a seventy-eight-year-old former federal judge and a former head of the Federal Bureau of Investigation but a man with no expertise in finance. Webster had had an admirable public career, but he had devoted his most recent decade to developing a lucrative law practice and, indeed, had occasionally traded on his public record on behalf of narrow and rather self-seeking causes.[41] His selection was roundly criticized; however this merely hardened Pitt in his determination. Though his fellow SEC commissioners, a group accustomed to ruling by consensus, were bitterly divided, Pitt mustered a three-to-two vote in favor, and Webster was approved.

And then it developed that Webster, who was supposed to set the rules, or at least the tone, for auditing public companies, had until recently served as head of the audit committee at one very troubled corporation: an Internet incubator called U.S. Technologies. The company was insolvent, and its chief executive, C. Gregory Earls, was under criminal investigation. (In 2003, Earls was indicted for swindling investors.) When the outside auditor had warned Webster of problems at the Internet company, Webster had fired the *auditor*—an action seemingly inconsistent with the qualities hoped for in the nation's new guardian of accounting.

Another SEC chairman would have demanded Webster's resignation and begun another search. However, it emerged that Pitt had known about Webster's involvement in U.S. Technologies and the investigation of the company and had decided it was irrelevant to Webster's selection—so irrelevant that Pitt had neglected to tell either his fellow SEC commissioners or the president. This was an inconceivable lapse. Representative Edward Markey, a Massachusetts Democrat, remarked, "Just when you think Mr. Pitt's judgment can't get any worse, he surprises us."[42] The president, by now, had begun to tire of Harvey Pitt. He was weary of corporate governance and of the incessant scandals that kept the issue alive, and Pitt had reached the moment that is fatal for any bureaucrat—when he becomes identified not with the resolution of a crisis but with its prolongation. Hoping to quell the uproar, Pitt announced an investigation of how Webster had come to be nominated—that is to say, Pitt would investigate Pitt's own selection process. This was tragedy disguised as farce, for it suggested that the many lessons in conflict of interest, so plentiful in the year past, were as yet unlearned by the chairman of the SEC. Even the gatekeeper was tainted, and this—if the system were ever to recover—the country could not abide. On election night 2002, Pitt resigned. There was no rejoicing nor was there a glimpse of dawn—only a muted sigh.

TEN

Epilogue

Financial collapses are as old as markets, but the *fin de siècle* breakdown ranks among the broadest and most systemic in history. The speculation was epochal, the abuse of investors was pervasive, and the fraud was more widespread than at any time under the present system of federal regulation. It was not merely that many companies, or many Wall Street operators, misbehaved; it was that the very culture encouraged the misbehavior and was, in large measure, its accomplice. It was not merely a matter of rogue executives and bankers but a failure of America's markets—its institutions, its financial community. The crash itself was one of Wall Street's worst.

People demand an explanation for crashes, but their origins are invariably to be found in the boom years that precede them.[1] The collapse of communism at the end of the 1980s and the daunting advances made in Silicon Valley throughout the '90s gave the public a heady appetite to invest in shares and ultimately to speculate. However, these factors alone do not explain the headlong abandonment of moral standards.

Nor does the refrain, popularized by Alan Greenspan, that America had suddenly become infected by greed.[2] People have always been greedy, and they have always been subject to speculative frenzy.

What gave the period its special license was the credo of shareholder value, a philosophical approach designed to pull America out of its previous period of malaise. During the '90s, even as, by one name or another, the credo was widely adopted, its meaning was increasingly distorted. It became a maxim not for enhancing business values, a process that occurs only over years, but for enhancing day-by-day quotations of shares, a far more ephemeral thing. Virtually every transgression flowed from this simple corruption. Corporate executives rewarded for short-term advances in their stock pocketed truly obscene and undeserved sums; accountants whose charter it is to demand honest reporting instead blessed any stratagem that would win applause on Wall Street; and fund managers and analysts, each of which group was supposed to search for good, enduring companies—shareholder value in its true sense—instead pumped the stocks that might win fleeting popularity. And Congress joined the chorus.

A sort of mass conspiracy, or mass delusion, ensued. Securities were worshipped regardless of the assets they represented; the market price—no matter how transitory—was honored whatever the underlying value. This obsession with appearances, with the market snapshot as opposed to the enterprise in the flesh, caused horrendous mischief. In a memo that surfaced after the crash, a J. P. Morgan Chase vice chairman was seen to admit, "We are making disguised loans, usually buried in commodities or equities derivatives."[3] Speaking broadly, the entire culture was in disguise. There was a general campaign to prettify the picture, to doctor the market profile.

Nowhere was this more evident than in the research churned out by Wall Street. In one of the e-mails unearthed by the Spitzer inquiry, Henry Blodget, the Merrill Internet analyst, weary of the unceasing pressure from bankers to paint his stocks in bullish colors, threatened nothing less than to utter his true opinion. ("We are going to just start calling the stocks . . . like we see them, no matter what the ancillary business consequences are."[4]) This was the ultimate irony of shareholder value. In a society honored around the world for its system of disclosure, truth had become a heresy.

Any ranking of market implosions must begin with the collapse of 1929, which ushered in the Depression. No similar cataclysm followed this time, yet the systemic failure was arguably as grave. Now, as then, frenzied speculation begat terrible losses and subsequent revelations of serious abuse. The boom periods themselves were remarkably parallel. The generation that rose to prominence after World War I, like the one that followed the cold war, felt it was living in a uniquely propitious time for business. The New Era doctrine of the '20s implied that modern management techniques had done away with the economic cycle; the new economy of the '90s implied a similar nirvana courtesy of the Internet. Moreover, in each era, faith in businessmen and in markets ran high, and government regulators were banished to a submissive, backstage role.

Contemporary investors suffered less than those in 1929 (though the legend of brokers jumping from skyscrapers was a myth[5]) thanks to a series of safeguards designed to prevent, or at least to mitigate, a repeat. Thus, investing on margin debt, which in '29 had led to chain-reaction selling and panic, was in later decades greatly restricted.[6] (CEOs who borrowed from their corporations, such as Bernie Ebbers, were an exception; one may imagine the calamitous state of affairs had every investor in WorldCom or, for that matter, Yahoo, been as leveraged as Ebbers.) Second, bank deposits were now federally insured, averting the prospect that bank runs would add to the anguish of market losses. In this and other ways, society has become better able to cushion the shock of market upheavals.

However, given that half of Americans now own stocks, the pain was indisputably more widespread. In the '20s, relatively few Americans owned stocks. As Galbraith observed, "The collapse in securities values affected in the first instance the wealthy and the well-to-do."[7] In the 1990s, by contrast, common stocks were no less a part of everyday life than minivans. It had become easier to check stock scores than baseball scores and, when the scoreboard darkened, tens of millions of Americans shared in the pain, and the economy suffered immediate harm.[8]

It is true that if one gauges the bubbles mathematically—that is, by the subsequent contraction in shares—the earlier debacle was more horrific. From the market peak in '29 to the lows of '32, the Dow fell 89 percent. But this ghastly decline reflected the coincident plunge in industrial output, employment, and so forth, not just the pricking of an investment bubble. A better measure of the speculation is that during the Great Crash per se—meaning the swift correction that occurred, despite little change in the economy, in October and November of '29—stocks fell by half. Coincidentally, in 2000–02, the S&P 500 fell by exactly the same amount; the Dow, a little less; the Nasdaq, considerably more.

It had been thought that the modern investor's access to information would temper his tendency to speculate, but the mania of '99 was absolutely breathtaking. Notwithstanding the Pollyannaish optimism of the late '20s, there was nothing in the Jazz Age (or in any other period in American life) to compare with the dot-com phenomenon, in which scores of companies that were *worthless* from start to finish came to be valued in the billions of dollars and, indeed, at vast premiums to established, profitable enterprises. The harm done was massive. The first purpose of markets, after all, is to properly allocate capital. In this, markets failed. Billions upon billions were squandered in an array of redundant industries: dot-coms, energy, telecoms, and so forth.

Fraud was also more widespread in the latter period. In the '20s, when little was prohibited and little was disclosed, one would have expected mischief. As it was, the scandals from that era, though alarming, were mostly confined to a handful of brokers, bankers, and stock-pool operators. In the '90s, despite the greater burden of regulatory supervision, the abuse spread beyond Wall Street to Main Street corporations, such as Enron, WorldCom, Rite Aid, Tyco, and Lucent. And these offenders were only the leading edge of a far broader cultural debasement, by which scores of companies routinely gamed their numbers and shaded their disclosures.

One explanation was that new financial instruments, in particular derivatives, made it easier for executives to cover their tracks.[9] Derivatives do explain many of the offenders' choice of tactics, and there can be no doubt of the need for more meaningful disclosure, a point that was already clear in 1998, after the fall of the hedge fund Long-Term Capital Management. Yet the fraud at WorldCom, the most massive in terms of dollars, was simple and conventional; it could have occurred as easily in 1901 as in 2001. And if one takes a longer view, each financial bubble is distinguished by some new wrinkle, some innovative technique, yet they are less the cause than the interesting detail.

The excesses of the '90s were, in any case, too diverse to admit to a single classification. For every WorldCom set of management cheats, there was a dot-com propelled by some seeming lunacy in the ozone. For every Tyco in which the villainy was brazen, there was a Xerox in which the wrongdoing was found, more subtly, in management's dissembling and less-than-frank reports to investors. Nonetheless, anyone who lived through the era rightly senses a coherence in its varied forms of excess. The progression from LBOs to stock options to a market bubble was nurtured by a consistent ethos; there was a common pattern behind each increment of speculation and episode of abuse. What the pattern describes is not a trait, such as greed, or an innovation, such as derivatives, but a cultural devolution—a generalized decline in standards. Sadly, even investors were guilty of it. Indeed, absent the eagerness of the shareholding public to applaud earnings management and similar window dressings, there would have been no reason for executives to spin their stocks. And this, finally, is what connects Enron and World-Com to the more bubbly speculations of the Internet. In one case, executives hid or altered their numbers so that their disclosures became a kind of fantasy; in the other, Wall Street sold shares on the basis of projections that were literally fantastic. Both the Enrons *and* the dot-coms depended on selling their respective fantasies to a gullible public.

Galbraith noted that economic writers carry a unique burden.[10] The military historian must merely recount his tale; he is never asked whether the slaughter of Gallipoli, the bombing of Dresden, is apt to recur. Only the economic historian is expected to opine on the likelihood of another debacle. For securities and the stock market in particular, the question is easy. Stocks are different from other investments—say, real estate. They're intangibles; we can't live in them or even touch or see them, and so their price depends largely on what the future holds or what it is perceived to hold. Your neighbor will not believe that his house is a future castle, but he may become convinced that a stock is one. The only link to reality is the information provided by management—whose interest will always be to garnish their particular castles. To seal the matter, stocks trade wholly in what we call a secondary market. There is speculation in, say, copper or wheat, but at the end of the day, someone actually acquires the wheat, bakes the bread, and so forth. In stocks, the day of reckoning is ever delayed, so that success, or profit, turns on the willingness of others to pay a higher price.

So, yes, there will be more bubbles and more crashes. And given the nature of the beast, Wall Street may be incapable of genuine reform. Investment banks have a long history of humbly accepting responsibility for whatever wrongdoing and then returning to their business. But have the specific corruptions associated with the cult of shareholder value been put to rest, or at least discouraged?

The legal and legislative response to the crash has been significant. WorldCom was assessed a record $500 million fine by the SEC. More astonishing, still, Citigroup agreed to pay $2.65 billion—one of the largest such awards ever—to settle claims by WorldCom shareholders that they had been duped by Jack Grubman, Citigroup's former analyst. Meanwhile, indictments have piled up against former executives at Enron, WorldCom, Tyco, Qwest, Cendant, and many others, including HealthSouth, where a major accounting fraud was belatedly uncovered in 2003. And the various prosecutions kept the scandals prominently in front of the public well into 2004.

Frank Quattrone, the marquee Internet banker, was convicted of obstructing justice. The trial of Dennis Kozlowski went on for six months, with prominent media coverage of his lurid lifestyle and wild spending. Saved by a lone sympathetic juror, Kozlowski gained a mistrial and had to prepare for trial yet again. Meanwhile, Jeffrey Skilling, the architect of Enron's rogue transformation, was indicted. Two months later, New York City cops detained Skilling, who was inebriated and had been making wild statements about being trailed by phantom FBI agents, at 4 A.M. outside an East Side bar—a pitiful coda to his fall. An even bigger fish, former WorldCom CEO Bernie Ebbers, was indicted for manipulating the company's results. Scott Sullivan, WorldCom's former chief financial officer, pleaded guilty and agreed to cooperate with Ebbers's prosecution. Then, in the summer of 2004, Ken Lay, the biggest fish of all, was charged with conspiracy.

Even though the stock market was finally on the rebound, the sheer number of prosecutions reinforced the public impression of the late '90s as an era of values gone awry. And on the prosecutions rolled: Marty Grass, the former Rite Aid chief, pleaded guilty. John Rigas and his two sons, the former Adelphia stewards, chose to stand trial. Martha Stewart, whose cookbooks, articles, and television shows had made her a familial-seeming tutor to millions of American homemakers, did so as well. Though the charge against her—obstructing the investigation of federal agents into her stock sale—was relatively trivial, her trial became a public spectacle. Tabloids feasted on accounts of what Stewart wore to court, and average investors were spellbound at the sight of the famously blond executive facing a jury. Whether Stewart was a proper target for prosecutors or a scapegoat selected for her sex was endlessly debated on talk shows and, indeed, in American living rooms. Her conviction, and the likelihood that she would serve time in prison, underscored a central point of the prosecutions: no executive is above the law.

True, the politically wired Gary Winnick seems to have been subjected to only the most cursory investigation. But prosecution is by nature selective and somewhat arbitrary. Enough CEOs and their underlings have been photographed in handcuffs to at least temper the next generation of would-be offenders. Deterrence is served if executives fear a high probability of punishment; absolute certainty isn't required.

Sarbanes-Oxley exposes future miscreants to both a greater likelihood of prosecution and longer sentences in the event of a conviction. The SEC's powers have been greatly reinforced and, not least, its budget has been roughly doubled. This simple step may be as important as any other; more and better-equipped cops generally mean more safe streets. In addition, the truth serum provision of Sarbanes-Oxley should be a potent disincentive. It speaks to the many executives who circumvented the rules rather than expressly violated them—who dissembled rather than outright lied. As the investor George Soros recognized, by compelling executives to swear to the accuracy of their disclosures, the law "reasserted the supremacy of broad principles over particular rules." Soros is probably too optimistic in declaring that "officers are likely to err on the side of caution and reveal all questionable practices," but there is no doubt that the requirement to sign, *personally,* will give many an executive pause.[11]

The changes relating to corporate governance are also significant. Corporate lawyers have been put on notice, and outside directors must operate in a climate that is, truly, more independent. As a result of Sarbanes-Oxley, auditors will also have to meet a higher standard of independence. The dismal end of Arthur Andersen is a deterrent in itself.

As for underwriters, the mostly likely outcome of the Spitzer crusade will be a diminution in the role of analysts. Indeed, the era of the superstar analyst and deal-maker, à la Grubman, may be over. This is all to the good.

And yet the reforms leave significant unfinished business. There is no evidence that boards have gained either wisdom or restraint with respect to executive compensation; in particular, there is no evidence that directors even understand the destructive impact of serial option grants and especially of those that allow executives to exercise their options and sell their stock in short order. In a telling postcrash example, no sooner did Citigroup's stock plunge by 25 percent, largely as a result of the embarrassing Grubman affair, than the company bestowed upon its chairman and CEO, Sandy Weill, a monster package of 1.5 million options—which would reward this already enormously wealthy mogul simply for recouping his losses.[12] The following year, Citigroup, as if to confirm that it was sticking to its old, extravagant ways, awarded Weill, who was retiring as CEO, a $29-million bonus.

That many companies (including Citigroup) have agreed to deduct the cost of options from their earnings does not address the central problem: the conventional stock-option program, besides being too lavish, continues to align the interests of CEOs with short-term results (or with a sequence of short-term results) in the stock market. This misplaced incentive is at the root of all that went wrong, the engine that drove executives to manage their earnings, to pressure analysts, to focus on the stock and not the business. It is the period's original sin.

In a more general sense, the CEO remains an imperious, too powerful figure. This points to a continuing serious deficit in governance, which is the twinning of the job of CEO and chairman. Surely, the recent scandals have shown that CEOs are not equipped to be their own guardians. The British system, which relies on an independent chair, is better.

In addition, the audit rules remain far too vulnerable to trickery and obfuscation. The main risk is not that auditors will break the rules but that, given the numbing complexity of modern finance, they will comply with the rules in such a way as to conceal larger truths. A worthy task of the newly formed public accounting board would be to find a way to implement the Soros doctrine: that accurate, full, and meaningful disclosure should take precedence over compliance with specific rules.

Given the disaster that befell their stocks, it might have been hoped that public companies would forswear the game of forecasting quarterly results and otherwise managing Wall Street's expectations—a hope expressed in the title of Professor Jensen's paper, "Just Say No to Wall Street." However, corporate departments of investor relations have it in their blood that their purpose is to seduce investors, no matter all the past seductions that have come to grief. This short-term approach is, confoundingly, encouraged by professional investors (mainly mutual funds), who ever exhibit a finger-on-the-trigger approach to their portfolios. The culture's obsession with near-term results was noted by John

Maynard Keynes, who observed in the '30s that professional investors were concerned "not with what an investment is really worth to a man who buys it 'for keeps,' but with what the market will value it at, under the influence of mass psychology, three months or a year hence."[13] He would not need to rewrite a word today.

Can some coherent picture, then, be drawn from the impressive but incomplete reforms that have followed the crash? In general, the provisions to deter specific offenses and crimes have been well conceived. On the other hand, efforts to reform the financial culture may prove to be notably less successful. There is a deadly symmetry that reinforces the culture's every unfortunate tendency, be it the short-term holding periods of mutual funds, the incentives of brokers to keep customers trading, or the fact that CEOs get rewarded for making mergers, even dumb ones. And it is a chief lesson of the scandals that the culture of a community, more than any laws, provides the moral determinant for its behavior. The customs that govern how executives, auditors, and bankers do their jobs, interact with each other, are motivated, and so forth, ultimately lead to specific deeds or misdeeds. In particular, we should not be surprised if in a culture that tolerates lying, even in seemingly marginal ways, public reports and disclosures become unreliable. It is worth repeating that very few executives or bankers in the '90s set out to commit fraud but that a great many set out to project a favorable and, if need be, enhanced image to Wall Street. Such activity was widely encouraged, and it fed on itself. Thus, the humbling of 2002—of Enron and Blodget and all the rest—had its origins in the long-running and widespread pursuit of higher shares. The cycle began, hopefully and almost innocently, with people attempting to promote their stocks; it ended with bankers disguising loans and analysts having to threaten to tell the truth.

NOTES

CHAPTER ONE: ORIGINS OF A CULTURE

1. "Ford Derides Reagan's Idea of Investing Social Security Funds in the Stock Market." *The Wall Street Journal,* Feb. 11, 1976.

2. "The Death of Equities." *Business Week,* Aug. 13, 1979.

3. Berkshire Hathaway Inc., 1978 *Annual Report,* 5.

4. "The Death of Equities." *Business Week,* Aug. 13, 1979.

5. Joel Seligman, *The Transformation of Wall Street: A History of the Securities and Exchange Commission and Modern Corporate Finance* (Boston: Northeastern University Press, 1982; revised 1995), 28–29.

6. Louis D. Brandeis, *Other People's Money and How the Bankers Use It* (New York: Frederick A. Stokes, 1914), 92.

7. Louis V. Gerstner Jr., *Who Says Elephants Can't Dance? Inside IBM's Historic Turnaround* (New York: HarperCollins, 2002), 117.

8. Leslie Wayne, "Focus on: Stock Prices: A Look at New Corporate Tactics." *The New York Times,* Feb. 26, 1984.

9. Daniel Yergin's "Awaiting the Next Oil Crisis," which appeared in *The New York Times Magazine* on July 11, 1982, is an example, if less alarmist and better written than most. According to Yergin, who said his aim was

"not to be apocalyptic," there was a "high probability of another oil shock, which could trigger [grave] economic and political consequences" in which even "the basic legitimacy of our political system might be called into question. . . ." It was excerpted from Yergin, *Global Insecurity: A Strategy for Energy and Economic Renewal* (1982).

10. Alan Greenspan, *Challenge,* March/April 1980.

11. Ezra F. Vogel, *Japan as Number One: Lessons for America* (Cambridge, Mass.: Harvard University Press, 1979).

12. Connie Bruck, *The Predator's Ball: The Inside Story of Drexel Burnham and the Rise of Junk Bond Raiders* (New York: American Lawyer/Simon & Schuster, 1988), 194. Bruck's is the first word, and remains the last word, on Milken.

13. Ibid., 198.

14. Louis Lowenstein [the author's father], *Sense and Nonsense in Corporate Finance* (Reading, Mass.: Addison-Wesley, 1991) 74.

15. Michael C. Jensen, "Eclipse of the Public Corporation." *Harvard Business Review,* Sept.–Oct. 1989.

16. Henry Kravis, "LBOs Can Help Restore America's Competitive Edge." *Financier,* August 1989.

17. Quoted in Steve Swartz and Randall Smith, "Quick Study: How Nelson Peltz Cleared $520 Million on the Sale of Triangle." *The Wall Street Journal,* Dec. 6, 1988.

18. Louis Lowenstein, "Pruning Deadwood in Hostile Takeovers." *Columbia Law Review* 249 (1983).

CHAPTER TWO: EARLY NINETIES—A CULTURE IS RICH

1. Michael C. Jensen and Kevin J. Murphy, "CEO Incentive—It's Not How Much You Pay, But How." *Harvard Business Review,* May–June, 1990.

2. Reprinted in Berkshire Hathaway, Inc. 1990 *Annual Report,* 22–23.

3. Ira Kay, interview with author.

4. Graef Crystal, interview with author.

5. Jeffrey H. Birnbaum, "Campaign '92: From Quayle to Clinton, Politicians

Are Pouncing on the Hot Issue of Top Executives' Salaries." *The Wall Street Journal*, Jan. 15, 1992.

6. "Paying the Boss." *The Economist*, Feb. 1, 1992.

7. Interview with author.

8. Jensen and Murphy, op. cit.

9. Wayne, "Focus on: Stock Prices."

10. Jeremy J. Siegel, *Stocks for the Long Run* (New York: McGraw-Hill, 1998 edition). The original 1994 edition uses different language but, by implication, makes a strongly similar point.

11. A famous *Ladies' Home Journal* article of 1929 was entitled "Everybody Ought to Be Rich."

12. Anthony Bianco, "The Prophet of Wall Street," *Business Week*, June 1, 1998.

13. See Eric Schurenberg, *401(k) Take Charge of Your Future: A Unique and Comprehensive Guide to Getting the Most Out of Your Retirement Plans* (Waltham, Mass.: Warner Books, 2003), and Roger Lowenstein, "Securities Blanket: How Joe Smith's Faith in the Market Mirrors the Passion of Millions," *The Wall Street Journal*, Sept. 9, 1996.

14. Interview with author, quoted in Lowenstein, "Securities Blanket."

15. James M. Poterba, "The Rise of the 'Equity Culture:' U.S. Stockownership Patterns, 1989–1998," preliminary (unpublished) draft, January 2001. Poterba calculates the percentage of adults that owned stocks "in any form" at 36 percent in 1989, 40 percent in 1992, 44 percent in 1995, and 52 percent in 1998. See also Lowenstein, "Securities Blanket."

16. Interview with author.

17. Joseph Stiglitz, "The Roaring Nineties." *The Atlantic Monthly*, Oct. 2002.

18. Jeff Madrick, "Enron, the Media and the New Economy." *The Nation*, Apr. 1, 2002.

19. Paul Krugman, "For Richer." *The New York Times Magazine*, Oct. 20, 2002.

20. Richard A. Brealey and Stewart C. Myers, *Principles of Corporate Finance* (New York: McGraw-Hill, 1981; 1984 edition), 268–273.

21. See Bob Woodward, *Maestro: Greenspan's Fed and the American Boom* (New York: Simon & Schuster, 2000).

22. Alfred P. Sloan, *My Years with General Motors* (New York: Doubleday, 1990; 1st ed., 1968).

23. Lowenstein, "Securities Blanket."

24. Lois Therrien, "Sara Lee: No Fads, No Buyouts, Just Old-Fashioned Growth," *Business Week*, Nov. 14, 1988.

25. This occurred in 1997, slightly after the other events in this chapter.

26. Roger Lowenstein, "Intrinsic Value: Remember When Companies Made Things?" *The Wall Street Journal*, Sept. 18, 1997.

27. ———, "Intrinsic Value: Rethinking the Latest Economic Elixir." *The Wall Street Journal*, Feb. 13, 1997.

28. This theory that the cost of equity capital varies with the volatility of a company's stock price is one of the oldest canards of finance. It is known as the capital asset pricing model. Intellectually, it has no merit, and, in practical terms, it has been discredited by numerous academic studies.

CHAPTER THREE: ENLIGHTENMENT GETS OUT OF HAND

1. John Cassidy, "The Greed Cycle." *The New Yorker*, Sept. 23, 2002.

2. Adam Smith, *The Wealth of Nations* (New York: Bantam, fifth edition, 2003; originally published 1776), 572. (Words have been deleted from the quotation for continuity.)

3. Ibid., 23.

4. For a fuller treatment of Smith's moralism, see Peter J. Dougherty, *Who's Afraid of Adam Smith* (New York: John Wiley & Sons, 2002).

5. Steve Swarz and Randall Smith, "Quick Study: How Nelson Peltz Cleared $520 Million on the Sale of Triangle." *The Wall Street Journal*, Dec. 6, 1988.

6. The portions on Whitacre borrow from Roger Lowenstein, "Heads I Win, Tails I Win." *The New York Times Magazine*, June 9, 2002.

7. Roger Lowenstein, "Intrinsic Value: Peltz's Pay and the Spirit of the Age." *The Wall Street Journal*, June 12, 1997.

8. Again, this is from Lowenstein, "Heads I Win, Tails I Win."

9. This was calculated from year-end 1989 through year-end 2002.

10. Lowenstein, "Heads I Win, Tails I Win."

11. Joann S. Lublin, "Pay for No Performance: CEOs Were Supposed to Get Top Dollar Only When They Got Top Results." *The Wall Street Journal*, Apr. 9, 1998.

12. Berkshire Hathaway Inc., 1988 *Annual Report*, 13.

13. Bruce Orwall and Joann S. Lublin, "If a Company Prospers, Should Its Directors Behave by the Book?" *The Wall Street Journal*, Feb. 24, 1997.

14. Justin Fox, "The Next Best Thing to Free Money," *Fortune*, July 7, 1997.

15. Opensecrets.org, Web site of the Center for Responsive Politics.

16. "Executive Excess 2002: CEOs Cook the Books, Skewer the Rest of Us." Joint Report of Institute for Policy Studies and United For a Fair Economy, Aug. 26, 2002.

17. Pearl Meyer Associates.

18. Paul Krugman, "For Richer." *The New York Times Magazine*, Oct. 20, 2002.

19. "Recent Changes in U.S. Family Finances: Results from the 1998 Survey of Consumer Finances." Federal Reserve Board Bulletin, January 2000, 15.

20. Krugman, "For Richer."

21. Jennifer Reingold, "Executive Pay: Tying Pay to Performance Is a Great Idea." *BusinessWeek*, Apr. 21, 1997. The methodology is a bit suspect; *BusinessWeek* counts income from options as earned in the year they are exercised, not the year they are granted.

22. David Cay Johnston, "Executive Pensions Eclipse Years on the Job." *The New York Times*, Dec. 17, 2002.

23. Executive Compensation Advisory Services.

24. Jennifer Reingold, "Executive Pay." *BusinessWeek*, Apr. 21, 1997.

25. Thomas A. Stewart, "The Leading Edge: Can Even Heroes Get Paid Too Much?" *Fortune*, June 8, 1998.

26. "Compensation Fit for a King," *Forbes*, May 17, 1999.

27. Roger Lowenstein, "Intrinsic Value: On the Difficulty of Hiring Good Help." *The Wall Street Journal*, Mar. 27, 1997.

28. Through December 31, 2002. This calculation includes the cash value of Eisner's option exercises but not (to avoid double counting) the value

of new option grants. The Treasury bond yielded 7.9 percent at the end of 1989. Over thirteen years it would have returned about 168 percent. According to Bloomberg, Disney's stock, over that span, rose at an annual rate of 5.12 percent, for a total return of 92 percent, including dividends.

29. Roger Lowenstein, "Unconventional Wisdom: Is Greed Good?" *Smart-Money*, June 1999.

30. Floyd Norris and Alex Berenson, "Conseco Files for Bankruptcy Protection." *The New York Times*, Dec. 19, 2002.

31. Matt Murray, "Bankers Trust Is Hit by $488 Million Loss." *The Wall Street Journal*, Oct. 23, 1998. Paul Beckett, "Former Chairman of Bankers Trust Is Expected to Quit Deutsche Bank Post." *The Wall Street Journal*, June 25, 1999 (Newman); Dean Foust, with Louis Lavelle, "CEO Pay: Nothing Succeeds like Failure." *BusinessWeek*, Sept. 11, 2000 (Ivester and Barad).

32. Lowenstein, "Intrinsic Value: On the Difficulty of Hiring Good Help."

33. Ibid.

34. John A. Byrne, "The CEO and the Board." *BusinessWeek*, Sept. 15, 1997.

CHAPTER FOUR: NUMBER GAMES

1. Betsy Morris, "Robert Goizueta and Jack Welch: The Wealth Builders." *Fortune*, Dec. 11, 1995.

2. John F. Welch, Jr., with John A. Byrne, *Jack: Straight from the Gut* (New York: Warner Books, 2001), 20.

3. Stratford Sherman, "A Master Class in Radical Change." *Fortune*, Dec. 13, 1993.

4. From 1992–2001. This calculation includes the cash value of Welch's option exercises but not (to avoid double counting) the value of new option grants.

5. Jon Birger, "GE's Glowing Numbers." *Money.com*, Nov. 15, 2000.

6. Ibid.

7. Ibid.

8. Interview with author.

9. Robert Friedman, interview with author.

10. Interview with author.

11. Quoted in Birger, "GE's Glowing Numbers."

12. Quoted in Cassidy, "The Greed Cycle."

13. Roger Lowenstein, "Unconventional Wisdom: Within the Letter." *Smart-Money,* May 2002.

14. ———, "Make Pinocchio CEOs Pay." *The Wall Street Journal,* Aug. 16, 2002. Arthur Levitt, *Take On The Street* (2002), 116. The SEC counted seven hundred restatements from 1997 through 2000.

15. ———, "Intrinsic Value: Earnings Not Always What They Seem." *The Wall Street Journal,* Feb. 15, 1996.

16. Francois Degeorge, Jayendu Patel, and Richard Zeckhauser, "Earnings Manipulation to Exceed Thresholds." Reported in the author's "Intrinsic Value: How to Be a Winner in the Profits Game." *The Wall Street Journal,* Apr. 3, 1997.

17. Howard Schilit, *Financial Shenanigans: How to Detect Accounting Gimmicks and Fraud in Financial Reports* (New York: McGraw-Hill, second edition, 2002), was enormously useful on Lucent, especially 18–22.

18. Jonathan Weil, "A CEO's Candid Speech May Come Back to Haunt Lucent." *The Wall Street Journal,* Nov. 20, 2002.

19. Interview with author.

20. Frank Partnoy, *Infectious Greed: How Deceit and Risk Corrupted the Financial Markets* (New York: Times Books, 2003), 155.

21. Roger Lowenstein, "Intrinsic Value: You Want Earnings? We've Got 'Em." *The Wall Street Journal,* Apr. 24, 1997.

22. Lynn Turner, interview with author.

23. Ibid.

24. Russ Banham, "Andrew S. Fastow—Enron Corp." *CFO Magazine,* Oct. 1, 1999.

25. Daniel Altman, "The Taming of the Finance Officers." *The New York Times,* Apr. 14, 2002.

26. Russ Banham, "Andrew S. Fastow—Enron Corp." *CFO Magazine,* Oct. 1, 1999.

27. Joseph Fuller and Michael C. Jensen, "Just Say No to Wall Street." *Journal of Applied Corporate Finance,* vol. 14, no. 4, Winter 2002, 41–46.

28. Michael C. Jensen, "Paying People to Lie: The Truth About the Budgeting Process." Harvard Business School working paper, Sept. 6, 2001, an executive summary of which was published as "Corporate Budgeting Is Broken, Let's Fix It." *Harvard Business Review,* November 2001.

29. Roger Lowenstein, "Intrinsic Value: Sipping the Fizz in Coca-Cola's Profit." *The Wall Street Journal,* May 1, 1997.

30. "Top IR Concerns for 1999—Will Whispered Earnings Die?" *Investor Relations Business,* Jan. 4, 1999.

31. See the excellent exposé by Anthony Bianco, William Symonds, and Nanette Byrnes, "The Rise and Fall of Dennis Kozlowski." *BusinessWeek,* Dec. 23, 2002.

32. Jonathan R. Laing, "Tyco's Titan: How Dennis Kozlowski Is Creating a Lean, Profitable Giant." *Barron's,* Apr 12, 1999.

33. Warren Buffett observed in the 1981 annual report on Berkshire Hathaway, Inc., that many managers, believing in the transformative powers of mergers, "apparently were overexposed in impressionable childhood years to the story in which the imprisoned handsome prince is released from a toad's body by a kiss from a beautiful princess."

34. Herb Greenberg, "Does Tyco Play Accounting Games?" *Fortune,* Apr. 1, 2002.

35. William C. Symonds with Heather Timmons and Diane Brady, "Behind Tyco's Accounting Alchemy." *BusinessWeek,* Feb. 25, 2002.

36. Daniel Golden, Mark Maremont, and David Armstrong, "Alarming Tactics: How Tyco Pushed ADT Dealers into Poor Areas to Boost Growth." *The Wall Street Journal,* Nov. 15, 2002.

37. *SEC v. Xerox Corp,* SEC Litigation Release No. 17465 / Apr. 11, 2002. Mark Maremont and James Bandler, "Xerox Restates Past Three Years' Results." *The Wall Street Journal,* June 1, 2001. Floyd Norris, "Xerox Will Battle SEC over Rules on Accounting." *The New York Times,* Jan. 8, 2002.

38. *SEC v. Xerox Corp.,* SEC Litigation Release No. 17465 / Apr. 11, 2002. John Hechinger and James Bandler, "Angry Investors Focus on Xerox's Romeril—Amid Company's Problems, CFO's Reputation Falters." *The Wall Street Journal,* Feb. 22, 2001.

39. Bernard Wysocki Jr., "Change Machine: Xerox Recasts Itself as Formidable Force in Digital Revolution." *The Wall Street Journal,* Feb. 2, 1999.

40. "Xerox Corporation." Report of the Center for Financial Research and Analysis, Apr. 19, 1999.

41. Ibid.

42. James Bandler and John Hechinger, "Leading the News: SEC Says Xerox Misled Investors by Manipulating Its Earnings." *The Wall Street Journal,* Apr. 12, 2002.

43. James Bandler and Mark Maremont, "Seeing Red: How Ex-Accountant Added up to Trouble for Humbled Xerox." *The Wall Street Journal,* June 28, 2001. Bandler and Hechinger, "SEC Says Xerox Misled Investors."

44. Bandler and Hechinger, "SEC Says Xerox Misled Investors."

45. John Hechinger and James Bandler, "Former Xerox Officials in Mexico Assert Headquarters Ignored Fiscal Warnings." *The Wall Street Journal,* Feb. 7, 2001.

46. James Bandler and John Hechinger, "Executive Challenges Xerox's Books, Was Fired." *The Wall Street Journal,* Feb. 6, 2001.

47. Claudia H. Deutsch and Reed Abelson, "Xerox Facing New Pressures over Auditing." *The New York Times,* Feb. 2001.

48. *SEC v. Xerox Corp.,* SEC Litigation Release No. 17465 / April 11, 2002.

49. James Bandler and Mark Maremont, "Xerox to Pay $10 Million in SEC Case." *The Wall Street Journal,* Apr. 2, 2002.

CHAPTER FIVE: DOORMEN AT NOON

1. Joel Seligman, *The Transformation of Wall Street* (1995; 1st ed. 1982), 104.

2. Michael R. Beschloss, *Kennedy and Roosevelt* (New York: W. W. Norton, 1980), 88.

3. Seligman, *Transformation,* 111.

4. Louis Lowenstein, "Financial Transparency and Corporate Governance: You Manage What You Measure." *Columbia Law Review,* Vol. 96, No. 5 (1996), 1342.

5. Seligman, *Transformation,* 277.

6. The other was John Shad, an executive at E. F. Hutton, who was appointed

by President Reagan. Though Harry McDonald, appointed by Truman, was a member of a Detroit investment bank, his primary business experience was in the dairy industry.

7. Levitt, *Take on the Street*, 4–6.

8. Ibid., 6, 8.

9. The cases were *Lampf* v. *Gilbertson* (1991) and *Central Bank of Denver* v. *First Interstate Bank of Denver* (1994).

10. Joel Seligman, interview with author.

11. James Chanos, interview with author.

12. Roger Lowenstein, "Intrinsic Value: House Aims to Fix Securities Laws, But, Indeed, Is the System Broke?" *The Wall Street Journal*, Aug. 10, 1995. Michael Schroeder, "Guess Who's Gunning for the SEC." *BusinessWeek*, Aug. 14, 1995.

13. Scott Sipprelle, interview with author.

14. SEC. Percentages are for 1993–2000.

15. Joel Seligman, interview with author.

16. Levitt, *Take on the Street*, 6.

17. Peter Elstrom, "The Power Broker." *BusinessWeek*, May 15, 2000.

18. Faye Landes, interview with author.

19. Gretchen Morgenson, "See No Evil, Speak No Evil." *Forbes*, Dec. 15, 1995. Anderson's firm is Atlantis Investment of Parsippany, New Jersey.

20. Levitt, *Take on the Street*, 67, 71.

21. The rule was conceived by Harvey Goldschmid, a Columbia law professor who was then the SEC's general counsel. Goldschmid's long interest in corporate governance dates to the 1970s, when, anticipating many of the concerns of the post-Enron era, he proposed that the United States require that corporate boards be composed entirely of independent directors. In 2002, he became an SEC commissioner.

22. Levitt, *Take on the Street*, 86, 92.

23. George Gilder, "The Outsider Trading Scandal." *The Wall Street Journal*, Apr. 19, 2000.

24. The SEC chief was William Cary.

25. Seligman, *Transformation*, 537.

26. Ibid., 538.

27. D. Jeanne Patterson and Nell Minow, "Blame Directors for Accounting Practices, Managing Earnings." *Pensions & Investments*, May 28, 2001.

28. Ibid.

29. Levitt, *Take on the Street*, 218.

30. Ibid., 113–14.

31. "Special Report: Accounting In Crisis." *Business Week*, Jan. 28, 2002. Peter Beinart, TRB From Washington, "Accounting." *The New Republic*, Feb. 11, 2002.

32. James G. Castellano, "Let's Play to Our Strength." *Journal of Accountancy*, February 2002.

33. Ken Brown and Jonathan Weil, "How Andersen's Embrace of Consulting Altered the Culture of the Auditing Firm." *The Wall Street Journal*, Mar. 12, 2002.

34. Peter Beinart, "Accounting."

35. Ianthe Jeanne Dugan, "Depreciated: Did You Hear the One About the Accountant? It's Not Very Funny." *The Wall Street Journal*, Mar. 14, 2002.

36. "Waste Management, Inc. Founder and Five Former Top Officers Sued for Massive Earnings Management Fraud." SEC Litigation Release No. 17435, Mar. 26, 2002.

37. SEC, Litigation Release No. 17039, June 19, 2001 [the settlement of Arthur Andersen LLP and three partners on charges of "knowingly or recklessly" issuing false and misleading unqualified audit reports on Waste Management's annual financial statements for the years 1993 through 1996]. The figure for consulting includes $11.8 million billed by Andersen directly and $6 million billed by its sister firm, Andersen Consulting.

38. Peter Beinart, "Accounting."

39. SEC Litigation Release No. 17435.

40. SEC Litigation Release No. 17039.

41. The author's father served on the SEC panel on audit effectiveness, which recommended restrictions on nonaudit work for audit clients.

42. Letter of Kenneth Lay to Arthur Levitt, quoted in Levitt, *Take on the Street*, 299.

43. Center for Responsive Politics.

44. Levitt, *Take on the Street*, 130–31, 292, 294.

45. Bernard Wysocki Jr., "Overview—Where We Stand." *The Wall Street Journal*, Sept. 27, 1999.

46. See Roger Lowenstein, "Into Thin Air." *The New York Times Magazine*, Feb. 17, 2002.

47. James K. Glassman, "Is Government Strangling the New Economy?" *The Wall Street Journal*, Apr. 6, 2000.

48. David Cay Johnston detailed the problems of the IRS in numerous articles for *The New York Times;* for example, "Departing Chief Says IRS Is Losing War on Tax Cheats," Nov. 5, 2002.

49. Partnoy, *Infectious Greed*, 147.

50. International Swaps & Derivatives Association. Figure represents notional dollars.

51. In 1994, P&G suffered major derivative losses and sued its dealer, Bankers Trust, for recovery. The same year, as a result of risky bets on interest-rate derivatives, Orange County became the largest government entity in U.S. history to file for bankruptcy.

52. Greenspan's support for derivatives is detailed in the author's *When Genius Failed* (New York: Random House, 2000).

53. Jacob M. Schlesinger, "The Deregulators: Did Washington Help Set Stage for Current Business Turmoil?" *The Wall Street Journal*, Oct. 17, 2002.

54. Lowenstein, *When Genius Failed*, 231.

55. Joseph Stiglitz, "The Roaring Nineties." *The Atlantic Monthly*, October 2002.

56. "United States: Too Triumphalist by Half." *The Economist*, Apr. 25, 1998.

57. See Paul Blustein, *The Chastening: Inside the Crisis That Rocked the Global Financial System and Humbled the IMF* (New York: PublicAffairs, 2001).

58. Joseph Stiglitz, "What I Learned at The World Economic Crisis." *The New Republic*, Apr. 17, 2000.

59. The loans figure is from Stiglitz, "What I Learned." The other figure is anecdotal.

Chapter Six: New Economy, Old Errors

1. Jay Ritter, interview with author.

2. Remarks by Chairman Alan Greenspan, Haas Annual Business Faculty Research Dialogue, University of California, Berkeley, Sept. 4, 1998.

3. This description is adapted from an article by the author in *ecompany.com*, "Who's to Blame for the Dot-com Insanity," April 2001.

4. Jonathan Cohen, "Amazon.com Inc: The World's Leading Internet Commerce Company Is Too Expensive." Merrill Lynch, Sept. 1, 1998.

5. As of the time of the eBay IPO.

6. George Gilder, "The Faith of a Futurist." *The Wall Street Journal,* Dec. 31, 1999.

7. Ibid.

8. James K. Glassman and Kevin A. Hassett, *Dow 36,000: The New Strategy for Profiting from the Coming Rise in the Stock Market* (New York: Three Rivers Press, 1999), 3, 18.

9. Ibid., 9.

10. Merrill Lynch Global Equity Fund Research, Feb. 14, 2000, quoted in Jeremy Siegel, *Stocks for the Long Run* (New York: McGraw-Hill, 2002), 147.

11. Daniel Pearl, "Futurist Schlock: Today's Cyberhype Has a Familiar Ring." *The Wall Street Journal,* Sept. 7, 1995.

12. Frank Quattrone, interview with author.

13. For accounts of Amazon's founding, see Joshua Quittner, "An Eye on the Future," *Time,* Dec. 27, 1999, and Peter de Jonge, "Riding the Wild, Perilous Waters of Amazon.com," *The New York Times Magazine,* Mar. 14, 1999.

14. David Perry, interview with author.

15. Randall E. Stross, *Eboys: The True Story of the Six Tall Men Who Backed eBay, Webvan, and Other Billion-Dollar Startups* (New York: Ballantine, 2000), 63.

16. Gary Dahl, Bud Grebey, Peter Relan, and other former Webvan employees, interviews with author.

17. Paul Gompers and Josh Lerner, "The Venture Capital Revolution." *Journal of Economic Perspectives,* vol. 15, no. 2 (Spring 2001), 146.

18. Thomson Financial / Venture Economics.

19. Mary Meeker, "Amazon.com (AMZN): Initiating Coverage." Morgan Stanley Dean Witter U.S. Investment Research, Sept. 22, 1997.

20. Jay Ritter, interview with author.

21. Susan Pulliam and Randall Smith, "Silicon Touch: For Frank Quattrone, with a Fief at CSFB, Tech Was a Gold Mine." *The Wall Street Journal*, May 3, 2001.

22. The kickback was in the form of higher commissions on future stock trades. See Pulliam and Smith's groundbreaking articles in *The Wall Street Journal*. In addition to "Silicon Touch," "CSFB Official Set Quota for Repayment Of IPO Profits in Form of Commissions," Aug. 10, 2001; "Sharing the Wealth: At CSFB, Lush Profit Earned on IPOs Found Its Way Back to Firm," Nov. 30, 2001, and, with Anita Raghavan and Gregory Zuckerman, "Coming to Terms: CSFB Agrees to Pay $100 Million to Settle Twin IPO Investigations," Dec. 11, 2001. See also Peter Elkind and Mark Gimein, "The Trouble with Frank." *Fortune*, Sept. 3, 2001.

23. John Heilemann, "Letter from Silicon Valley: The Networker." *The New Yorker*, Aug. 11, 1997 [italics in original].

24. Levitt, *Take on the Street*, 120.

25. Christopher Byron, "Cisco's Web of Deals." nypost.com, Feb. 18, 2002.

26. Jamis MacNiven, interview with author.

27. Dyan Machan, "An Edison for a New Age?" *Forbes*, May 17, 1999.

28. Bernard Wysocki Jr., "Funny Money: Rethinking a Quaint Idea: Profits." *The Wall Street Journal*, May 19, 1999.

29. Matt Krantz, "Young at Helm Riding the Wacky Net Waves Solo." *USA Today*, Aug. 18, 1999.

30. David Wessel, "Bold Estimate of Web's Thirst for Electricity Seems All Wet," *The Wall Street Journal*, Dec. 5, 2002.

31. Rafe Needleman, "Idealab Launches Free-PC.com." *Red Herring*, Feb. 8, 1999.

32. Spring 2000.

33. Jerry Useem, "Dot-coms: What Have We Learned." *Fortune*, Oct. 30, 2000.

By 1990, close to $400 billion was invested in 401(k)s. By 1995, the total had doubled. Unlike a traditional pension, which provided a fixed, guaranteed stipend, a 401(k) pegged one's retirement to the stock market. This raised people's interest profoundly, for it was the employee himself, not some distant pension manager, who was making the investment choices. Employees typically added to their plans every month, with a rhythmic precision that bred a deceptive aura of steadiness.

Gina Giacomazzi, a vice president of marketing for an outfit known as 401k Forum, which provided advice to employees, had a vivid way of describing the dream of millions of new investors. "If everyone in America could add 1% to their return, that would add a tremendous amount to our retirement savings," she proclaimed in a mid-'90s interview.[14] Of course, the ultimate return from a security is derived by the earnings of the underlying asset—which will not be affected by the enthusiasm of 401(k) investors. The dubious notion that everyone could raise their return by investing in stocks that, collectively, the country already owned, was a profound testimony to the country's new faith in the market.

A parallel misconception gripped Washington, where Democrats and Republicans alike rushed to proclaim their support for the idea that President Ford had mockingly dismissed two decades earlier: putting Social Security funds into stocks. The politicians were headily encouraged in such sentiments, as PaineWebber, Merrill Lynch, and virtually anyone who took the subway (or limousine) to Wall Street were lobbying for Social Security reform, and contributing to the politicians' coffers. Nonetheless, the pols truly believed that such reform would "add" to the country's savings. By the mid-'90s, close to half the country (up from a mere fifth in the 1960s) was invested in either stocks, mutual funds or both.[15] Naturally, politicians were eager to enlist the other half. What the pols forgot was that, ultimately, society's wealth derives from the products that companies sell and the profits they earn—not from the appeal of their securities to investors. Shuffle some stocks from existing shareholders to retirees and somebody would wind up richer, somebody poorer, but not society as a whole.

W ashington's enthusiasm for privatizing Social Security was emblematic of a general promarket tilt. In fact, save Ronald Reagan, Clinton was the most market-oriented president since the Roaring Twenties. He made a fateful decision in his first term to subject social spending to the higher priority of balancing the budget. It was a bipartisan goal, but the Democrats' support was particularly telling. For Congressional Republicans, led by Newt Gingrich, cutting government was simply an act of dogma. For Clinton Democrats it was about calming the fears of bond traders, thus, it was hoped, lowering interest rates and making development more affordable. Liberalism was not forgotten— but the bond market came first. James Carville, a Clinton campaign consultant, quipped that in his next life he wanted to be reborn as the bond market—for it was there, and not in the White House, where Carville had deduced that real power lay.

The quip had a deeper implication: government had been diminished. The collapse of the Berlin Wall and the end of communism had put the lid on socialism; unexpectedly, it had diminished liberal government as well. The nation-state was said to be vestigial, part of an historical process that now had ended. Mario Gabelli, a well-known mutual fund manager, marveled at the new Europe: barbed wire and welfare statism were out, Hollywood, McDonald's and all things American were in.[16] America's ascendancy bred an insouciant optimism, a Coolidge-esque notion of the paramount role of business and of government's only function being to grease the wheels.

Clinton did not go that far, but as Joseph Stiglitz, a skeptical member of his economic cabinet, argued, decisions were filtered through a market-

34. K. C. Swanson, "Lessons from the Folly: Opening the March 10, 2000, Time Capsule." *TheStreet.com,* Mar. 9, 2001.

35. Michael Nol, "The Optimist." *Bloomberg Markets,* October 2002.

36. "E-strategy brief: GE. While Welch Waited," *The Economist,* May 19, 2001.

37. Edward Horowitz, interview with author.

38. "Clayton Christensen on 'Innovator's Dilemmas and Innovator's No-Brainers.'" *BusinessWeek Online, e.biz,* Mar. 15, 1999.

39. John Kenneth Galbraith, *The Great Crash* (Boston: Houghton, Mifflin, 1988; 1st ed. 1954), 60–65.

40. Technically, CMGI was not itself the venture fund. Rather, it invested and controlled funds, dubbed CMG@Ventures and the like, which in turn bought stakes in start-up companies.

41. Bill Martin and Rusty Szurek, interviews with author.

42. The one exception was CMGI's original business of marketing book lists to college professors—the one business that was not dependent on the Internet.

43. Paul C. Judge, "The Web Giant Nobody Knows." *Business Week,* July 27, 1998.

44. James Surowiecki, "Barry Diller Is No Visionary," *Fortune,* Apr. 12, 1999. Surowiecki was the first to appreciate Diller's metamorphosis from Hollywood to direct marketing and the Internet.

45. Barry Diller, interview with author.

46. Quoted in Bob Davis, *Speed Is Life: Street Smart Lessons from the Front Lines of Business* (New York: Doubleday, 2001) 77–78.

47. Jay Ritter, interview with author.

48. Thomson Financial. The figure for Quattrone is an estimate, but he was widely reported to have earned in the neighborhood of $100 million in a single year alone (see Pulliam and Smith, "Silicon Touch.")

49. Patrick Byrne, CEO, Overstock.com, interview with author.

CHAPTER SEVEN: ENRON

1. Julian E. Barnes, Megan Barnett, Christopher H. Schmitt, and Marianne Lavelle, "How a Titan Came Undone." *U.S. News & World Report,* Mar. 18, 2002.

2. Ibid.

3. Ibid.

4. "Earlier Scandal Pointed to Need for Controls." *Financial Times,* Jan. 16, 2002.

5. Barnes et al., "Titan."

6. Interview with former Enron employee.

7. Barnes et al., "Titan."

8. Toni Mack, "Hidden Risks." *Forbes,* May 24, 1993. Cited in John D. Martin, "An Analysis of the Failure of Enron Corp.," unpublished, Aug. 28, 2002, 27.

9. Barnes et al., "Titan."

10. Ed Michaels, Helen Handfield-Jones, and Beth Axelrod, *The War for Talent* (Boston: Harvard Business School Press, 2001), 43, 47.

11. Tom Fowler, "The Pride and the Fall of Enron." *Houston Chronicle,* Oct. 20, 2002. April Witt and Peter Behr, "Dream Job Turns into a Nightmare: Skilling's Success Came at High Price." *The Washington Post,* July 29, 2002 [second of a five-part series; hereafter WP II].

12. Harlan S. Byrne, "Hello, New Economy." *Barron's,* Mar. 27, 2000.

13. Anita Raghavan, Kathryn Kranhold and Alexei Barrionuevo, "Full Speed Ahead, How Enron Bosses Created a Culture Of Pushing Limits." *The Wall Street Journal,* Aug. 26, 2002. Wendy Zellner, "Jeffrey Skilling." *BusinessWeek,* May 15, 2000. WP II.

14. Vincent Kaminski and John Martin, "Transforming Enron: The Value of Active Management." *Journal of Applied Corporate Finance,* vol. 13, no. 4, Winter 2001 [italics added].

15. Barnes et al., "Titan."

16. John R. Emshwiller and Rebecca Smith, "Joint Venture: A 1997 Enron Meeting Belies Officers' Claims They Were in the Dark." *The Wall Street Journal,* Feb. 1, 2002. "Andrew S. Fastow—Enron Corp." *CFO Magazine,* Oct. 1, 1999.

17. Report of the special investigation committee of the Enron board, chaired by William Powers Jr., Feb. 1, 2002 (hereafter, the Powers report) 43–44.

Ellen Joan Pollock, "Limited Partners: Lawyers or Enron Faulted Its Deals, Didn't Force Issue." *The Wall Street Journal,* May 22, 2002.

18. Powers report, 8, 45–46, and 64. The return was shared with a Kopper friend and coinvestor.

19. Powers report, 44–45; Pollock, "Limited Partners."

20. Powers report, 41.

21. Powers report, 45–52.

22. Powers report, 42.

23. John Martin said the conversation took place between Skilling and a third party.

24. Enron Corp., *2000 Annual Report,* 16.

25. Interview with former Enron employee.

26. Partnoy, *Infectious Greed,* 306.

27. Enron, *2000 Annual Report,* 45.

28. John Olson, interview with author.

29. Powers report, 4, 97.

30. Interview with former Enron employee. Powers report, 84–85. Peter Behr and April Witt, "Visionary's Dream Led to Risky Business." *The Washington Post,* July 28, 2002 [hereafter WPI].

31. Powers report, 150–55; 162, 166.

32. Raghavan, Kranhold, and Barrionuevo, "Full Speed Ahead."

33. Stuart L. Gillian and John D. Martin, "Financial Engineering, Corporate Governance, and the Collapse of Enron," unpublished draft, Sept. 17, 2002, 22.

34. John Martin, interview with author. "The Five Best Boards." *Chief Executive,* October 2000.

35. Gillian and Martin, "Financial Engineering," 23, 24, 48.

36. Powers report, 153.

37. Powers report, 72, 166; Raghavan, Kranhold and Barrionuevo, "Full Speed Ahead."

38. Kurt Eichenwald, "Enron's Collapse: The Partnerships; Investors Lured to Enron Deals by Inside Data." *The New York Times,* Jan. 25, 2002.

39. Powers report, 73. The report says, "We understand LJM2 ultimately had approximately 50 limited partners, including" Merrill, J. P. Morgan, Citicorp, and GE Capital. "We are not certain of this [the names] because LJM2 declined to provide any information to us." Eichenwald, "Enron's Collapse."

40. Powers report, 68, 134, 140, 141; *U.S. vs. Andrew S. Fastow*, U.S. District Court, Southern District of Texas, criminal complaint filed Oct. 1, 2002.

41. Quoted in testimony of Frank Partnoy, U.S. Senate Committee on Governmental Affairs, Jan. 24, 2002, 12.

42. *"SEC v. Merrill Lynch & Co., et al."* U.S. Securities and Exchange Commission, Litigation Release No. 18038, Mar. 17, 2003. Kurt Eichenwald, "1999 Transaction With Enron Keeps Dogging Merrill Lynch." *The New York Times*, Oct. 3, 2002.

43. Harrison, vice chairman of Alliance Capital Management, ran the organization's large-capitalization growth stock team. In seeking to explain his investment to a Senate subcommittee, Harrison testified, on May 16, 2002, that "Enron's management had been widely heralded as among the brightest and most visionary management teams in the world." The Lay quote is from David Kirkpatrick, "Enron Takes its Pipeline to the Net." *Fortune*, Jan. 24, 2000.

44. "Business: A Matter of Principals." *The Economist*, June 30, 2001.

45. Partnoy, *Infectious Greed*, 357–58.

46. Interview with former Enron employee.

47. Rebecca Smith and John R. Emshwiller, "Prosecutors Probe Skilling's Role in Enron's Failed Telecom Venture." *The Wall Street Journal*, Dec. 13, 2002.

48. Brian O'Reilly, "The Power Merchant." *Fortune*, Apr. 17, 2000.

49. Tom Fowler and Mary Flood, "Broadband Claims Investigated as Fraud." *Houston Chronicle*, Jan. 2, 2003.

50. O'Reilly, "The Power Merchant." See also Robert Preston and Mike Koller, "Enron Surges into E-markets." *Information Week*, Nov. 6, 2000.

51. Andrew Odlyzko, interview with author.

52. Peter Behr, "Technology Investors Have a New Specter to Worry About: The Bandwidth Glut." *The Washington Post*, Sept. 24, 2000.

53. Philip S. Bagwell, *The Transport Revolution from 1770* (1974), 94.

54. Andrew Odlyzko and Tom Stluka, interviews with author. "The Power of WorldCom's puff." *The Economist,* July 20, 2002. Yochi J. Dreazen, "Behind the Fiber Glut: Telecom Carriers Were Driven by Wildly Optimistic Data on Internet's Growth Rate." *The Wall Street Journal,* Sept. 26, 2002.

55. Allan Tumolillo, interview with author.

56. G. Christian Hill, "The Wireless World—The Spoils of War." *The Wall Street Journal,* Sept. 11, 1997.

57. Paul Starr, "The Great Telecom Implosion." *The American Prospect,* Sept. 9, 2002. Andrew Odlyzko, interview with author.

58. Joanna Markis, "Bandwidth Barons." *Data Communications,* July 1998.

59. Scott Cleland, interview with author.

60. Thomson Financial; figures are for 1996–2002.

61. Thomson Financial; 1996–2002. The term "Wall Street" is used loosely, as the figures include sales by foreign issuers and also sales to overseas investors. Although fees on telecom issues dwarfed those on Internet and dot-com stocks, they were only marginally ahead of the fees for all technology issues.

62. First interim report of Dick Thornburgh, bankruptcy court examiner, U.S. Bankruptcy Court, Southern District of New York. In re: WorldCom Inc., Case No. 02-15533, Nov. 4, 2002 [hereafter the Thornburgh report], 58.

63. Indeed, a former WorldCom executive said, "The boost from postacquisition accounting was like a drug. But it meant bigger deals had to come along to keep the ball rolling." Kurt Eichenwald, "For WorldCom, Acquisitions Were Behind Its Rise and Fall." *The New York Times,* Aug. 8, 2002.

64. George Gilder, "Manager's Journal: The Fiber Baron." *The Wall Street Journal,* Oct. 6, 1997.

65. Michael E. Kanell and Russell Grantham, "WorldCom CEO Had Great Run, Hard Fall." *The Atlanta Journal-Constitution,* June 30, 2002. Catharine Yang with Peter Elstrom, "Doc Ebbers' Miracle Diet." *Business-Week,* Mar. 1, 1999. Nelson D. Schwartz, "How Ebbers Is Whipping MCI WorldCom into Shape." *Fortune,* Feb. 1, 1999.

66. Steven Rosenbush, "Inside the Telecom Game." *BusinessWeek*, Aug. 5, 2002.

67. Dreazen, "Behind the Fiber Glut."

68. Julie Creswell with Nomi Prins, "The Emperor of Greed." *Fortune*, June 24, 2002.

69. Thornburgh report, 91, 97–8.

70. Thornburgh report, 98.

71. According to the September 2002 complaint filed by New York State against five telecom chief executives, *State of New York and Eliot Spitzer v. Philip F. Anschutz, Bernard J. Ebbers et al.*, 23, between 1997 and 2002 Salomon Smith Barney advised WorldCom on approximately twenty-three investment banking deals and received fees of $107 million. Thornburgh report, 83, 85.

72. Laurie P. Cohen, "Winnick Is Told He Must Testify in Milken Case." *The Wall Street Journal*, Dec. 11, 1989. Kurt Eichenwald, "Prosecutors Said to Shorten Milken Presentencing Case." *The New York Times*, Oct. 10, 1990.

73. Center for Responsive Politics. Daniel Gross, "How Global Crossing Spun Political Gold." *Business 2.0*, Mar. 24, 2002.

74. Creswell, "Emperor of Greed."

75. Ibid.

76. Ibid.

CHAPTER EIGHT: BANKRUPT

1. John Cassidy, "Striking It Rich: The Rise and Fall of Popular Capitalism." *The New Yorker*, Jan. 14, 2002.

2. The figure is a rough estimate that takes into account both the venture money invested in dot-coms and the vastly greater sums that were borrowed by the telecoms.

3. Dennis K. Berman and Deborah Solomon, "Optical Illusion: Accounting Questions Swirl Around Pioneer in the Telecom World." *The Wall Street Journal*, Feb. 13, 2002. The "salmon" memo, dated June 5, 2000, was presented in hearings held by the House Energy and Commerce Subcommittee on Oversight & Investigations on Sept. 24 and Oct. 1, 2002. See its

report, "Capacity Swaps by Global Crossing and Qwest: Sham Transactions Designed to Boost Revenues?" See also Simon Romero, "Global Crossing Memo Indicates Early Warning of Downfall." *The New York Times*, Oct. 1, 2002.

4. Dennis K. Berman, Julia Angwin, and Chip Cummins, "Tricks of the Trade: As Market Bubble Neared End, Bogus Swaps Provided a Lift." *The Wall Street Journal*, Dec. 23, 2002. John D. Martin and Akin Sayrak, "Did Earnings Management Contribute to the Overvaluation of Enron's Stock." [unpublished], Aug. 7, 2002.

5. See *Roy L. Olofson vs. Gary C. Winnick, et al.*, Superior Court, County of Los Angeles, Central District, Case No. BC 274033. See especially 6–7 and 9–10 for Olofson's allegations relating to Global's presentation of its cash flow.

6. Global Crossing Ltd. Form 10-Q, May 15, 2001, 15.

7. Berman and Solomon, "Optical Illusion."

8. *Olofson vs. Winnick*, 18–20, 21. Robert Lenzner and Victoria Murphy, "Global Crashing." *Forbes*, Oct. 29, 2001. Berman and Solomon, "Optical Illusion." Dennis K. Berman, "Study Questioned Global Crossing Deals." *The Wall Street Journal*, Feb. 19, 2002.

9. This is a favorite line of the mutual fund manager Martin Whitman.

10. Dennis K. Berman, "Andersen's 'Swaps' Method Draws Scrutiny." *The Wall Street Journal*, Mar. 19, 2002.

11. Berman, Angwin, and Cummins, "Tricks of the Trade."

12. *Olofson vs. Winnick*, 6–8. 10–12, 24. Berman and Solomon, "Optical Illusion." Berman, Angwin, and Cummins, "Tricks of the Trade."

13. Berman and Solomon, "Optical Illusion."

14. "Bush Sr.'s Profitable Crossing," *BusinessWeek Online*, Feb. 22, 2002. "Global Crossing: Where's the Outrage on Capitol Hill?" *BusinessWeek Online*, Feb. 25, 2002. Gross, "How Global Crossing Spun Political Gold." According to *BusinessWeek*, the price paid by Bush for his stock isn't known. The stock may have been payment for two speeches Bush made on behalf of Global. His customary speaking fee was $80,000.

15. Dennis K. Berman, "Dialing for Dollars: Before Telecom Industry Sank, Insiders Sold Billions in Stock." *The Wall Street Journal*, Aug. 12, 2002.

16. Thornburgh report, 105.

17. Sullivan was indicted for conspiracy to commit securities fraud, filing false statements with the SEC, and other criminal violations of the securities laws on Aug. 28, 2002. Charges are pending.

18. Thornburgh report, 109.

19. Thornburgh report, 72.

20. Thornburgh report, 74, 79.

21. Thornburgh report, 74, 77.

22. Thornburgh report, 80–81.

23. James Chanos, the Wall Street investor, was a notable exception. He began to short (bet against) Enron stock because, among other reasons, its optimism about broadband seemed inconsistent with the industry's general decline.

24. David Rynecki, "Ten Stocks to Last the Decade." Aug. 14, 2000. Market mavens may be curious about the others on the list. They were Broadcom, Charles Schwab, Genentech, Morgan Stanley, Nokia, Nortel Networks, Oracle, Univision, and Viacom. The 80 percent decline was calculated from the prices in the magazine to December 31, 2002.

25. Enron disclosed $1.47 per share in "operating results" for 2000; after a loss of $.35 for "items impacting comparability," net income was $1.12. The comparability item is explained in the Management's Discussion and Analysis section of the 2000 *Annual Report*, 25.

26. Randall Stross, "Googlewhacking Enron." usnews.com, Feb. 9, 2002.

27. Enron Corp., 2000 *Annual Report*, 4–5, 6.

28. John Martin, interview with author. Testimony of Partnoy, 29.

29. David Barboza, "Despite Denial, Enron Papers Show Big Profit on Price Bets." *The New York Times*, Dec. 12, 2002.

30. Ronald Barone, "Enron Corp." UBS Warburg Research Note, Jan. 26, 2001. Curt Launer, "Enron Corp." Credit Suisse First Boston Equity Research, Jan. 26, 2002.

31. Barone said of Enron's ability to take gains from selling assets: "This is an enormous earnings vehicle, which can often be called upon when and if

market conditions require." Bethany McLean, "Is Enron Overpriced?" *Fortune,* Mar. 5, 2001.

32. "Kenneth Lay: The Energetic Messiah." *The Economist,* June 3, 2000.

33. Enron bankruptcy filing. See also Kurt Eichenwald, "Enron Paid Huge Bonuses in '01; Experts See a Motive for Cheating." *The New York Times,* Mar. 1, 2002.

34. The figures were compiled by Milberg Weiss Bershad Hynes & Lerach, counsel to the consolidated class-action complaint against Enron in U.S. District Court, Southern District of Texas. Sales were tabulated from 1996 onward.

35. Center for Responsive Politics. Enron's employees donated $736,800 to Bush campaigns and to the Bush presidential inaugural.

36. Kurt Eichenwald, "Company Man to the End, After All." *The New York Times,* Feb. 9, 2003. The description of the headquarters is from Partnoy's testimony, 2. Enron Field opened on Apr. 7, 2000.

37. Permanent Subcommittee on Investigations, Committee on Governmental Affairs, U.S. Senate, "The Role of the Board of Directors in Enron's Collapse." July 8, 2002, 53.

38. Testimony of Partnoy, 13–15; Enron Corp. 2000 *Annual Report,* 49.

39. Kurt Eichenwald, "The Findings Against Enron." *The New York Times,* Sept. 23, 2002.

40. Senate Governmental Affairs Committee Permanent Subcommittee on Investigations, hearings of July 22, 2003. Kurt Eichenwald, "Enron Hid Big Loans, Data Indicate." *The New York Times,* Feb. 27, 2002.

41. Senate Governmental Affairs Committee Permanent Subcommittee on Investigations, hearings of Dec. 11, 2001. A statement by Senator Carl Levin lays out the basics of the Bacchus partnership. The e-mail was disclosed in the subcommittee's Report on Fishtail, Bacchus, Sundance, and Slapshot: Four Enron Transactions Funded and Facilitated by U.S. Financial Institutions, Jan. 2, 2003. See also Richard A. Oppel Jr. and Kurt Eichenwald, "Inquiry Said to Examine Citigroup Role in Enron Deal." *The New York Times,* Dec. 9, 2002.

42. Report on Fishtail, Bacchus, Sundance, and Slapshot; Oppel and Eichenwald, "Inquiry Said to Examine Citigroup Role in Enron Deal."

43. Peter Behr and April Witt, "Concerns Grow Amid Conflicts." *The Washington Post,* July 30, 2002 [hereafter WP III]. Barbara Ley Toffler [cowritten with Jennifer Reingold], *Final Accounting: Ambition, Greed, and the Fall of Arthur Andersen* (New York: Broadway Books, 2003), 167. The Andersen memo went out in October 1998.

44. See especially Toffler, *Final Accounting.*

45. Alexei Barrionuevo, "Documents Show How Enron-Andersen Ties Grew." *The Wall Street Journal,* Feb. 26, 2002. Ianthe Jeanne Dugan, Dennis K. Berman, and Alexei Barrionuevo, "On Camera, People at Andersen, Enron Tell How Close They Were." *The Wall Street Journal,* Apr. 15, 2002.

46. Powers report, 97, 100. Jonathan Weil, "Andersen's Auditors Debated Partnership Losses." *The Wall Street Journal,* April 3, 2002.

47. Powers report, 128-29.

48. Powers report, 97-98, 129-32.

49. Powers report, 106.

50. Powers report, 133.

51. Interview with former Enron employee.

52. Powers report, 98, 121, 122.

53. WP III. Weil, "Andersen's Auditors Debated Partnership Losses." Powers report, 98, 120, 122.

54. Aside from the aforementioned Vince Kaminski, Jeffrey McMahon, Enron's treasurer, testified to Congress that he was transferred after complaining to Skilling about Fastow's dual role as CFO and LJM partner. Another employee, Stuart Zisman, a lawyer, wrote in a memo that Raptor "might lead one to believe that the financial books at Enron are being 'cooked' in order to eliminate a drag on earnings. . . ." Zisman was chastised by his supervisor for using "unnecessary inflammatory language."

55. WP I.

56. McLean, "Is Enron Overpriced?" One other publication deserves mention for its skepticism of Enron. In its issue of June 3, 2000, *The Economist,* in

"The Energetic Messiah", while generally praising Enron for being "as re-markable as it seems," cannily observed that Enron's "great failing" was its arrogance—even its "hubris."

57. Jonathan Friedland, "Enron's CEO, Skilling, Quits Two Top Posts." *The Wall Street Journal*, Aug. 15. 2001.

58. Letter from Sherron Watkins (unsigned) to Kenneth Lay.

59. Powers report, 172, 174. Watkins's letter to Lay. Max Hendricks III, of Vinson & Elkins, letter to James V. Derrick Jr. of Enron, Oct. 15. WP III.

60. Powers report, 125–27. WP III. April Witt and Peter Behr, "Losses, Con-flicts, Threaten Survival." *The Washington Post*, July 31, 2002 [hereafter WP IV].

61. Powers report, 127–28, 133.

62. Richard Grubman, interview with author.

63. The Powers report (164) found that Fastow's partnership capital increased by a total of $31 million in 1999 and 2000 and that, in addition, he received distributions of $18.7 million in 2000. However, the calculation of his gains has been something of a moving target. *The Wall Street Journal* first reported, a week before Fastow's resignation, that $35 million of the charge taken by Enron raised "vexing conflict-of-interest questions." (John Emshwiller and Rebecca Smith, "Enron Jolt: Investments, Assets Generate Big Loss," Oct. 17, 2001.) Two days later, the *Journal* said Enron had "estimated" that Fastow had earned more than $30 million from LJM (Smith and Emshwiller, "Enron CFO's Partnership Had Millions In Profit"). Finally, *The Washington Post* (WP IV) later concluded that Fastow earned $45 million from the partnerships. In addition to his profits from LJM, Fastow sold about $34 million worth of Enron stock.

64. Jeanne Cummings and Michael Schroeder, "Enron's Lay Sought Cabinet Officials' Help." *The Wall Street Journal*, Jan. 11, 2002.

65. Center for Responsive Politics.

CHAPTER NINE: YEAR OF THE LOCUSTS

1. WP II. WP IV. Peter Behr and April Witt, "Hidden Debts, Deals Scuttle Last Chance." *The Washington Post*, Aug. 1, 2002 [hereafter WP V].

2. Bridget O'Brian, "Enron Backer Gets $2 Million for 2001." *The Wall Street Journal*, Apr. 3, 2002.

3. Greg Ip, "Mood Swings in Favor of Regulation." *The Wall Street Journal*, Mar. 29, 2002.

4. Jared Sandberg and Joann Lublin, "Questioning the Books: Adelphia Draws Market Criticism Over Debt, Loans." *The Wall Street Journal*, Mar. 29, 2002.

5. "The Swamp Fox on Enron's Tail." *BusinessWeek Online*, Feb. 4, 2002.

6. U.S. Senate Committee on Governmental Affairs, "The Fall of Enron: How Could It Have Happened?" Jan. 24, 2002.

7. Various conservative writers, including Robert Novak ("The Trial of Harvey Pitt," *TownHall.com*, July 18, 2002), have suggested that the "kinder, gentler" quote was taken out of context to wrongly suggest that Pitt was promising to make the SEC a friendlier place for his former accounting clients. With the caveat that the chairman made a ritual plea for accountants to, in turn, deal more openly with the SEC, that is *exactly* what he proposed. In the Miami Beach address, which was directed to the governing board of the American Institute of Certified Public Accountants, on Oct. 22, 2001, Pitt began: "In recent years, the unremarkable notion—of an SEC chairman meeting with this group—has taken on considerable mental, if not physical, risk. To put a fine point on it, as accountants often say, the agency I am privileged to lead has not, of late, always been a kinder and gentler place for accountants; and the audit profession, in turn, has not always had nice things to say about us! Given that recent history, I am especially pleased to have this chance to be with you today." He continued a few moments later: "Somewhere along the way, accountants became afraid to talk to the SEC, and the SEC appeared to be unwilling to listen to the profession. Those days are ended."

8. Charles T. Munger, letter to United States League of Savings Institutions, May 30, 1989, quoted in the author's *Buffett: The Making of an American Capitalist* (New York: Random House, 1995), 349.

9. Roger Lowenstein: "Auditor Independence: The SEC Chairman Doesn't Get It." *The Wall Street Journal,* Jan. 23, 2002.

10. "Harvey Pitt's Credibility." *The Wall Street Journal,* May 8, 2002.

11. James Surowiecki, "Bush's Buddy Economy." *The New Yorker,* Sept. 2, 2002.

12. The Harken affair has often been explored. Though the preponderance of evidence suggests that Bush was aware of Harken's distress at the time of the stock sale (this was also the conclusion of the SEC), Bush has advanced a counterargument that he was selling in advance of what he expected would be *good* news—the announcement of a new drilling contract with Bahrain. In light of Harken's problems and the fact that the purchaser of the stock was never identified, conspiracy theorists have suggested that the purchase was a politically motivated favor. Bush's spokesman has said Bush does not know who the buyer was and calls the suspicion "farfetched." Bush has never explained his reporting lapse, but here there is conflicting evidence as to whether carelessness or some more sinister motive was at work. For a neutral summary of the facts, see Jackie Calmes, "Questioning the Books: The President Speaks: Bush's Résumé May Be Obstacle in Corporate Fight." *The Wall Street Journal,* July 10, 2002. A more detailed examination appears in Anthony York, "Memos: Bush Knew of Harken's Problems." *Salon.com,* July 12, 2002.

13. J. P. Morgan Chase news release, Jan. 22, 2003.

14. Deborah Lohse, "E*Trade CEO made $50 million last year." *San Jose Mercury News,* May 1, 2002. The figure in the headline does not include stock-based compensation. Susanne Craig, "No Discount: E*Trade CEO Gets Pay Deal of $80 Million." *The Wall Street Journal,* May 1, 2002. Craig, "For E*Trade's CEO, The Pay and Perks Are Just E*Normous. 'A Runaway Gravy Train.'" *The Wall Street Journal,* May 10, 2002. Craig, "High-Paid E*Trade CEO Agrees To Ratchet Down Compensation." *The Wall Street Journal,* May 13, 2002.

15. Michael C. Jensen, "How Stock Options Reward Managers for Destroying Value and What to Do About It," incomplete draft, Apr. 17, 2001.

Fuller and Jensen, "Just Say No to Wall Street." The Jensen interview is with the author.

16. Gretchen Morgenson, "Business Lobby Seeks to Limit Investor Votes On Options." *The New York Times*, June 6, 2002.

17. Galbraith, *The Great Crash*, 108.

18. Concurrent SEC charges are detailed in SEC release 2002-92, "SEC Announces Fraud Charges Against Former Rite Aid Senior Management," June 21, 2002. Also see Paula Dwyer and Dan Carney, "Year of the Whistleblower." *BusinessWeek online*, Dec. 16, 2002.

19. Thornburgh report, 23–30.

20. John Harwood, "Public Esteem For Business Falls In Wake of Enron." *The Wall Street Journal*, Apr. 11, 2002. Senator Paul Sarbanes, "Public Company Accounting Reform and Investor Protection Act of 2002," a statement released by his office, July 8, 2002.

21. Sarbanes, release of July 8, 2002.

22. David Wessel, "What's Wrong?—Venal Sins: Why the Bad Guys of the Boardroom Emerged en Masse." *The Wall Street Journal*, June 20, 2002. Sarbanes, press release of July 8, 2002. Joel Seligman, interview with author.

23. "What Cleanup?" *BusinessWeek*, June 17, 2002.

24. "Record Number of Financial-Reporting Cases Opened by SEC Staff in January, February." *Securities Regulation & Law Report*, Apr. 8, 2002.

25. Cassidy, "The Greed Cycle."

26. Alex Berenson and Lowell Bergman, "Under Cheney, Halliburton Altered Policy on Accounting." *The New York Times*, May 22, 2002. Alex Berenson, "Halliburton And Inquiry By the SEC." *The New York Times*, May 30, 2002.

27. Jeanne Cummings, Jacob M. Schlesinger, and Michael Schroeder, "Securities Threat: Bush Crackdown On Business Fraud Signals New Era." *The Wall Street Journal*, July 10, 2002.

28. Alex Berenson, "A U.S. Push on Accounting Fraud." *The New York Times*, Apr. 9, 2003.

29. Statement of Representative Michael Oxley, committee chairman, Oct. 2, 2002.

30. Dennis K. Berman, "Innovation Outpaced the Marketplace." *The Wall Street Journal*, Sept. 26, 2002. The Conference Board.

31. Andrew Ross Sorkin, "Tyco Details Lavish Lives of Executives." *The New York Times*, Sept. 18, 2002. Gretchen Morgenson with Andrew Ross Sorkin, "Tyco Rewarded an Executive During a Grand Jury Inquiry." *The New York Times*, Sept. 26, 2002. Laurie P. Cohen, "Tyco's Former Top Lawyer Joins CEO on Hot Seat." *The Wall Street Journal*, Sept. 13, 2000. "The Tyco Mystery." *The Wall Street Journal*, Mar. 25, 2003.

32. Geraldine Fabrikant, "GE Expenses for Ex-Chief Cited in Divorce Papers." *The New York Times*, Sept. 6, 2002; Rachel Emma Silverman, "Here's the Retirement Jack Welch Built: $1.4 Million a Month." *The Wall Street Journal*, Oct. 31, 2002.

33. Leslie Wayne and Alex Kuczynski, "Tarnished Image Places Welch in Unlikely Company." *The New York Times*, Sept. 16, 2002. "Courtside Tickets for Life." *The New York Times*, Sept. 15, 2002. *The New York Times*'s 1933 editorial quoted in Seligman, *Transformation of Wall Street*, 37.

34. Greg Ip, "The Economy: New York Fed President Chides CEOs on Hefty Compensation." *The Wall Street Journal*, Sept. 12, 2002. Reingold, "Executive Pay."

35. Deborah Solomon and Dennis Berman, "Global's Winnick Is Tied to Swap." *The Wall Street Journal*, Aug. 30, 2002.

36. Alexei Barrionuevo, Jonathan Weil, and John R. Wilke, "Enron's Fastow Charged with Fraud." *The Wall Street Journal*, Oct. 3, 2002.

37. Jay Ritter, interview with author. Ventro had been renamed Nexprise, and the stock was reverse split, raising the nominal price.

38. The 92nd Street Y episode was widely reported. A brief summary appears in "The Prekindergarten Connection." *The New York Times*, Nov. 16, 2002.

39. Attorney General of the State of New York, "In the Matter of Morgan Stanley Co. Inc.," Assurance of Discontinuance Pursuant to Executive Law, 63 (15), 20.

40. SEC Release 2002-179.

41. Webster, in 1992, was hired by the Air Transport Association, an industry

group, to lobby against fingerprinting and background checks for airport screeners. Webster later served on the board of NextWave Telecom, an upstart wireless company that aggressively bid for airwave licenses and subsequently defaulted on billions of dollars owed to the Federal Communications Commission. Alex Berenson, "Webster's Public Service Image Not Duplicated in Private," *The New York Times,* Nov. 6, 2002.

42. John R. Wilke, "Webster Says He Will Likely Quit As Head of New Accounting Board." *The Wall Street Journal,* Nov. 12, 2002. Stephen Labaton, "Audit Overseer Being Challenged by Firm He Dismissed at Old Job." *The New York Times,* Nov. 8, 2002. Michael Schroeder, "Regulator Under Fire: As Pitt Launches SEC Probe of Himself, Criticism Mounts." *The Wall Street Journal,* Nov. 1, 2002.

CHAPTER TEN: EPILOGUE

1. Galbraith makes this point in *The Great Crash,* 169.

2. On July 16, 2002—just after the revelations of wrongdoing at World-Com—Greenspan testified to the Senate Banking Committee, "An infectious greed seemed to grip much of our business community."

3. *J. P Morgan Chase & Co.* v. *Liberty Mutual Insurance Co.*

4. In the Matter of An Inquiry by Eliot Spitzer, Attorney General of the State of New York, with regard to the acts and practices of Merrill Lynch & Co., Inc., Henry Blodget, et al., Affidavit in support of application for an order pursuant to General Business Law section 354, 19.

5. Galbraith, *The Great Crash,* 128–30.

6. Sophisticated investors continue to leverage equity investments by resorting to puts and calls and other derivatives.

7. Galbraith, *The Great Crash,* 180.

8. Although the amount of the so-called wealth effect (the impact of market movements on the economy) cannot be pinpointed, most economists agree that it exists and that it has grown as more Americans have come to own shares.

9. See, for example, Partnoy, *Infectious Greed.*

10. Galbraith, *The Great Crash,* 188.

11. George Soros, "Why the Markets Can't Fix Themselves." *The New Republic*, Sept. 2, 2002.

12. Citigroup, press release, Feb. 12, 2003.

13. John Maynard Keynes, *The General Theory of Employment, Interest and Money* (New York: Cambridge University Press, 1973; first edition 1936), 154–55.

INDEX